DATE DUE

LIVES ON THE LINE

Dispatches from the U.S.-Mexico Border

LIVES ON THE LINE

Dispatches from
the U.S.–Mexico Border

MIRIAM DAVIDSON

PHOTOGRAPHS BY JEFFRY SCOTT

The University of Arizona Press

Tucson

The University of Arizona Press
© 2000 The Arizona Board of Regents
First Printing
All rights reserved

∞ This book is printed on acid-free, archival-quality paper.
Manufactured in the United States of America

05 04 03 02 01 00   6 5 4 3 2 1

Library of Congress Cataloging-in-Publication Data
Davidson, Miriam.
Lives on the line: dispatches from the U.S.–Mexico border / Miriam Davidson;
photographs by Jeffry Scott.
p. cm.
Includes bibliographical references and index.
ISBN 0-8165-1997-8 (cloth: alk. paper)—ISBN 0-8165-1998-6 (pbk.: alk. paper)
1. Nogales (Nogales, Mexico)—Social conditions.   2. Nogales (Ariz.)—Social
conditions.   3. Mexican-American Border Region—Social conditions.   I. Title.
HN120.N64 D38   2000
306′.0972′62—dc21   00-008566

British Library Cataloguing-in-Publication Data
A catalogue record for this book is available from the British Library.

TO DAVID *again, and always*

CONTENTS

ILLUSTRATIONS

LIVES ON THE LINE

Dispatches from the U.S.-Mexico Border

The Two Faces of Nogales

For most of the afternoon of Sunday, November 23, 1997, all was quiet along the U.S.–Mexico border at Nogales. A steady stream of Mexican shoppers filled the streets on the Arizona side, and on the Sonora side, long lines of cars waited at the downtown plaza to enter the United States. The usual weekend throngs of begging children, teenage windshield washers, and adult vendors roamed between the cars. The vendors' arms were laden with a wide variety of goods both hand and machine made, including snacks, sweets, sunshades, seat covers, cassette tapes, string puppets, and large papier-mâché figures of Tweety Bird and Christ crucified. Around 5:30 P.M., as darkness and the evening chill began to descend into the valley, a red van with Arizona license plates crossed into Mexico. The van drove up to one of the three inspection lanes, stopped, and pulled slowly over the speed bump. Nine times out of ten the light turns green, and the driver may proceed, but this time the signal turned red, and a bell sounded. Mexican customs officials motioned the van to pull over for further inspection. According to the official story, Mexican authorities searched the van and found $123,000 in U.S. currency in a box in the back. They then took the driver, a twenty-five-year-old Nogales, Sonora, man, into the booth for questioning.

An hour passed. Suddenly, like a scene from a movie, a white pickup truck came speeding the wrong way up the plaza and screeched to a halt in front of the inspection booth. Seven men armed with pistols and AK-47 rifles jumped out and opened fire. The Mexican cops shot back, and a ferocious gun battle ensued. Beggars and vendors and tourists ran screaming from the plaza. Cars trapped in lines to enter the United States were peppered with fire, their windows and windshields smashing to pieces as the people inside ducked and prayed. Inspectors on the U.S. side frantically began waving the terrified drivers across the border. Some witnesses later claimed they heard shots coming from Buenos Aires, the hillside neighborhood overlooking the port of entry that is a notorious haven for smugglers and drug dealers. At least eighty shots streaked across the darkened plaza during the ten-minute battle. Then, as suddenly as it began, the shooting stopped. One of the Mexican customs inspectors lay dead, hit in the head at close range, and two of the gunmen and several bystanders were injured. The two injured gunmen and the driver of the van were arrested. All the others escaped—several of them, witnesses said, up the streets of Buenos Aires. Authorities closed the port of entry for hours afterward as officers from Customs, the Immigration and Naturalization Service (INS), and other U.S. agencies joined Mexican police in investigating.

For weeks afterward, the incident was the talk of both Nogales, Arizona, and Nogales, Sonora. People claimed there was much more money in the van than officials reported, a million or more in drug profits. Some said the shoot-out had in fact been a diversion and that other vehicles loaded with cash or drugs had crossed unimpeded during the melee. Rumors swirled that it was an inside job after a plainclothes cop on the scene was arrested, although he was released and returned to duty several days later. Mexican authorities remained characteristically tight-lipped about their investigation, saying only that the captured gunmen were known drug traffickers and that at least one had served time in a U.S. prison. The true story of what really happened may never be known.

Violence like this hadn't been seen in Nogales for eighty years, and it prompted law enforcement agencies on both sides of the line to beef up inspections. The already long lines of cars, trucks, and people who crossed everyday slowed to a virtual standstill, resulting in many complaints from local residents. After the shoot-out, the new mayor of Nogales, Sonora, proposed that the Mexican military start patrolling downtown. The idea of armed and uniformed soldiers on the streets evoked "war zone" images certain to harm local businesses, though, so most community leaders quickly rejected the mayor's proposal. Such a move, they believed, would only increase the likelihood of more shoot-outs and of more innocent bystanders being killed and injured.

On the cusp of a new century, Nogales seemed to be returning to its Old West past. The community was founded as a freewheeling, frontier town built on trade of all kinds, and it had a violent history. Smugglers and bootleggers had favored its hills for generations, and the plaza had been the scene of several pitched battles during the Mexican Revolution, two of which involved the U.S. side. Yet things were different now. "Nogales just isn't the same anymore," people said, shaking their heads, and they weren't talking about drug trafficking only. Like many other cities along the two-thousand-mile-long U.S.–Mexico border, Nogales, Sonora, had undergone rapid industrial and population growth during the previous twenty years. Starting in the early 1980s, hundreds of foreign, mostly U.S.–owned factories known as *maquiladoras* moved to the border to take advantage of Mexico's low wages and lax environmental regulations. Poverty and pollution followed. At the same time, the U.S. government launched a series of crackdowns on drugs and illegal immigration that put pressure on smugglers and led to increasingly violent confrontations between locals and authorities on both sides of the line. The combination of the maquiladora boom and the law enforcement crackdown brought big changes all along the border. For the twin towns of Nogales, Arizona, and Nogales, Sonora, the impact was overwhelming.

When I first arrived in Nogales in the early 1980s, the maquiladora boom was just getting under way, and the community still retained the close-knit, small-town character that lifelong residents now recall fondly. In those days, Nogales's main claim to fame was La Caverna, a restaurant that occupied an airy, rock-walled cave just a few feet from the fence on the Mexican side. For decades, La Caverna's food, drink, music, and floor shows attracted everyone from John Dillinger to John Wayne to this remote border outpost. It burned down in a spectacular fire in 1983 and never reopened. The loss of La Caverna symbolized the death of the charming tourist town that was the old Nogales. A new Nogales has been built in its place, an industrial city full of conflict and despair, but also hope. This book is about the new Nogales and the future it represents.

Nogales, Arizona, and Nogales, Sonora, known as Ambos (Both) Nogales, lie nestled together along a seasonal stream in a narrow, high desert canyon sixty miles south of Tucson. Early Indians believed this place was enchanted, with its abundant birds and wildlife and thick stands of cottonwood, willow, and walnut trees (*nogales* is Spanish for walnuts). From the beginning, the community prided itself on being open to outsiders. The first settler on the U.S. side was a Jewish peddler from Russia who established a post office and general store in 1880. Two years later, the young wife of Raymond Morley—chief location engineer of the Atchison, Topeka, and Santa Fe—put Nogales on the map by tapping home the silver spike that linked U.S. and Mexican railways for the first time. The trains ran through the valley along the Nogales Wash and served as the community's lifeblood for its first half-century, sparking a lively cross-border trade in minerals, cattle, produce, and other commodities. The railroad also brought in settlers from such faraway places as China, France, Spain, Italy, Germany, Greece, and Palestine. One of the most distinguished early citizens of Nogales, Arizona, was Lt. Henry Flipper, the first black graduate of West Point. He came in 1891 and stayed until 1906, surveying the town and helping to settle land claims. Flipper said he found the people of Nogales more accepting than others he had met, a sentiment later echoed by the great Mexican revolutionary general Alvaro Obregón, who owned several businesses on the Mexican side and lived for a time on the U.S. side. "If I could spread the genuine friendship and unity of the people of Ambos Nogales throughout the world," Obregón once said, "it would go far in abolishing war and hatreds and would establish a reign of universal peace."

As a young reporter unfamiliar with this part of the border, I experienced the friendliness of Nogales firsthand. People on both sides welcomed me, opened their homes to me, and fed me delicious beans, soups, tamales, and homemade tortillas. Even those who owned nothing were incredibly generous. I had to be careful not to admire something in their homes because they would insist on giving it to me. Everyone was patient with my Spanish, which was awful at first, and no one made me feel humiliated for saying something dumb. I met wonderful people who told me their stories and entrusted me to share them with the world. For their encouragement and inspiration, and for many more gifts, I will always be grateful.

Yet even while I was made to feel so at home, I couldn't help thinking about others who were less privileged. What if, instead of being a fair-haired and fair-skinned American, I were a dark-haired and dark-skinned Mexican? Most people who had come to Nogales in recent decades to work in the factories or to cross into the United States had encountered far different receptions than I had. The more time I spent there, the more I learned about the other face of Ambos Nogales. Starting with the brutal struggle to rid the land of Apache and Yaqui Indians in the nineteenth century, through the expulsion of the Chinese from Sonora during the Depression and the deportation of thousands of Mexican migrant workers from the United States under Operation Wetback in the 1950s, and on up until the present day, currents of racism and violence have always flowed through Nogales like water beneath the border. Some people have been welcomed with open arms, but many more have been rejected, captured, deported, and even killed for being the wrong color or on the wrong side of the line. Thus, Ambos Nogales is a place of both opportunity and despair, new beginnings and the death of dreams.

The contrast between the welcoming and rejecting faces of Nogales turned out to be a central theme in the story that originally brought me there: the sanctuary movement. Sanctuary was a nationwide network of faith communities and others who helped refugees fleeing civil wars and death squads in Central America during the early 1980s. At the time, the U.S. government considered the refugees to be "illegal aliens" and was deporting them to their home countries. Some of these deportees were later found dead. Sanctuary supporters maintained that the refugees should be given at least temporary safe haven in the United States. In Tucson and Nogales, where the movement was born, a number of clergy and lay people from both sides of the line took considerable risks to shelter the refugees, help them sneak across the border, and drive them to sanctuary churches around the country. The movement generated much favorable media attention; I was only one of many reporters who came to Arizona to interview sanctuary workers and participate in "border runs" to pick up refugees.

Dismayed at all the sympathetic coverage, immigration officials decided to put a stop to sanctuary. They sent undercover informants into churches to secretly record the group's meetings, and in 1985, the U.S. attorney for Arizona indicted twelve people, including two Catholic priests and two church lay workers from Ambos Nogales, on alien-smuggling charges. The well-publicized trial took place in the federal courthouse in Tucson later that year. It was the first big story I ever covered, and I remember being impressed with the courage and commitment of the sanctuary workers as well as surprised by the lengths the government was willing to go to in order to prosecute them. The evidence showed that the sanctuary workers had helped only a handful of refugees, all of whom had suffered rape, torture, or the murder of close family members at the hands of Salvadoran, Guatemalan, and Mexican security forces. But the jury convicted eight people anyway, including the two priests and one of the church lay workers, a sixty-year-old housewife from Nogales, Sonora. The judge sentenced all eight to probation. Not long after, immigration authorities admitted in a lawsuit that they had unfairly denied the refugees' asylum claims and agreed to offer temporary safe haven to Guatemalans and Salvadorans in the United States.

The sanctuary trial, like the loss of La Caverna, heralded the changes beginning to engulf Ambos Nogales. During the next ten years, as I worked as a reporter in Nogales, I saw the brutal, ugly side of those changes—the violence, poverty, and environmental devastation. Yet I also saw the beautiful side—caring families, welcoming of newcomers, and the optimism of young people striving for a better life. Through my own reporting and that of others, I saw the community receive a notoriety far beyond its size. It became known as a place where all the troubles of the border were magnified. At the same time, Nogales also benefited from media attention to its problems. The stories, as negative as they were, raised national attention to and concern for this community, especially during the debate over the North American Free Trade Agreement (NAFTA). True, Nogales was a microcosm of the border, but of the good as well as the bad. I wanted to write a book that revealed both faces.

This book tells five stories, each of which describes different aspects of the impact of the maquiladora boom and the law enforcement crackdown on the people of Ambos Nogales. The stories portray individuals—some well known, some not—whose lives represent larger issues and who have in some way shaped the cities' recent history. Telling the tales of a maquiladora worker family, an environmental activist, a tragic confrontation between a Border Patrol agent and a local man, a teenage gang member, and two maquiladora managers, the book takes a personal approach to five current border issues: the living and working conditions of maquiladora workers, the environment, the law enforcement crackdown, youth, and the social responsibility of maquiladora owners and managers. Together, these stories illustrate the many contradictions of the region. They look at both the costs and benefits of the industrial boom as well as at the rising tension over whether the border should be open or closed. The questions of whom to welcome and whom to turn away, what to let in and what to keep out, have always been reflected in the two faces of Nogales, but never have they been more clearly revealed than now.

The driving force behind the transformation of Nogales—and the main subject of this book—is the maquiladora boom. The U.S. and Mexican governments first established the maquiladora program in 1965 to help develop the border and to create jobs for former braceros, Mexican migrant workers who had been deported from the United States under Operation Wetback. The idea was to offer incentives to U.S. and other foreign-owned businesses to ship raw materials to assembly plants on the Mexican side, employ Mexican labor to do the work, and then reimport the finished goods to the United States for sale, practically duty-free. Maquiladoras took a while to catch on, especially in smaller cities such as Nogales. Only a handful of large corporations, including Motorola and General Instrument, opened maquiladoras here in the late 1960s and early 1970s. Although the maquiladora industry grew slowly throughout the latter decade, it didn't really take off until the early 1980s, when a series of financial crises and peso devaluations lowered the cost of Mexican labor to among the cheapest in the world. After that, the race to the border was on. The number of maquiladoras grew spectacularly throughout the 1980s, and in the early 1990s, the passage of NAFTA and another big peso collapse made the industry even more attractive to foreign corporations. By the end of the century, more than four thousand maquiladoras had been established in Mexico, almost one hundred of which were in Nogales.

The maquiladoras, or *maquilas* for short, attracted large numbers of jobless people to cities that did not have the housing or infrastructure to support them. This situation was especially true in Nogales, where an estimated 80 percent of the workers were new arrivals. Between the early 1980s and the mid-1990s, the population of Nogales, Sonora, tripled to some 350,000—at least fifteen times the population of Nogales, Arizona, which remained steady at about 20,000. More than half the entire workforce of Nogales, Sonora, toiled in the facto-ries, a higher percentage than in any other city on the border. Most of those coming to work were teenagers and young adults from southern Sonora and the nearby state of Sinaloa. They found that though maquiladora jobs were plentiful, salaries were so low—about thirty-five to forty-five dollars for a forty-eight-hour week—and costs so high that they could not afford to pay rent or utilities. They lived, for the most part, as squatters in shacks constructed from tin, wood pallets, plastic sheets, and cardboard boxes salvaged from the factories and the dump. Few had indoor plumbing; some had no water or electricity. Crime, disease, and family breakdown were rampant in the squatters' camps. But it was a reflection of the depth of poverty in Mexico that most of these workers felt they were better off in Nogales than they were in their hometowns.

This book first looks at the life story of one of these workers, Yolanda Sánchez, and her family. I met Yolanda in the fall of 1996, when she had been living in Nogales for ten years. Like so many oth-ers, Yolanda was a single mother who had fled rural poverty and a drunken, abusive husband to make a new life for herself and her chil-dren on the border. In a series of interviews in 1997 and 1998, she told me why she came to Nogales, what it was like for her when she arrived, and how she was able to build a home and survive. The stories she and her daughters, Guadalupe and Bobbi, told me are stories of courageous daily struggles for rights and dignity as workers, women, and human beings. Their stories are presented against the background of the de-velopment of the maquila industry and the history of worker-organiz-ing efforts in Nogales and along the entire border.

The maquiladora and population boom, combined with inad-equate infrastructure and Mexico's lax environmental enforcement, led inevitably to widespread pollution on the border. Problems were espe-cially acute in Ambos Nogales due to the region's lack of water, steep hills, and northward-sloping topography. This community, in fact, has a long history of complex environmental issues requiring close binational planning and cooperation. In the past, the two sides had worked well together to ensure an adequate supply of drinking water and to control flooding in the Nogales Wash. The crowning achievement of their cooperation was the unique and elaborate tunnel system of the twin cities—a system that houses the wash and its tributaries as the water flows north across the border. The tunnels were originally built in the 1930s by the U.S. Civilian Conservation Corps and Works Progress Administration, and have been expanded several times since. Both cities also worked together to manage wastewater by constructing a joint sewer system and binational treatment plant in the 1950s. Inevitably, however, sewer repair and construction in Mexico, not to mention road paving and other infrastructure development, failed to keep up with population growth. By the mid-1980s, air, water, and soil pollution from factories, trucks, unpaved streets, and squatters' camps in Nogales, Sonora, was flowing downhill and downwind toward the much smaller Nogales, Arizona. The situation quickly developed into one of the worst environmental crises on the border.

Just as contamination in Nogales reached a critical stage, residents on the U.S. side began to fall ill from cancer and other diseases at alarming rates. Many suspected cross-border pollution was to blame. Jimmy Teyechea, a Nogales, Arizona, produce broker diagnosed with a rare bone-marrow cancer at age forty, was one local who transformed his pain into a national campaign against border pollution. I was fortunate enough to meet and interview Jimmy in early 1994, when he was at the height of his crusade. His fearlessness in confronting business leaders, government officials, scientists, and journalists was legendary, and he helped change history by calling public attention to the crisis in his hometown. Through Jimmy's story, I look at what has and has not been done to address pollution and health problems in Ambos Nogales, at the impact of the free-trade agreement, and at the troubling implications of environmental destruction here and elsewhere on the border.

The next story turns away from the maquiladora industry to look at the other main engine of change in Nogales, the law enforcement crackdown. Smuggling contraband through these hills is a practice as old as Nogales itself. At the turn of the twentieth century, a brisk trade existed in the importation of Chinese immigrants from Mexico to work illegally in U.S. mines and farms. In what would later become a familiar pattern, many of the would-be immigrants were robbed and beaten before being abandoned on the border, and there were reports of atrocities and unsolved killings. During the 1920s, smugglers turned to the lucrative liquor trade. Customs agents on horseback chased strings of pack mules loaded with barrels of rum and tequila through the back country, and shoot-outs between rival bootleggers were common. In 1926, just two years after the Border Patrol was formed, two of its agents were killed by liquor smugglers in Nogales, Arizona. The area calmed down considerably in the decades after Prohibition. What smuggling there was consisted mostly of marijuana, a primarily local trade that was controlled by the scar-faced Somoza brothers of Nogales, Sonora—known as Los Quemados, or "the burnt ones." By the 1980s, however, the U.S. war on drugs had driven Columbian cartels away from Florida and toward the southwest border, where they hooked up with Mexican drug lords familiar with the best routes. Such large amounts of drugs were coming through the desert around Nogales that federal agents took to calling it "cocaine alley."

Drug smuggling may have heated up in the hills, but people-smuggling was not yet a big enterprise in Nogales. Most immigrants preferred to cross into California or Texas, where they could be closer to jobs and large cities. When I first saw the Nogales border fence in 1985, it was a ramshackle, chain-link affair full of gaping holes and makeshift patches. Undocumented immigrants tended to be local day-crossers who would step through the fence to visit relatives or shop on the other side. In many cases, border-crossers and Border Patrol agents knew each other by name, and the atmosphere was almost relaxed. (During the sanctuary trial, Central American refugees who crossed through

Nogales said it wasn't the Border Patrol who scared them the most, but the young toughs who stood next to holes in the fence and demanded money before they would let them through.)

The scene changed dramatically for the worse in the early 1990s, when the Border Patrol began cracking down in Texas and California. Word went around that the passage was easier through Nogales, and the town quickly became a major smuggling route; some thirty thousand arrests a month took place in 1993. With Nogales overrun by immigrants, the Border Patrol soon turned its attention to the area. Beginning in 1994, the agency tripled the number of agents; installed cameras, sensors, and lights; and, most notably, replaced the border fence with a two-mile-long, fourteen-foot-tall steel wall. Although the crackdown drove border-crossers away from town and sharply lowered crime on the U.S. side, the community was divided over it in more ways than one. Most locals accepted the need to combat crime and violence associated with smuggling, but they also believed Nogales could handle only so many Border Patrol agents, and they were concerned about violations of their own and their neighbors' rights. They resented the ugliness and implied hostility of the wall, and many were convinced it had damaged the town's character and economy. As one businessman said, "The Berlin Wall went down and our Nogales wall went up."

Whenever people in Nogales talked to me about the Border Patrol, they inevitably brought up the case of Dario Miranda Valenzuela. One of the most infamous episodes in the history of law enforcement on the border, Miranda's story is important for understanding how local residents view the current crackdown. In 1992, a U.S. Border Patrol agent named Michael Elmer shot and killed Miranda, a twenty-six-year-old undocumented immigrant from Nogales, Sonora, in a canyon west of town. Elmer tried to cover up the fact that he'd shot an unarmed man in the back, but his partner turned him in, and he was arrested and charged with murder. Elmer's trial and its outcome caused a sensation on the border by calling attention to what critics said was a

A view from the U.S. side shows the western edge of Ambos Nogales before the wall was built.

longstanding pattern of Border Patrol abuses. The story of Miranda and Elmer is intertwined with a look at the impact of the crackdown in Nogales from several perspectives, including those of the Border Patrol, local residents, and immigrants. It also examines the controversy over the use of the military on the border.

Stories of the new Nogales are stories of youth, so I turn next to that subject. It's impossible to spend any time on the border—or in Mexico for that matter—without noticing how young everyone is. The country's burgeoning population has had major consequences for cities such as Nogales, Sonora, which are struggling to provide jobs, services, and education for people under the age of twenty, estimated at nearly half the population. Although birthrates are now declining all across Mexico, the large number of young families will continue to have profound implications for at least the next thirty years. Throughout the book, I look at what the future holds for Nogales and the border by examining what young peoples' lives are like. I am particularly interested in the condition of women, who make up the majority of the maquiladora workforce and who face early pregnancy and childbearing amid the loss of traditional Mexican family support structures. I wanted to show the ways in which the lives of teenage girls on the border are different from their mothers' and the ways in which they are the same.

Chapter four looks at a particular group of young people in Nogales, the infamous "tunnel kids." In the early 1990s, this gang of homeless children living in the city's underground drainage tunnels brought more negative national attention to Ambos Nogales. Local officials themselves pointed to the kids' criminal violence in order to force the U.S. government to do something about the tunnels. The National Guard installed giant steel doors in the tunnels in 1994, and stepped-up law enforcement on both sides helped bring the kids under control. At the same time, Nogales community leaders established a drop-in shelter on the Mexican side, Mi Nueva Casa, that helped put some tunnel kids on a more productive path. I tell the story of one of these kids, a girl named Cristina, who, with help from Mi Nueva Casa, aspired to get away from gang life in the tunnels. In addition to Cristina's story, I describe a visit I made to the tunnels in early 1998 and look at what other services exist to help troubled young people in Nogales and elsewhere on the border.

The final chapter returns to the impact of the maquiladora boom, but from a different perspective. In Nogales, as in other cities, industry has given rise not only to vast slums but to a small, professional middle class. Most of these managers and engineers are Americans who have moved to the border in the past twenty years or so. Don Nibbe, one of the first managers to arrive in Nogales, came down from Chicago in 1970 to run the new General Instrument plant. "Nogales was a nice, sleepy little town then," he told me. "You had to be careful who you talked to, because all the families were interrelated. People would say, 'Nogales isn't a place; it's a state of mind.'" Nibbe lived in Kino Springs on the U.S. side, near the rolling grasslands of the San Rafael ranch where the movie *Oklahoma!* was filmed. "I used to look across the desert, at the mountains and all God made, and think, 'How lucky I am.'"

Nibbe left Nogales in the mid-1970s and later founded the maquiladora trade magazine *Twin Plant News*. Most of the managers who came after him also lived on the U.S. side, either in Kino Springs or Rio Rico, a suburban enclave about ten miles north of the border. These men (and occasionally women) were business people who defended maquiladoras as good for both countries, yet they were also confronted daily with the desperate poverty of their employees. I wanted to explore what it was like for them to work in a situation of such inequality. I found that, for the most part, they were decent and conscientious, and that they cared about their workers, even if most of them believed there was not much they could do. A couple of managers distinguished themselves, however, for personally having done a great deal to lessen the suffering of workers' families. I wanted to include their stories as a counterpoint to the negative coverage the maquiladoras generally receive.

Chapter five tells two stories of maquiladora managers who have made unique and lasting contributions to the Nogales community. The first is about Hope Torres, a top-level manager at a maquiladora, and her husband José. Together, this couple gathered hundreds of dollars of monthly contributions from the maquiladoras and other sources to establish a free lunch program for children in the Nogales, Sonora, shantytowns. Their story is interwoven with that of another manager, Tom Higgins, who helped pioneer an innovative program that helps workers buy their own houses in Nogales. The program was so successful that it was expanded to numerous other border cities. The Torres and Higgins stories, and other acts of charity and social concern on the part of maquiladora managers, show that questions of whether this industry is good or bad are not easy to answer.

This book focuses on a particular place, Ambos Nogales, during a particularly eventful period in its history, the 1990s. It is a *gringa* reporter's account of individual lives and deaths. At the same time, I hope it reveals larger truths about conditions on the U.S.–Mexico border at the end of the twentieth century. Through these stories, I hope to show the rising tension between free trade and militarization that characterizes the growing economic integration of the first and third worlds. I also hope to portray some positive aspects of the changes that have transformed this fast-growing region. The border presents both challenges and opportunities not only for the people who live here, but for all Americans. These are some of the stories of the new Nogales.

CHAPTER 1

"God Made My Dream Come True"

On a cold January morning in 1987, Yolanda Sánchez arrived in the valley of Nogales with one peso in her pocket, a single change of clothes, and a determination to make a new home for herself and her children. "The thing I most remember," she told me years later, "was how afraid I was." As the bus pulled into the station at dawn that day, Yolanda said a prayer, asking God to please protect and guide her in the unfamiliar city. She thought about the four children she had left behind with her mother in southern Sonora and how much she missed them, and she wondered what might await her on the border. Whatever it was, Yolanda prayed that things would go better than they had during the first thirty-three years of her life.

Yolanda was born in 1953 in Bacobampo, Sonora, a village that lies about 350 miles south of the border on a fertile plain along the Rio Mayo as it flows toward the Gulf of California. She was the fourth of six children of a troubled farmworker who eked out a living in the corn, cotton, wheat, and vegetable fields around the town. Yolanda's father was a good and gentle man who would go out of his way to help others, but he also drank heavily. What little he earned often disappeared in two or three days, forcing his family to live with his mother and sisters and to rely on them for money. The day after Christmas 1956, drunk and depressed over his inability to support his family, he put a bullet in his brain. He was just thirty-two years old.

Yolanda was too young to remember her father's suicide, but from that day on, her childhood was over. Her mother took her older siblings and moved out of the house, leaving Yolanda to be raised by her grandmother and aunts. They put her to work almost immediately. "They gave me a basket that got bigger and bigger the older I got, and sent me out to sell tomatoes and chili peppers in the street. No matter what the weather, if I was sick or if I didn't feel like it—I had to go. I could not come back to the house unless my basket was empty. If I did, I'd get a beating with a belt." Her aunts also punished her by withholding food. "We had to earn every bite we ate. Many nights I went to bed hungry."

Yolanda tried to run away several times during her childhood. She had ideas of walking the twenty or so miles to Navajoa, the closest city to Bacobampo, but never made it that far. When she was fifteen, she ran away again, this time determined to succeed. As she reached the edge of town, she passed a house with a water well and decided to stop and play in the canal. Yolanda was thin but pretty, with high cheekbones and dark, deep-set eyes, and a man who worked at the pump house came out to talk to her. He was twenty-nine—almost twice as old as she—part Yaqui and part Mayo Indian. Yolanda was attracted. "He made a good salary, but I wasn't thinking of that. I just wanted someone to take me away from the suffering I'd been experiencing. I thought he was a good man, but I didn't know him that well. I was still a little girl who liked to play with dolls."

Yolanda married the man from the pump house. Within a week of their marriage, he got drunk and beat her up, and she knew she had made a terrible mistake. She tried to go home to her mother, who by this time had more mouths to feed (Yolanda is one of thirteen children), but her mother refused to take her back. "She told me, 'You chose him; you have to stay with him.'" Yolanda stayed with her husband, hoping that maybe if she got pregnant he'd quit beating her. He didn't. Despite his abuse, her small and malnourished body bore three healthy children—Ramiro, Guadalupe, and Ramón—during the next few years. "The hunger was even worse than before, if that's possible, because now I had my children to worry about. My husband drank grain alcohol daily. He'd spend all his money at the cantina, buying rounds of drinks for everyone, hiring mariachis and paying for taxis. Then he would come home at three, four in the morning, and demand that I fix him dinner. If I didn't jump up right away, he hit me. I was too afraid to ask him for money. I'd lie awake at night, counting the lines on the ceiling and wondering, 'How am I going to feed my kids tomorrow? What am I going to do?' I was so low. My life wasn't life." She attempted suicide, although the memory of her father's death kept her from cutting her veins too deeply. "I knew I didn't want to do that to my children. I just wanted someone to help me."

Yolanda endured more than ten years of abuse before her deliverance finally came. One afternoon in the late 1970s, she was washing clothes in her yard when the supervisor of a nearby construction project stopped by to introduce himself. Yolanda and El Gordo, as the contractor was called, hit it off at once. "He saw how I was living, with no money to feed my children, and he helped me. He gave me a job fixing food for his workers. He would come with bags of fruit, meat, all kinds of food neither I nor my kids had ever eaten. He was very generous." Although El Gordo already had a wife and kids in Ciudad Obregón, he and Yolanda fell in love. "The love that grew between us was very pure. I never felt taken advantage of, like he was expecting me to do anything." When Yolanda's husband discovered the relationship, he beat her up. "That was the last time he ever beat me. El Gordo told him, 'You hit her again, you'll have to deal with me.'"

Taking her children, Yolanda went with El Gordo to a village in the Sierra Madre not far from the Spanish colonial capital of Alamos. She lived there for a year while El Gordo worked on another construction project and went back and forth between her and his family in Obregón. She knew the affair couldn't last, but she didn't care. "He was the first and only man in my life who ever really loved me. He touched me in my soul, in the deepest, cleanest part of my being." Toward the end of her year with El Gordo, Yolanda became pregnant. It was her way of making a final break from her husband, who had been begging her to come back. "'Don't tell me the baby isn't mine,' he said.

'I want to give her my name.' I said, 'Why should I give her your name when you don't take care of the three you have?'" Yolanda gave birth to her youngest child, Eva, the following summer, in a house in Bacobampo that El Gordo had built for her. She nicknamed the little girl Bobbi, which was her pronunciation of the English word *baby*. Perhaps inevitably, El Gordo soon began to lose interest. "He still visited us, but not as often. He started to say vulgar things to me." After a while, he quit coming around.

Despite the end of the affair, El Gordo's love had planted a seed of self-worth in Yolanda, a seed of belief that, no matter what her circumstances, she could heal the wounds of her childhood. She began to study the Bible. "Before, I was sure no one loved me, and that I deserved everything that had happened to me. From the Bible, I learned a different way of looking at myself and my life. I was happier in my house. I appreciated my children more. Little by little, the hand of God, and my own will, brought me up. God gave me the strength to keep on struggling."

For the next six years, Yolanda lived on her own in Bacobampo, working as a maid, a field hand, and whatever else she could be in order to feed her children. Jobs were scarce, especially for women, and few paid more than two or three dollars for ten hours of backbreaking labor. She reluctantly concluded that she had to leave her hometown. "A girl from my town had moved up to Nogales and was telling me there were jobs, that I should come. I was afraid, though. I was very much a woman of my pueblo. I still am. If I could have found a decent man there to be a father for my kids, I never would have left." By the time Bobbi entered kindergarten, Yolanda was ready to make the move. She arranged for her mother to care for her children while she went ahead to get settled, sold a propane tank for twenty pesos, and bought a one-way ticket to the border.

At first, things went well in Nogales. Yolanda's friend from home gave her a place to stay, and the day after she arrived, her friend's sister took her to the maquiladora where she worked, Jefel de Mexico. Yolanda was hired on the spot. She went to work twisting wires together and assembling inductors for about four dollars a day. With her first paycheck, she bought secondhand clothes, shoes, and toys to send to her kids, and gave money to the family who had taken her in. By June, when Bobbi finished kindergarten, Yolanda was able to bring her to Nogales to live. "I began to feel like there was a place for me.

"I lived with my friend a couple of months, and everything was fine. Then one Saturday morning, I was lying in bed, sleeping, when I felt something on top of me. Something heavy. I woke up, and I saw it was the father of my friend. He said, 'Quiet, or you'll wake the baby.' I pushed him off. I knew I had to leave, but I couldn't tell them why." With no other place to go, Yolanda moved in with a man to whom her friend had recently introduced her, a professional photographer in his midforties. Elias Ortiz was quiet and serious, a sort of self-taught intellectual and a far cry from the violent, macho men she had known. She hoped he was the one she had been looking for. "But I crashed on the rocks again." Elias, it turned out, wasn't interested in fatherhood. "He refused to let my older kids come live with us. He didn't even want Bobbi there." He also continued to see other women. "He didn't respect me or the women he paraded in front of me. Once he had one in bed with him in one room while I was in the other with my daughter." Despite the humiliation, Yolanda stayed in Elias's house for most of her first two years in Nogales. She could not afford a place of her own and was tired of looking for someone to take care of her. "I already had one child out of wedlock. What was I supposed to do, go from man to man? I stayed with him, but I promised myself two things: I would not fall in love, and I would not have children with him."

In the fall of 1989, Yolanda finally got the break she needed when a friend told her about a land invasion or squatter settlement taking place over by the new highway. By this time, she had moved out of Elias's house, was living in an apartment she couldn't afford, and was desperate to find a home of her own. She took a bus over to where the new *colonia* was going up and talked to the man who was in charge of distributing *terrenos,* or plots of land. "You can have one up there," he said, pointing to a small, steep hillock overlooking the highway, "but you better build on it quick before someone else does." The next morning at dawn, Yolanda arrived with a water jug and a pick ax, set Bobbi down to play under a mesquite tree, and went to work chopping cactus and leveling the ground for her house. She worked all day and went back to the apartment at night, where she lay awake worrying that when she returned to the terreno in the morning, someone else would have claimed it. After a few days, she began staying on the land all the time, sleeping amid the snakes and scorpions on a bed she made for herself and Bobbi in a fold in the ground. "It rained, and I had to cover Bobbi with my body so she wouldn't get wet. I wrapped a rope around her and tied her to me in case someone came along during the night and tried to steal her."

Yolanda shook her head at the memory. "I think God made me suffer a lot, so I would appreciate his mercy more."

In the beginning, the maquiladora industry was hardly the sure thing it turned out to be in retrospect. The American and Mexican businessmen who built the early factories were considered great risk takers; Richard Campbell Sr., the California strawberry basket manufacturer who developed the first industrial park in Nogales, was known around town as "the crazy gringo." The first maquila in Nogales, Motorola, was opened in the mid-1960s by the Dabdoubs, a prominent local family of Palestinian descent, but it was Campbell who saw the potential for large-scale development. He found a suitable place for an industrial park south of town, in what was then open country, and used his wife's invaluable family connections to General Alvaro Obregón to persuade the city to extend the border free-trade zone to include the new park. Campbell also arranged for the city to lease the land to him—later to the maquiladora association—for the next thirty years. Dick Bolin, a consultant for Arthur D. Little, who did one of the first feasibility studies on maquiladoras, recalled the day in the late 1960s when he went with Campbell out to the site. "There was nothing there but pasture and the little crosses by the roadside where people had had accidents. We saw a cow giving birth."

At first, Campbell had trouble convincing companies to move into the park. American businessmen were suspicious of the Mexican government, fearing their investments might be expropriated as foreign rail, oil, and mining companies had been after the revolution. The cost of labor, about fifty cents an hour, was lower than in the United States, but not so low as to justify the hassle and expense of setting up a foreign corporation. They also had doubts about transportation and communications, fears about language and cultural barriers, and questions about the abilities of Mexican workers. "We were dealing with a lot of stereotypes, a lot of prejudice," said Duane Boyett, a former Singer executive whom Campbell tapped to manage the park.

One American businessman who didn't have doubts was Richard Bosse, owner of the Artley flute and saxophone company in Nogales, Arizona. In the early 1960s, Bosse had moved his company down from Elkhart, Indiana, in order to compete with cheaper Japanese imports. Satisfied with the eager and talented employees he had found in Nogales, many of whom were from Mexico, he built a large manufacturing facility about five miles north of the border, in an area of grassy meadowlands known as Potrero Hills. He employed several hundred people there, turning copper, chromium, and other metals into finely crafted instruments. After meeting with Campbell, he agreed to move some of the work to the new industrial park on the Mexican side.

Coin-Art, as the new musical instrument maquiladora was called, was the first tenant in the park. A few others joined it, but not enough to pay off the loans. "We went bankrupt about four times," Boyett said. Finally, while sharing a six pack of beer with Boyett in 1971, Campbell hit on an idea that would save not only his park, but the entire maquiladora industry. "He was a financial genius," Boyett said. "He said, 'Why don't we tell them we'll provide the building, the workers, the necessary paperwork, communications, and transportation—everything but the manufacturing."' The idea, called the "shelter plant" concept, made it easy for Americans to invest in Mexico and soon caught on all along the border.

With vigorous local boosters such as Campbell and the Dabdoubs, Nogales attracted a number of large companies throughout the 1970s. They included Memorex, which made computer wiring; Avent, a hospital clothing manufacturer; office-supply maker Wilson-Jones; Foster Grant (sunglasses); Samsonite (suitcases); and Chamberlain, which made garage door openers for Sears. Chamberlain, started by a group of former Sears executives in the early 1970s, soon grew to become the biggest maquiladora in Nogales. After a truck bypass highway, called the *periferico,* opened west of downtown in 1976, Chamberlain moved over there to be closer to the new Mariposa port of entry, and several other maquiladoras opened nearby. The traditional economic base of mining, ranching, and tourism in Nogales faded into irrelevance as the city was transformed into a maquila center. By the early 1980s, Nogales was home to more than twenty-three large factories.

At first, workers were plentiful in Nogales and all along the border. "One time in Chihuahua City we put out an ad calling for ten workers and had five thousand lined up the next morning," Boyett said. "A woman came up to me and said, 'I'll do anything for a job. Anything.'" The maquilas preferred to hire young, single women who still lived at home with their families rather than unemployed braceros. Women supposedly were better at fine finger work and tedious tasks, and they were less likely to complain or cause trouble than men. "They were better workers," shrugged Boyett, adding that the men were more interested in chasing women than in working. The jobs were grueling and unfamiliar, and turnover rates were high, more than 100 percent a year at some companies. "They didn't know to wrap tape around their fingers or that their backs would hurt at the end of the first week, so they'd quit. We weren't very good at preparing them for the kind of work they'd be doing or responding to their concerns."

The entry of teenage girls into Mexico's paid workforce caused social upheaval as well. The girls listened more to their fathers than to their bosses, so the personnel manager had to go around to their homes and tell their fathers what time they needed to be at work each day. If a worker was sick or needed time off, she would bring a note from home like a schoolchild. Boyett told the story of one man who waited outside the factory for nine hours every day, rain or shine, while his daughter worked inside, so he could escort her home. The American managers also had some trouble adjusting to the new regime. "The most common complaint we had was, 'Tell them to quit eating their tacos on top of my car,'" Boyett said.

With the creation of the maquiladora industry, hopes were high that as Mexico developed an industrial base, wages and living standards would rise, just as they had in the United States. A 1972 article in *Newsweek* sang the praises of maquiladoras in Nogales. "People used to eat meat once a week, but now they're eating it five times a week, and there's bread and milk, too," one local official boasted. "Many people have been able to move out of their cardboard shacks into decent homes," said another.

Yolanda collected wood pallets, cardboard boxes, plastic sheets, and discarded pieces of corrugated tin to build a leaky home for herself and Bobbi on the hill beside the highway. The one-room shack had no electricity or running water, and for the first few months, before she was able to afford a propane stove, she cooked outside over an open fire. Like her neighbors, she used oil lamps and candles to light the house, and got her water from a truck that chugged along the highway every day, filling up fifty-gallon drums that people had salvaged from the maquilas or the dump. Most of the drums had previously contained toxic chemicals, and residents knew they shouldn't store drinking water in them. "But what choice did we have?" said Yolanda, who kept her water in a Johnson Wax barrel. Even boiling the water cost money.

As primitive as conditions were, she was thrilled to be on her own and immediately made plans to bring her three older children to the border.

By this time, Ramiro, the oldest, had completed school in Bacobampo and was engaged to a local girl. Yolanda encouraged the couple to come to Nogales, and shortly after they were married, they did, settling nearby in Los Encinos. Yolanda's other two children, sixteen-year-old Guadalupe and fourteen-year-old Ramón, came to live with her. At first, Guadalupe (or Lupe, for short) wasn't too thrilled about the idea. "It's too ugly," she said. "You can go live in Colonia Kennedy if you don't like it," Yolanda retorted, referring to the richest neighborhood in Nogales, a hilltop enclave of mansions behind high walls. As soon as they arrived, both Ramiro and Guadalupe went to work in the maquiladoras: Ramiro at Jefel, the same company that had given Yolanda her first job, and Lupe at Foster Grant, making sunglasses.

Yolanda was closer than ever to her dream of independence, yet she still found herself under the control of a tyrannical man—this time, the neighborhood leader who had given her the plot of land. Like almost all Nogales colonias that began as land invasions, Yolanda's new neighborhood was led by a political activist for the Partido Revolucionario Institucional (PRI), Mexico's ruling party. These self-appointed leaders served as intermediaries among the squatters, landowners, and the city government to hand out terrenos, collect payments, and get utilities installed, enabling them to wield tremendous power over the lives of people such as Yolanda. "Some of the leaders are good, but others really take advantage," she said. "People are so desperate, if you tell them the land is theirs, they'll run up and stay through hunger, thirst, heat, cold, rain, snow, whatever. Many people came up here thinking they were going to get land, but the leaders have the power to give it or take it away and sell it to someone else."

After overhearing that the leader of her neighborhood planned to take away her terreno, Yolanda moved one last time. Halfway up a steep hill on the other side of the highway stood an empty, one-room hut on a small, sloping plot surrounded by mostly vacant land. The place belonged to a man named Angel who told her she could stay there if she kept an eye on it for him. Although a good half-mile from the nearest water, this terreno was quieter and safer than the one on the highway, and, most important from Yolanda's perspective, it was registered in Angel's name, which meant neither a neighborhood leader nor even the city itself could evict her. As soon as she moved in, she set about building more rooms, using pallets and boxes from Wilson-Jones and other maquilas that gave away scrap materials. Angel, whose family owned several tracts of land around town, saw the effort she was making and gave her the title. In the spring of 1991, she went down to Bacobampo, sold her house to her mother for about two thousand dollars, and used the money to pay off the Sonoran state agency that held the lien on the terreno. After three years of struggle, Yolanda finally owned her own land and home in Nogales. "I felt like the queen of the hill."

The neighborhood grew up quickly around her. Every day, it seemed, new families appeared in Los Encinos, staking out terrenos and collecting scrap wood to build a little house. Most came from southern Sonora, although a few were from Sinaloa or Nayarit or Jalisco or other nearby states. None were from Nogales itself. Many were single mothers, as homeless and afraid as Yolanda had been when she first came to the border. Seeing an opportunity, she added more rooms onto her house to rent to the newcomers. She also made money by selling used clothes and kitchen utensils and by babysitting for her neighbors while they went to work in the maquiladoras. Now a grandmother nearing forty, she herself was too old to get a job in the factories, which generally did not hire women older than thirty-six. "The maquilas are the first option, the most immediate way to establish yourself here. But I always had a little higher aspiration for myself. Depending on who we

Yolanda, age 43.

are, we can be closed inside a factory for the rest of our days, or we can use it as a means to survive while we look for a better way to sustain ourselves."

Yolanda also reconciled with Elias, who was down on his luck after having lost his home and business following the death of his father. She was lonely and needed the money, so she agreed to let him move in for thirty dollars a week in room and board. Now that he was living in her house, he was more respectful than before, but he still didn't treat her, as she said, "like a man is supposed to treat a woman. He expects me to cook and give him companionship, but he doesn't lift a finger around here."

With the population of the colonias booming, pressure built on the city to provide services. In late 1991, Yolanda and hundreds of others joined a series of protest marches demanding water and electricity for two of the longest-standing settlements, Los Encinos and

Los Tapiros. At one rally, neighbors went down to the periferico that ran below Los Encinos and blocked traffic for several hours while they waved signs and shouted slogans. Pictures of the protestors lying down in the middle of the highway appeared on the local TV news that evening. Because the endless parade of semis loaded with fruits, vegetables, and consumer goods for Americans was now threatened with disruption, Nogales officials were forced to take action. They promised to bring public services to Los Encinos.

It was not until the summer of 1993, almost two years after the protest on the periferico, that utilities finally reached Yolanda's neighborhood. The sewer installation, like many such projects in Nogales, was a do-it-yourself affair: the city donated the pipes, and residents themselves dug the trenches. The water lines were another matter. The many hills and chronic water shortages in Nogales meant that each family had to kick in about seventy-five dollars to build the lines, plus another fifteen dollars or so in monthly fees, despite the fact that the water flowed only a few hours each day and was still considered unsafe to drink. Those residents with money put in indoor plumbing, plus a tank on the roof to use during the frequent outages, but the rest, including Yolanda, made do with a hose connected to a tap in front of the house, stored water in discarded chemical barrels, and continued to use an outhouse and to bathe and wash clothes and dishes outdoors. Even this state of affairs was a big improvement over scrambling to meet water trucks and having to hand carry jugs of water up the hill. Yolanda was able to start a garden, something she had wanted to do since coming to the border. She planted herbs and flowers, including mint, calla lilies, geraniums, marigolds, and aloe vera, in an assortment of tin cans, glass jars, cooking pots, and other containers gathered in rows on either side of her front door. Soon her whole yard bloomed with color, a tiny patch of beauty amid the bare wood and cardboard.

The long-awaited arrival of electricity brought even more joy. Installation was cheap, about ten dollars per family, and an electrician who lived in the colonia helped wire Yolanda's house for free. She was delighted when the city put up a fluorescent orange streetlight right below her front step. "When I was a kid, my grandmother would take us to our aunt's house in Navajoa. It was hot, and we'd sleep outside on the porch, near this streetlight that made a buzzing sound. I'd fall asleep to that noise. I'd think, one day, if I have money and a house, I'd like to have a light like that. And now, here I have one. I can't believe how God made my dream come true."

By the early 1980s, labor trouble was brewing for the maquiladora industry. In many cities, especially small ones such as Nogales, the available supply of young girls had been used up, and the maquilas were forced to begin hiring married women in their twenties and early thirties, as well as men. The maquila workforce in Nogales was, in fact, more than half men, one of the highest percentages of any city. Managers complained frequently about the labor shortages and high turnover on the border, and some companies, including Motorola, responded by moving farther south into Mexico. But they refused to do the one thing sure to solve labor problems—raise wages. The reason was simple: they didn't have to.

The Mexican government, anxious not to drive away this desperately needed source of jobs and capital, helped maquila owners keep worker demands in check. When the U.S. recession eliminated thousands of maquila jobs in the mid-1970s, Mexico revived the industry by exempting it from the country's strict labor laws. Probationary periods, during which workers didn't have to be paid minimum wage or given benefits, were extended from thirty to ninety days, and maquilas were given the power to fire people without having to show cause or pay severance. Legal minimum wages were kept low, and although the factories paid somewhat more than the minimum, managers in each city apparently agreed among themselves not to compete for workers on the basis of salary. "We all participated in a salary survey and agreed to offer the same starting wage," one Nogales manager later admitted to a reporter. Managers also insisted they were under pressure from both the Mexican government and Mexican-owned businesses not to raise wages.

Workers were essentially powerless to stop these cozy arrangements between the maquiladoras and the Mexican government. In some cities, they had little or no representation; Nogales, for example, historically had one of the least-organized work forces on the border, which was one reason it was attractive to maquilas. Even workers who did belong to one of Mexico's official unions—which were essentially an arm of the state—often didn't know it. "White" or "phantom" unions, as they were called, existed more to keep workers under control than to fight for their rights. This arrangement was made clear in 1981, when Mexico's main official union, the Confederación de Trabajadores de México (CTM), signed a contract with the fourteen largest maquiladoras in Nogales without even bothering to consult the workers. The contract allowed companies not only to hire and fire employees at will, but to change their hours, job assignments, and days off without notice, and to determine the speed of machinery and number of workers needed. When workers heard about it, they were angry, but most believed there was nothing they could do.

Alberto Morackis, now a well-known mural artist in Nogales, was one maquiladora worker who refused to go down without a fight. In the late 1970s and early 1980s, he was a young operator at Jefel, the factory that later employed Yolanda and her son. "Jefel was a very dirty factory," Morackis told me. "People were working with asbestos. I heard on the news that asbestos was dangerous and banned in the United States, but nobody would believe me. People don't know the kinds of things they're working with, and the companies don't tell them." Morackis also believed Jefel's severance and profit-sharing policies violated the law, and he helped organize a committee to present the workers' concerns to management. Instead of meeting with the committee, company officials fired everyone on it. After that, Morackis and other workers tried to launch organizing drives at Chamberlain and Minsa, a clothing manufacturer. "We had to work from outside the factories, and it was very difficult. We were fighting against both the CTM and the government."

These initial organizing efforts and the simmering anger over the CTM contract lit the fuse for what happened after the 1982 peso devaluation. As Morackis described it, "The government recommended to companies that salaries be raised to compensate, but the maquilas here didn't want to do it, so people mobilized." In February of that year, hundreds of workers took to the streets behind the banner of the Socialist Workers' Party. "The strikes went from factory to factory, three one day, two another," Morackis said. "There were protests and actions in about twenty different factories. It was very spontaneous." Workers marched through the streets almost every day to demand that companies raise pay and provide severance for laid-off workers.

The maquilas responded to the protests by raising salaries a little, but they also took advantage of the crisis to get rid of troublemakers. Some smaller companies went out of business altogether and larger ones cut back their staffs. In June, Samsonite fired fifteen workers who had led a work stoppage at the plant in protest against company job cuts. In most cases, fired workers were blacklisted, which meant they couldn't find work at any other factory in Nogales. Protests in other cities usually ended similarly, although some turned violent. In 1988, all twelve hundred workers at a Eureka vacuum cleaner plant in Juárez walked off the job after the company fired twenty workers who tried to form an independent union. "While the workers were outside," one organizer said, "the company security force started beating them up, hitting the women with baseball bats, and then they tear-gassed them." In 1994, after NAFTA was implemented, police in riot gear broke up a strike at the Sony plant in Nuevo Laredo. According to Tijuana human rights monitor Victor Clark Alfaro, maquila workers who have tried to form their own unions have been arrested, tortured, and killed. Yet even in the face of threats and intimidation, firings, blacklistings, and plant closings, the protests in Nogales and elsewhere were not a failure, Alberto Morackis insisted. "The maquilas have changed. Now there are cafeterias and child care in a lot of companies. There've been improvements, although working conditions and salaries are still not what we'd like them to be."

With the workers tamed and the peso devalued, the way was open for the maquiladora boom. During the 1980s, the number of maquilas in Nogales went from twenty-three to almost seventy. Nationwide, a new maquila opened every five days, not only in traditional centers, but in smaller cities as well. Automobile manufacturers such as Ford and General Motors moved aggressively into Mexico, and companies from Europe and Asia opened maquilas to serve as export platforms to the United States. The number of workers swelled to more than half a million, and as it did, so grew the shantytowns ringing the factories, along with all their accompanying environmental problems.

The days of dreaming that maquilas would lift Mexicans out of poverty were over. Now the only expectation the country had was that they would provide jobs for at least some of the million new young people entering the workforce each year.

In her own house with her children around her, Yolanda finally could relax a little. She had achieved a major goal of her life, which was to give her kids, especially her daughters, more choices and more opportunities than she had known. On the border, women were able to earn their own money and not have to depend on men for their survival. They had more freedom to decide when and if they would marry, and to leave abusive men. These were not small advantages. Yet Nogales was also full of temptations and bad influences. Sex, drugs, dirty money—everything was more available and out in the open here than in Bacobampo. Yolanda knew she would have to work hard to keep her children from falling into the many traps that had been set for them.

Already, Yolanda had lost most of her influence over Guadalupe, who had become quite independent after being on her own for much of her adolescence. Lupe had lived for a while with an aunt in Tijuana before coming to Nogales, and in many respects, she was more worldly than her mother. Unlike Yolanda, she knew how to drive. Although she had inherited her mother's slight frame, strong voice, and stronger will, she seemed to lack the fear and shame that stalked Yolanda. When she was eighteen, she had a child out of wedlock and soon afterward began living with a man who was not the child's father. She had no trouble at all finding and keeping jobs in the maquiladoras. Her first, at Foster Grant, paid thirty dollars for forty-eight hours of snapping sunglass lenses into frames as they moved past her on a conveyor belt. "I liked it, because I was making money and the work was easy. We were all girls, and we would talk on the line and become friends and then go out afterward."

After about a year at Foster Grant, Lupe quit to go visit her grandmother in Bacobampo. When she returned to Nogales, she worked a variety of jobs at a string of factories: assembling garage door openers at Chamberlain, ironing men's suits at Minsa, sewing hospital clothes at Avent, and soldering circuit boards at Delta. In a pattern typical of maquila workers, she would quit after a few weeks or months if she didn't like her boss or her work, if she got bored or sick, or if she wanted to go on vacation. She knew she could always get another job, and seniority didn't matter much. All of the jobs paid between thirty and forty dollars for a forty-eight-hour week, including attendance and production bonuses. At Minsa, where she ironed parts of suits, she was paid by the piece, which she preferred. "If you want to, you can work really hard and then rest. They wanted us to iron about 375 pieces a day. But I could iron up to 1,000, and sometimes I made up to three days' pay in one day."

Lupe was never fired from any job because she worked hard and didn't fight with other people. She wasn't afraid to stand up for herself, though. "There's a lot of abuses," she said. "The supervisors are always trying to take advantage of the power they have over the operators on the line. If a supervisor doesn't like a girl, or if she's rebellious, he sexually harasses her until she leaves. A lot of times, the supervisors or engineers will ask to go out with an operator, and usually she'll accept because she wants special advantages or she doesn't want to get fired. It happens to everyone. You have to be ready to fend them off." At Minsa, Lupe had to deal with a situation in which one of the girls on her line was dating a supervisor. "I saw him writing numbers on her time sheet, as if she had been producing during down time. I got mad, and about fifteen of us left our ironing and refused to work. I told the manager, 'Look at last week's time sheets. If they don't show she's being paid for work she didn't do, you can fire me.' The time sheets proved what we were saying. After that, they replaced the supervisor as the boss of that line."

Because Lupe had not been provided with protective gear at any of the factories where she worked, she also suffered her share of exposure to toxins and chemicals. At Avent, she broke out in severe rashes on her arms after working with fiberglass and had to go on disability for six months. At Delta, the air on the factory floor was filled with a fine silver dust that gave her pimples, as well as one cold after another. After four months on the line, she asked to be transferred to a secretarial position in the office, where the air was better and she made slightly more money. Her new boss, however, was a tyrant. "He was always yelling and throwing papers at me because I didn't bring him coffee or something." She went to the personnel director, who advised her to file a written complaint with the local labor conciliation board. "I brought the complaint to the boss who was harassing me. He refused to sign it. We talked, and I told him that the next time he yelled at me, I would take him to conciliation. After that, he was more polite." Many maquila workers were reluctant to speak out for fear of losing their jobs, but not Lupe. "I wasn't going to quit, and if they fired me, they'd have to pay severance. Also, I wasn't the first one to complain about this guy. I knew I was justified."

Before she was hired for a job and at the end of a three-month probationary period, every maquiladora where Lupe worked required her to take a pregnancy test. Women's rights groups attacked this practice as discriminatory and illegal, but Lupe said she understood why factories refused to hire pregnant women. "You can't get your money's worth out of them. They get sick, they have to go to doctor's appointments, and they can't work as hard, on top of the eighty days maternity leave the company has to pay." Each woman had to take a urinalysis test or, if she was menstruating, prove she was not pregnant by showing her bloody pad to the doctor or nurse. When Bobbi started work in the maquilas at fourteen, she too was tested. The doctor refused to take her word that she was a virgin. "He kept asking me, 'Are you a señorita? Are you *sure* you're a señorita?' He was a pig. The doctors who ask to see your Kotex are pigs."

Two years younger than the legal minimum to work, Bobbi actually had to lie about her age on her job application. "I looked older, and the companies never check," she shrugged. Although only halfway through eighth grade, she was already developed, and Yolanda decided it was time for her to quit school and go to work. The school was far away, necessitating long bus trips in the dark, and Yolanda worried about exposing her daughter to drugs and danger on the street. Moreover, the family needed the money. Elias, who had taught himself English and German and who often had a book in his hand, tried to convince Yolanda to let Bobbi stay in school. Yolanda couldn't see the use. After all, Ramiro had a secondary school diploma, and he didn't make more money than any other maquila workers. So Bobbi went to work at Minsa, where she was safe under her sister Lupe's watchful eye, but she was less able to tolerate the rigors of the job and quit after a few months. She worked at four different maquilas in the space of a year—ironing, inspecting, sorting coupons, and entering data. Eventually, she landed at Delta, a Taiwanese computer maker just down the hill from Yolanda's house, where all four of Yolanda's children worked at one time or another. Like Lupe, Bobbi was on the line for a few months until the silver dust in the air started giving her pimples, and she quit.

With so many teenage workers at the maquilas, the atmosphere in them resembled that of a high school. Some of the girls dressed in miniskirts, high heels, heavy makeup, and lots of jewelry, as if they were going to a party. As one maquila manager observed, "When they bend over, you can see the moon." During breaks and at the end of their shifts, the young people would go outside to have a soda and flirt, and a few, especially boys, would smoke tobacco or marijuana cigarettes. On weekends, some workers danced for hours at Coco Loco and other clubs in town that catered to the maquila trade, squandering most of their paychecks on drinks and cocaine. A few led double lives, augmenting their maquiladora salaries through prostitution.

Yolanda was ambivalent about the greater sexual freedom of the border. On one hand, she was grateful not to have to marry Elias. On the other, she refused to take communion because she believed she was living in sin, and she decried the lack of morals she perceived among young people. "Many girls now think that it's not losing their virginity that's the problem. They lose their virginity in the factory, with whatever guy. They think if they take the pills, they can go to bed with anyone they want and no one will know." The church and other social critics blamed the maquilas for the situation, but as Yolanda's son Ramiro pointed out, "The maquilas don't make girls wear miniskirts and makeup." Still, working at the maquiladoras involved some risks. Many workers had to go to work before dawn or return home after midnight, and some became targets of abuse. The most horrific examples of this violence were the brutal sex murders of more than one hundred maquiladora workers in Ciudad Juárez during the mid-1990s. The killings went on for years, despite the arrest of dozens of suspects. Finally, in early 1999, a ring of maquila bus drivers was implicated after police arrested one of them and he reportedly confessed. Outraged women's rights groups blamed the maquilas for allowing the crimes to occur. Managers in Juárez, however, insisted they weren't responsible because the bus drivers worked for a subcontractor.

Yolanda, at least, did not have to worry about such things. For the most part, her children grew up safe, decent, and hardworking, not *marijuaneros* or drug dealers like some young people in the neighborhood. Ramiro and his wife and two children lived nearby, as did Guadalupe, her child, and common-law husband; Bobbi still lived at home with Yolanda. It was Ramón, Yolanda's second son, who caused her the most grief. A drinker like his father, he was unable to hold down a job. When he was in his early twenties, he spent most of his days sleeping in a tiny closet he built in front of Yolanda's house, often getting drunk and threatening Yolanda, and once even brandishing a gun. Yolanda was reluctant to kick him out, but she was afraid and felt she had no choice. She tore down his closet and told him he couldn't live with her anymore. Ramón stayed with friends for a while before, much to Yolanda's relief, he decided to leave Nogales and go back to Bacobampo, where he moved in with his grandmother, got a job, and quit drinking.

As the maquila industry grew by leaps and bounds, so did the number of its critics. U.S. labor, human rights, and environmental groups condemned the factories as exploiters and polluters, and the media presented many stories that focused on the persistent poverty of the workers and the increasing degradation of the border. In the early 1990s, as debate over NAFTA reached its peak, so did the critics' attacks. One maquila manager recalled with disgust a visit to the border by Congressman Richard Gephardt in which Gephardt's staffers supposedly grabbed maquila workers' paychecks from their hands and waved them in front of reporters to show how little workers earned. In Nogales, the story that caused the biggest stir by far was a 1990 article by journalist Sandy Tolan in the *New York Times Magazine.* The article, titled "The Border Boom: Hope and Heartbreak," depicted a land invasion in a colonia and a family building a shack out of boxes and wood pallets salvaged from the maquilas. It also leveled accusations of toxic dumping at the industrial park. After the article appeared, most maquila managers in Nogales quit talking to reporters, and some sent security men to follow and videotape journalists who did stories anyway. A few managers also quit giving away boxes and pallets to workers. "We get criticized no matter what we do," one complained. Yet the bad publicity seemed to have little or no effect. As Don Nibbe of the *Twin Plant News* told me, "This is a Teflon industry. The criticism just slides off, and it keeps on growing."

And grow it did, especially after the implementation of NAFTA in 1994 and the disastrous devaluation of the peso later that year. The crisis forced many Mexican-owned firms to shut down, but U.S. and other foreign corporations were ready to take advantage of the rock-bottom labor costs, not to mention the increased stability and security for their investments that NAFTA represented. The peso dropped so much that the maquilas were able to almost double the size of their workforces with little increase in the total payroll. Three large, modern factories opened in Nogales, and five thousand new workers were hired the year after the peso collapse. Nationally, maquiladora industry employment more than doubled, from about half a million to more than one million in the 1990s; the number of shelter companies—the maquiladora subcontractors pioneered by Dick Campbell in Nogales—grew; and the trend of companies moving inland accelerated. Industrial parks opened or expanded in Magdalena, Imuris, Hermosillo, Guaymas, Obregón, and many other cities. Companies were tired of the constant search for workers in places such as Nogales. "The maquilas have gotten a black eye for creating problems on the border," Don Nibbe said. "A lot of companies have done really well by going inland. The little towns roll out the red carpet for them, give them free land. They say, 'We don't want our sons and daughters going to the border where there's no place for them to live, and the future is uncertain.' In the interior, people can go home for lunch and be with their families. They're more stable and happier." And, of course, their salaries were even lower than they were on the border.

Although a boon to employers, the 1994–95 peso crisis hit the workers hard. "A lot of us wish this hadn't happened because we feel our workers' pain," said Ken Lilley, a manager at General Electric in Nogales. Many managers who had lived through the 1982 peso collapse were ready to raise wages a little and provide food coupons, bus passes, and other incentives to help their employees through the crisis. Even so, inflation quickly ate up any increase. Food prices on the Mexican side equaled or surpassed those in the United States: a gallon of milk cost two dollars; a chicken, four dollars. Although there were no mass protests as before, an air of desperation filled the streets. Crime, especially thefts and robberies, rose sharply. As Roscoe Combs, general manager of the Walbro maquila, was getting ready to go home one afternoon, he was attacked by thieves wanting his car. "Three guys with knives came up to me. I tried to close the car door on the them, but they stabbed me in the chest, arm, and leg." Maquila executives in larger cities such as Tijuana were forced to buy armor-plated vehicles and hire bodyguards after several were kidnapped and held for ransom.

Nogales, Arizona, also took a big hit from the crisis. With the peso worth half its value against the dollar, Mexican shoppers who used to fill the streets on weekends stopped coming over the border. Retail sales downtown dropped by half in the year after the devaluation, and many places closed, including the Safeway and Capin's, one of the city's oldest department stores. The boarded-up storefronts and abandoned sidewalks, not to mention the rusty steel wall that replaced the border fence in 1994, gave Morley Avenue a "war zone" feel that city fathers were anxious to dispel. Yet, however bad the situation was on the border, it was worse in the interior of Mexico, and more hungry people kept arriving in Nogales every day.

Yolanda weathered the crisis with her usual faith and good humor, although when I first met her in the fall of 1996, she told me she just survived day to day. The thirty dollars she received from Elias's weekly salary at the print shop didn't go far, and she was constantly scrambling for more money. She babysat, cleaned houses, and made tortillas for a woman who lived across the line. She served as an informal *curandera,* or healer, for the neighborhood, giving shots of antibiotics to sick children and dispensing herbal treatments and hot-oil massages. For a while, she worked as a maid for a family who always paid her in American money and seemed to have endless stashes of bills around. Yolanda was suspicious—Nogales is awash in drug money that cannot be banked—so she quit. She knew many people who were involved in the drug trade—including Elias's brother, who was doing time in the federal prison in Tucson, and several neighbors who were building fancy two-story, brick, and concrete-block homes. She avoided them, saying, "I'm poor but honorable."

Drug money aside, Yolanda found other ways to benefit from her proximity to the United States. One day, some young, Spanish-speaking social workers from Tucson came by her house, looking for people who wanted to host American church and student groups taking "experiential education" tours of the border. The social workers were from an organization called Borderlinks that led Americans on such activities as Border Patrol ride-alongs and factory visits (often a tough sell with managers), as well as meetings with community leaders, activists, and maquiladora workers. Borderlinks offered Yolanda between five and ten dollars per person to prepare a meal, talk about her life, and once in a while have one or two overnight guests. She jumped at the chance to make money and, she hoped, to meet people who could help her. During the next few years, she became a regular Borderlinks hostess, sometimes feeding and entertaining dozens of gringos who filled her front room and yard in what amounted to an informal dinner party. She took pains to buy higher-quality meat and vegetables from across the border, to use bottled water to prepare dishes such as chicken mole or cheese enchiladas, and to fix stacks of flour tortillas by hand. During dinner, she jumped around like a bird, making sure everyone was fed, all the while talking in loud, clear Spanish, sometimes stepping outside for a cigarette, and, through a translator, regaling guests with her survival stories. She told several groups about the time a flood of water ran into her house from the house behind her. Instead of getting mad, she sat on her bed, took off her shoes, let her feet splash in the water, and raised her arms to thank God for letting her play like a little kid.

Through Borderlinks, Yolanda met several American journalists, including me, and we became friends. I came to know both her cheerful, optimistic side that loved God and her fearful, depressed side that appeared from time to time. Yolanda has an expressive face, sparkling eyes, and a wide smile, but her deeply lined skin and bad teeth mark her as poor. After I got to know her, I learned her husband had almost knocked her teeth out years before, and she never had been able to afford to get them fixed. She always made me feel at home when I went to visit her, and I reciprocated by inviting her to come stay with me in Tucson. Hesitant but excited about this new direction in her life, she accepted. On weekends we went around to yard sales and thrift stores, buying clothes, shoes, kitchen utensils, and other items she could re-sell to her neighbors. People often gave her stuff for free, and she was effusively grateful. "I think God is making up to me for all the suffer-ings of my childhood," she said after one large haul.

Yolanda also had a large network of friends in Nogales, and in the summer of 1997, one of them gave her another terreno in a new colonia a couple of miles west of Los Encinos. She began clearing the land and collecting materials to build a little house, just as she had done ten years before. One day around sunset I went out to where she, Bobbi, and some of their neighbors from Los Encinos were working on the new terreno. The property was nothing more than a sliver of dirt wedged between the road and a steep gully thick with mesquite and scrub oak trees. Yolanda and the others had leveled the ground with shovels and a wheelbarrow, and shored up the slope with several rows of old tires. I saw other families building homes on the surrounding hillsides, some quite nice, although the area was not yet densely settled and still had the feel of open country. Yolanda was tired but happy as we stood on the top of the hill and watched night fall and lights come on in the city to the east. "I'd like to rent my other house and move out here," she said. "It's clean, it's peaceful, and I have room for a real garden." I didn't mention that there was no water.

As it turned out, Yolanda found an even better use for the land. Bobbi, then seventeen, was dating her first serious boyfriend, a quiet twenty-one-year-old man named Gil whom she'd met at Delta. Yolanda had successfully defended her daughter's virtue from all the tomcats of the neighborhood and was anxious for Bobbi to find a decent young man so she could, as Yolanda said, "leave this house dressed in white." Gil was a good worker, he apparently didn't drink and wasn't violent, and he seemed to really love Bobbi. When he proposed, about six months after the couple met, both Bobbi and Yolanda were thrilled. Yolanda immediately began preparing for an elaborate, formal ceremony to which she would invite four hundred guests. She wouldn't hear of suggestions from some of her American friends that the wedding be small or, God forbid, potluck. With the help of everyone she knew, she managed to collect enough to have invitations printed, rent a hall, order food and a wedding cake, and buy a beautiful lace gown for Bobbi as well as a slinky mother-of-the-bride dress for herself. All in all, the wedding probably cost more than one thousand dollars. As her present to the young couple, Yolanda gave them the new terreno, and Gil, with help from his family, built a little two-room pallet house on it for his bride.

The wedding took place on a sweltering afternoon in July 1998. Yolanda had tried to contact El Gordo to tell him, but he never called back. If Bobbi was hurt by his rejection, she didn't show it. A few days before the wedding, Yolanda also had a fight with Elias, who was supposed to stand in as Bobbi's father, so he made himself scarce during the big event. Bobbi's older brother Ramiro ended up walking her down the aisle. The ceremony took place at the Church of the Purest Conception, on the main square downtown right next to the border. Smiling radiantly from behind the veil, her round face framed by long, dark corkscrew curls, Bobbi was the picture of virginal innocence. Gil wore formal cowboy attire with bolo tie, eelskin boots, and a white straw hat

Bobbi leaves her mother's house in Los Encinos on her wedding day.

that looked striking against his dark skin. At the altar, the couple kneeled before the priest, linked by a white cord called a *lazo* that symbolized their union. The priest's marital advice was the high point of the brief, solemn service. "You must never yell at your wife," he warned Gil, "unless it's to say, 'Sit down while I mop the floor!'" After the ceremony, the couple walked together down a side aisle to present Bobbi's bouquet to a statue of the Virgin of Guadalupe. The church was less than half full, and I wondered where the four hundred guests were. They didn't show up until five or six hours later, when the reception at the cavernous Moroco nightclub along the railroad tracks finally got rolling. Dozens and dozens of sharply dressed young men and women, many carrying beer, appeared at the door, so many that the bouncers had to check invitations. By midnight, the place was packed. A DJ played Mexican top forty, *norteños, conjuntos, cumbias,* and *rancheras,* and everyone danced, men with women, women with women, and men with men. Gil, wearing his white straw hat, remained sober and taciturn as he and Bobbi two-stepped around the floor. Friends and family members came up and pinned dollar bills to his jacket, and soon he had a string of money hanging from him like a tail.

After the wedding, the couple moved into the house Gil had built for them in Las Torres. The floor was raw dirt, the roof leaked, and there was no electricity or water, but Bobbi was delighted in her honeymoon cottage, surrounded by all the wedding presents, new glasses and dishes and pots and pans. When I went to visit about a month after her wedding, she told me she was thinking of postponing her first child and going back to work. She said she wanted to study English so she could make more money. Gil had a new job at Hasta Mex, owned by Otis Elevator and one of the better maquilas in town, where he was making seventy pesos (then seven dollars) a day, but Bobbi wanted to get electricity in the house—it would cost five hundred pesos to bring in a line—and water, maybe, before having a child.

Yolanda, however, had other ideas. "To have one is no big deal, and it's important to make sure everything is working properly," she told me, and then related a story about a cousin who had used birth control and later was unable to have children. Gil also wanted a baby right away. Even the doctor at the social security hospital advised Bobbi against contraception, saying, "You got married to have children, right?" Under pressure from him, her mother, and her husband, Bobbi gave up. Within two months of her wedding, she was pregnant.

Yolanda was relieved to throw herself into helping Bobbi get ready for the baby. With her youngest child out of the house, she had been feeling out of sorts, unaccustomed to concentrating only on herself. She seemed resigned to her relationship with Elias. "I'll stick with him out of inertia because that's the way life is, but my heart, my woman's heart, is dead. Life obligated me to think more about being a mother than a woman, anyway." She spent time reading the Bible and listening to religious music on her boom box. "For me, the first solution was to seek God. The second was to leave my pueblo and come here to Nogales, where I found tranquility and my future. I still don't have a peso, but I have a lot of affection, and the worries that used to obsess me—like what I was going to eat tomorrow—aren't that bad anymore."

Throughout the fall and winter, both Yolanda and Bobbi were giddy with anticipation over the baby. "It's all she talks about," Yolanda said. "It used to be, when I came home from the yard sales, she'd ask, 'What did you get me?' Now it's, 'What did you get the baby?'" Old women in the neighborhood told Bobbi they could tell it was a boy from the way she was carrying, and Gil made no secret of the fact that he wanted a son. At the Otis Christmas party, the expectant couple posed for pictures, glowing with pride, with Bobbi turned sideways to show her rounded stomach.

On January 15, Yolanda took Bobbi to the public hospital for a checkup. Bobbi had complained that she was having to pee constantly, which Yolanda assured her was normal, but both women were concerned as they waited for the appointment. The technician did the ultrasound and said that the baby was a girl who seemed to be progressing normally. Then Yolanda saw a funny look cross his face. "Doctor, what's the matter?" He excused himself, came back in with another doctor, and they checked the ultrasound again. Yolanda followed them out of the room. "There's something wrong with the placenta," they said. It wasn't big enough, so the baby was suffering and going to die; there was nothing they could do about it. All day Friday, as Bobbi's and Gil's families assembled at the hospital, Yolanda was in a daze, pacing the halls or sitting on the steps out front, smoking cigarettes. Evening fell. The doctors said the baby was dead, and they were going to induce a miscarriage. Bobbi was in labor the entire night, while all around her in the maternity ward, she could hear the cries of healthy children being born. As dawn broke, she finally gave birth to a five-month-old fetus. Gil held the perfectly formed baby in his hand and said a prayer as the little girl's mouth fell open, and she emitted a tiny sigh.

Yolanda was beside herself. At first, she believed the baby was born alive—that the doctors had induced labor and killed the baby by mistake. She also blamed the hospital for not giving Bobbi an ultrasound appointment in December, when perhaps the problem could have been detected and remedied. "Maybe if we didn't have to go to the poor people's hospital, things would have been different." After a while, she calmed down and accepted that the child had, in fact, been born dead. She decided the loss was no one's fault and that, for whatever reason, God hadn't wanted this baby to be born.

Bobbi recovered more quickly than Yolanda. When I saw her at her in-laws' house the Monday after the miscarriage, she was sad, but not crying as Yolanda and Guadalupe were. She was in bed, and though in pain, she was still able to giggle in amazement at her swollen, rock-hard breasts that were beginning to leak milk. After she recovered, Bobbi went back to the public hospital and went on birth control, as she had wanted to do before. She and Yolanda agreed she should wait a year (Bobbi told me she wanted to wait two) for her body to mature, for her and Gil to get to know each other and to prepare their home for a baby. In the spring, she went back to work, this time at a new maquila that made dentures, where Lupe also worked. She liked her job and with the money she made was able to install electricity in her house. She was still sad about losing the baby, especially around Mother's Day and the day the little girl was supposed to have been born. At the same time, she seemed relieved to be able to enjoy being a teenager a little while longer. "Don't worry, Mommy," she reassured Yolanda. "Next time I'll have twins."

CHAPTER 2

Living Is For Everyone

When I first met Jimmy Teyechea, he opened his front door and scowled at me. It was a bright, chilly morning in February 1994, and I was yet another reporter pestering the cancer-stricken man about his outspoken activism against environmental pollution in Nogales, Arizona. His mother had forgotten to give him the message I was coming. "I can't see you now," he said. "Come back later." Evidently having gotten out of bed to answer the door, Jimmy was wearing pajamas, and his hair was mussed. I had heard he could be difficult, and from his hunched over, wasted appearance, he was obviously ill. Still, I needed the interview. I gave him an hour to collect himself, and when I came back, he was a transformed man. He'd showered, combed his hair, and put on jeans and a Mickey Mouse sweatshirt. We spent the rest of the morning together, and he could not have been more gracious. Jimmy said that when he had been diagnosed with cancer four years before, doctors had given him only a year to live. He had outlasted their predictions, he believed, because he had found his purpose. "The battle is not between living and dying," he told me. "The battle is to give meaning to life."

The first thing Jimmy wanted to do was take me on a tour of Carrillo Street. He put on sunglasses and, leaning heavily on a cane, led me out the front door past a small magnolia tree in the yard to the curb. The street was a typical American cul-de-sac, lined with ranch-style homes and neatly trimmed trees and bushes. "Over here," Jimmy said, pointing to a house across from his own, "we have Mr. Bachelier, who died of myeloma. His twenty-three-year-old son died of leukemia. And down here," he said, shuffling forward, "is Jesse Partida, who's got throat cancer." We crossed Martinez Street and started up the block while Jimmy listed the names of victims and the types of cancer in each house. There were fourteen cases in all, at least one in half of the eighteen homes on Carrillo Sreet, and that didn't include the ones around the corner on Martinez. After about ten minutes, Jimmy was exhausted and wanted to return home. He was gaunt and pale, and out here in the bright light, his once-luxurious hair—"my sister used to be so jealous of me"—looked thin and wispy. We walked slowly back to the house.

In the living room of his childhood home, Jimmy showed me a pin map he'd help make to indicate the extent of disease in Nogales, as well as his scrapbook of clippings about environmental problems on the border. We talked about how getting cancer had changed his life. Jimmy had been a produce broker making a six-figure income, a party guy and a jock with a reputation for caring mostly about himself. He told me that in those days, he had thought nothing of farmworkers as he crossed their picket lines to buy grapes. "Where they slept, what they ate, whether they were being poisoned by pesticides were of no concern to me," he said. "It never hit me people were dying."

In the fall of 1989, it hit him. Jimmy was in Mexico, checking on produce in the field, when he offered to help stack crates of cucumbers that had rotted and were going to be thrown away. As he worked, fermenting cucumber juice seeped inside a broken blister on his palm, but because there was no clean water near the field, he had to wait until evening to wash up. By that time, the blister was infected. Jimmy came home to Nogales with a 105-degree fever and a bright red streak running from his wrist to his armpit. He checked into Holy Cross, the hospital where he had been born, with blood poisoning so severe it took eight days to bring it under control. Dr. George Comerci, Jimmy's internist, was surprised at the extent of infection in such a young and apparently healthy man, and he ordered a series of tests. The results were devastating. At age forty, Jimmy was diagnosed with an unusual form of cancer called multiple myeloma.

Myeloma is a type of leukemia or blood cancer that occurs when one of the cells in the bone marrow, which the body uses to manufacture blood, goes haywire and starts multiplying out of control. It rarely strikes people as young as Jimmy, and he was curious about what could have caused it. He had been a drinker and a smoker, but Dr. Comerci told him these habits are not associated with myeloma. His work in produce may have exposed him to pesticides, but, again, the doctor didn't think the exposure was high enough over a long enough period to do damage. "We really don't know what causes myeloma," Dr. Comerci said. Jimmy wasn't satisfied with that answer. He knew something had caused it, and he believed if he just looked hard enough, he could find out what.

At first, Jimmy didn't suspect an environmental link. For two years after his diagnosis, he had enough problems just keeping himself alive. He was of Basque ancestry and nothing if not stubborn, but he had some major trials in store. His wife divorced him, he lost his job, and he had to move back home with his parents on Carrillo Street. Not only was he sick all the time from the chemotherapy, but in 1991, when the drugs began to fail, he was forced to undergo a grueling and still-experimental transplant of his own bone marrow. Through months of intravenous chemotherapy that wiped out his immune system, he endured long stays at the hospital in Tucson and thousands of needle jabs. Jimmy was both a playful and combative patient, sometimes refusing to have his blood drawn or wearing a fake nose and glasses as he walked up and down the halls of the hospital, chatting and joking with other patients. One night, he played a trick on one of the nurses. Pretending to be asleep when she showed up to check his heart, he waited until she had hooked up the last lead to the monitor and then, as she turned to flip the switch, started jerking violently. The nurse almost fainted.

By the spring of 1992, Jimmy had recovered enough from the transplant to begin reaching out to other cancer victims and their families. At the hospital in Nogales, he met Sylvia Montañez, a widow whose

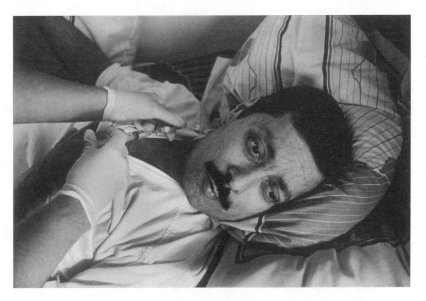

Jimmy Teyechea receives treatment for cancer at his home in Nogales, Arizona.

forty-three-year-old husband had died of renal cell cancer, and the two of them began dating. They went to church together at Sacred Heart each evening, and he called her at work every morning to tell her a joke. (Jimmy loved cancer jokes, such as this one by Henny Youngman: A guy goes to the doctor, learns he has cancer. The doctor gives him six months to live. The guy says, "But doc, I can't pay your bill in that time." So the doctor says, "Okay, I'll give you another six months.") Jimmy also loved to visit children, such as little Michelle Ramirez, a leukemia victim whose mother, Susan Thomas Ramirez, had been one of his childhood friends. He spent many hours with Michelle and with another boy, Fernando Espinoza, who'd been battling leukemia since he was four years old. Jimmy and Fernie passed the time trading jokes, talking about baseball, and keeping each other's spirits up. After one visit, Fernie told his mother, "Don't be so sad. I'm going to get well."

Although estranged from his own teenage son, Jimmy was extremely close to his daughter, Liana. He took "Shorty," as he called her, fishing with him at Patagonia Lake, his IV bottle hooked on a nearby tree. They played catch in the yard, and he accompanied her on guitar while she sang. He videotaped her school plays and recitals, and she wrote poems and letters to him. "I was a major, big-time daddy's girl," Liana said. The day I met him, Jimmy talked about how proud he was of his daughter and showed me a letter she had written a few years before, when she was ten. She had gone door to door, reading the letter and asking neighbors to donate a dime each to help with Jimmy's cancer treatment. "This is for all the sick people in the world. I know how hard it must be in a lonely, dark room where you are all alone. But actually you are not alone. God and Jesus are right there with you, taking care of you. Sometimes when you were the best you can be, God will take you to heaven where you will suffer no longer. When it's time to leave, say to yourself, 'God, I'm glad I got to live. I'm thankful you gave me life.' When you're sick, just remember what I'm telling you, never lose hope in yourself! Thank you."

Jimmy looked at me with his intense "frog" eyes, as Liana called them. "The world has to know what's happening in Nogales," he said quietly. "I'm speaking for the twelve-year-old kid I just visited who's got leukemia. I'm speaking for friends of mine who've died. What I want to know is, after I'm gone, who will speak for me?"

To look at Carrillo Street, you would never suspect there was anything wrong. Surrounded by a quiet neighborhood about a mile north of the border and a few blocks west of the Nogales Wash, it was one of the nicest streets in Nogales, Arizona. Jimmy's father, a decorated World War II veteran, was one of a number of returning soldiers who had built homes here in the 1950s. The new subdivison occupied the grounds of the former Camp Little, a U.S. Army fort that had been established in 1910 to protect the town during the Mexican Revolution. Jimmy had enjoyed an idyllic youth in this apparently clean, safe place. His childhood friend Susan Thomas Ramirez grew up closer to the border—her parents owned the old Montezuma Hotel and bar on Morley Avenue—and recalled how clean Nogales was in the 1950s and 1960s. It never occurred to her there might be a time bomb here.

Changes in the local environment were imperceptible until the 1980s, when residents began to notice that the once clear blue skies were turning yellow and brown. Prevailing winds blow south to north, and as cross-border trade and population on the Mexican side boomed throughout the decade, air pollution on the U.S. side gradually worsened. By the early 1990s, tests showed that on some days tiny Nogales had the worst air in Arizona, even worse than Phoenix, a city of more than two million that frequently violated federal air-quality standards. Every few weeks, the dump in Nogales, Sonora —which lay three miles south of the border—caught fire, and the stench of burning tires, plastic, and garbage filled the air. The smoke stung people's throats and eyes, and forced school officials to cancel outdoor activities. The air was especially bad in winter, when exhaust from hundreds of produce trucks waiting to cross the border shrouded the valley like a fog, held in place by the cold air overhead.

Although the air was as bad or worse on the Mexican side, the chief environmental and public health concerns—here as well as all along the border—were the inadequate water and wastewater systems. By the mid-1980s, the Nogales Wash flowed almost year round with wastewater from thousands of hillside shacks and outhouses as well as with the contents of many leaky, broken water·and sewer pipes. During rainstorms, runoff from the hillsides and overflow from the sewers ran into the wash, and tons of sewage- and garbage-filled water coursed into the United States. In 1990, after dozens of cases of hepatitis were reported in Nogales, Arizona, Santa Cruz County officials declared the water in the wash to be a public health threat. The U.S. government installed a chlorinator at the entrance to the tunnels on the Mexican side, which worked to kill bacteria before the water flowed into the United States. Of course, the chlorinator had no effect at all on the numerous metals, solvents, petroleums, and other hazardous wastes in the wash runoff.

The first sign of widespread industrial contamination of the Nogales Wash came in 1986, when the Arizona Department of Health

A woman walks on the U.S. side of the border as smoke that smells of burning plastic pours over the wall from Nogales, Sonora.

Services found high levels of toxins including trichloroethane, tetrachloroethane (PCE), chloroform, and trichloroethylene (TCE) in the water. Subsequent tests found high levels of lead, cyanide, mercury, chromium, copper, and other metals. In 1988, testing of wells along the wash found a plume of industrial solvents—including many of those found in the surface water—contaminating the groundwater for at least several miles north of the border. At the time, there were at least one hundred private wells along the wash on the Arizona side, plus an untold number on the Mexican side. Most of these wells were still in use by homes and businesses, including produce warehouses that shipped fruits and vegetables all over the country. In the late 1980s and again in 1994, the Santa Cruz County Health Department cautioned private well owners in Nogales, Arizona, not to drink or prepare food with the water, but it had no authority to shut down the wells and no way of knowing how many residents heeded the warning.

For Susan Thomas Ramirez, that warning came too late. In the mid-1980s, she and her family lived in a house along the Nogales Wash that was served by a private well. Susan drank water from the well while pregnant with her youngest child, Michelle. In 1987, the little girl, then only eighteen months old, was diagnosed with leukemia. Susan talked to her neighbors and learned that some of them also had cancer. Beginning to suspect the water, she had her well tested, and although the results came back clean, she still had doubts. The wells along the wash are shallow—fifty feet or less—and contaminants can appear and disappear quickly.

Susan and her family moved to another part of town, but after what had happened, she wondered if the water was safe anywhere in Nogales. She did some research and found that most of the public drinking water came from presumably safe wells along the Santa Cruz River five miles east of town. Yet she was alarmed to learn that, during droughts, the city had used wells along the wash to supplement its supply until at least the mid-1980s. Even more disturbing was her discovery that private water companies serving thousands of local residents continued to pump water from wells along the wash, as did the city of Nogales, Sonora. Susan began to speak out about the water at meetings and conferences and to anyone who would listen, including Jimmy Teyechea.

After talking with Susan Thomas Ramirez, Jimmy had his family switch to bottled water, but he still wasn't convinced there was an environmental link to his cancer. Then, in early 1992, while sitting in his living room on Carrillo Street, he made the connection. Multiple myeloma is supposed to be a relatively uncommon cancer. In a town the size of Nogales, the expected number of cases would be about one per year, yet the man across the street had died of myeloma. Around the corner, another man was suffering from the same disease, and the woman who lived in the house on the other side of the Teyechea's backyard fence had just been diagnosed with it. "Four cases of a rare form of cancer in this little two-block area," Jimmy told his mother. "That's too many. Something's going on here."

With the same tenacity he had brought to fighting his illness, Jimmy began to pursue the possibility of a disease cluster in Nogales. He and Sylvia went down to the local mortuary and spent several weeks examining 1,000 death certificates dating back to 1986. Four hundred gave no cause of death, but of the remaining 600, 290 listed cancer. The figure fueled Jimmy's suspicion that something was seriously wrong. He talked about his findings with Dr. Comerci and learned that the doctor also was concerned. Comerci had counted at least thirteen people—more than twice the expected number—who had either died from or been diagnosed with pancreatic cancer in Nogales, Arizona, during the late 1980s. Eight of those victims lived in the neighborhood of Noon and McNab Streets, on a ridge overlooking Carrillo Street that also had been part of the old Camp Little grounds.

Through Susan, Jimmy met Anna Acuña, another Nogales native alarmed about what was going on. Anna had been keeping a list of people in town with lupus, an autoimmune disease of unknown origin that usually strikes women and can cause painful weakening of the joints and damage to the kidneys and nervous system. Herself a lupus sufferer, Anna already had more than two dozen names on the list just from asking friends and neighbors. Jimmy, Susan, and Anna began meeting and sharing the material they had gathered. "It was amazing," Anna said. "We had all this information, but we didn't know what to do with it. It was kind of scary." They talked about what could be causing the diseases. Could it be, as Susan believed, the water? Or was it, as Anna believed, the air? It had to be something relatively recent because the illnesses had begun showing up only in the previous decade or so. Using a map of Nogales, they decided to plot the deaths they had recorded to see if a pattern emerged.

In November 1992, Jimmy, Anna, and Susan invited a dozen friends and neighbors to Anna's house to help make the map. They used different colored pins to mark the homes of victims: yellow for pancreatic cancer, red for blood cancers such as leukemia and multiple myeloma, orange for ovarian cancer, black for lupus, and green for other forms of cancer. By the time they finished late in the evening, the map was covered with pins. Although the pins revealed no clear pattern, most were clustered in neighborhoods near downtown and along the wash.

The map-making session became front-page news in the *Nogales International* and proved to be a turning point. Scores of people who were sick or whose family members were sick or dead from cancer or lupus began calling and coming to meetings. All were relieved to share their suffering and excited about the possibility of finding answers. Jimmy christened the new organization LIFE—Living Is For Everyone—and encouraged its members to let others know they weren't alone. He told a story about one cancer victim he'd visited who'd told him, "'You know, I didn't go by to see this man, and I didn't go by to see you, but what the hell, nobody came to see me either.' That's what this group is about, trying to change that."

The organization also had another, more contentious purpose. After discovering the extent of environmental contamination in Nogales, Jimmy, Anna, Susan, and other LIFE members had become convinced that pollution—not genes or lifestyle or God or fate—had made them sick. They founded LIFE not only to support each other, but to push scientists to find the cause of their diseases and, most of all, to demand environmental cleanup. Confronting and stopping polluters was, in Jimmy's mind, the group's main purpose, and he vowed to do that any way he could. "Jimmy didn't care who he pissed off," said his friend and fellow produce broker Glenn Saavedra. "He wanted to bust things up."

Right from the start, LIFE stirred up controversy. Local civic and business leaders, worried about bad publicity and anxious not to upset their counterparts in Nogales, Sonora, refused to meet with the group. Arizona state officials also dismissed LIFE's concerns by insisting that the claim that pollution was causing disease in Nogales didn't stand up to scientific scrutiny. "This is part of what the public has a gross misconception about," said Dr. Tim Flood, head of the Arizona Office of Chronic Disease Epidemiology. "The evidence is very poor that a contaminated general environment is associated with cancer."

Flood even doubted that the disease rates in Nogales were extraordinary. He pointed out the cancer death rate in Santa Cruz County was 142 for 100,000 residents in 1990, less than Arizona's overall rate of 185, and that the county's mortality rates for breast, prostate, and cervical cancer were no higher than average.

Despite the rebuff from public officials and experts such as Dr. Flood, LIFE's evidence of high rates of cancer and lupus in Nogales piqued the interest of two scientists at the University of Arizona. Doctors Joel Meister and Larry Clark met with the group and, impressed with the amount of work Jimmy, Anna, and Susan already had done, agreed to investigate further. Clark used LIFE's figures to make some preliminary calculations and found that rates of lupus, multiple myeloma, and leukemia in Nogales did appear higher than they should be. The two scientists said they believed the state cancer registry on which Dr. Flood had relied for his data was incomplete and that more study was needed. They proposed that LIFE get together a group of volunteers to start doing a systematic survey of five thousand households in Nogales.

Jimmy was happy and relaxed at the first few meetings. His cancer was in remission, Sylvia had helped him reconcile with his son, and people were beginning to pay attention to health and environmental issues in Nogales. Getting sick "took all the pressure off," he told one reporter. "If this were my last night on Earth, I'd pop some popcorn and watch a video of *The Evil Dead* or *The Attack of the Killer Tomatoes* with my kids." That same fall, Jimmy was asked to be master of ceremonies at his twenty-fifth high school reunion. Before his diagnosis, he had shunned such events, but this time he eagerly accepted.

The night of the reunion, Jimmy walked easily by himself to the podium. His hair and beard had grown back full and thick since the transplant, and he looked tall and handsome in his best white suit with a dark shirt and tie. At first, he joked about his predicament. One bad thing about having cancer, he noted, is getting people to repay money you've loaned them. "And if you think that's hard, try getting someone to loan you any." He teased classmates who had donated platelets to him, especially one whose nickname in high school had been El Grano (the pimple). "For a week afterward, I was standing in front of the mirror, popping zits." Then Jimmy turned philosophical. Cancer, he said, had taught him to live unconditionally. "It's not our job to turn life into what we want it to be. We can't do that. We don't have that kind of power. What life is about is trying to learn something from each event we're faced with and then in turn passing that on to others. 'Unconditional life' means letting go of things, and breaking their hold over us. When we do that, we can take our heart and give it to the people who really matter. All in all," he concluded, having cancer was "an absolutely amazing experience. I don't regret it, and there's nothing about it I would give back if I could."

As Jimmy collected information, he started a scrapbook of articles about environmental contamination in Nogales and elsewhere on the border. It was not a pretty picture. In 1990, journalist Sandy Tolan had taken water samples from a manhole near the industrial park in Nogales, Sonora, for his *New York Times Magazine* article about the maquiladora industry. The results showed dangerously high levels of toluene, xylene, benzene, and other carcinogens. That same year, an environmental group called the National Toxics Campaign took another sample from the spot where the former Coin-Art *maquila,* now owned by United Musical Instruments (UMI), discharged wastewater into the street. The water was found to contain sixty-six times the safe standard for copper and three hundred times the standard for chromium.

These samples, Jimmy was convinced, were the tip of a toxic iceberg. "They've been dumping for twenty years," he said. "I shudder to think what's over there." Since 1983, all *maquiladoras* were supposed to account for hazardous materials used in manufacturing and to return any waste to its country of origin, usually the United States, but studies done in the late 1980s and early 1990s found that only 30 percent of maquiladoras tracked their waste, and only 20 percent could prove they were complying with the law. Properly disposing of hazardous waste cost several hundred dollars a barrel, giving company officials a strong incentive to look the other way when someone offered to do it for less. One of Jimmy's friends who lived in Nogales during the early 1990s, Phil Bernake, said he witnessed routine dumping during the eighteen years he worked in the maquiladoras. "I saw 3,500 gallons of hazardous waste liquid, a slurry, go down the drain three to four times a week," Bernake said. "As long as the supervisor says, 'Yes boss, I took care of it; it was done right,' that's all they want to know."

Many maquiladoras relied on private hauling firms to dispose of their waste, which they then blamed when problems occurred. In one case in Ciudad Juárez in the late 1980s, rocks covered with Kaltex, an industrial solvent, turned up in the city dump. The chemical was traced to Outboard Marine de Mexico, a maquiladora that made parts for Johnson and Evinrude outboard engines. Company officials said their waste had been dumped "by accident." Several parents said their children were brain damaged from sniffing rocks covered with the bright-green solvent. In another case, after a small explosion in a Tijuana sewer line in 1993, investigators went to a nearby industrial park to check on a waste-recycling firm. They found the owner and two workers pouring chemicals down the drain, something they apparently had been doing for years. The industrial park sits on Otay Mesa, above a *colonia* of maquiladora workers called Chilpancingo that had experienced a rise in anencephalic births—babies born with missing or partially formed brains.

In fact, as Jimmy learned, cases of anencephaly were appearing all over the border. In Nogales, Sonora, there were two cases in 1990, six in 1991, and nine in 1992, alarming local doctors and prompting health officials to initiate a study. Although the study found the rate was in keeping with local population increases, Jimmy and Sylvia consulted some Mexican doctors who questioned the validity of the findings. They said health statistics in Mexico are notoriously inaccurate and that bad news is frequently suppressed, especially when delicate political issues, such as the approval of the North American Free Trade Agreement (NAFTA), are at stake. Nevertheless, at a conference in El Paso in 1993, researchers reported four- to tenfold rises in anencephaly throughout Mexico. Anencephaly and related defects were also occurring among women who lived on the U.S. side. In 1991, a Nogales, Arizona, resident named Patreese Randall, who lived in a house along the wash and had drunk water from a private well while pregnant, gave birth to a boy whose brain was only partially formed on the right side. The boy was blind in his right eye, paralyzed on the left side of his body, and suffered seizures. In Brownsville, Texas, across the Rio Grande from Matamoros, dozens of anencephalics were born in the early 1990s, including three in a thirty-six-hour period in the spring of 1991.

Since ancient times, anencephaly has been considered a harbinger of evil, and its presence on the border was not lost on environmentalists. Birth defects had been appearing among children born to maquiladora workers for decades; most notably, at least twenty children of women who worked at Mallory Capacitors in Matamoros in the 1970s had been born with severe mental and physical handicaps. It was not far-fetched to presume a link between the maquiladoras and the general rise in anencephaly on the border, even among children whose mothers had never worked in the factories. Matamoros was home to several pesticide-producing maquiladoras owned by Union Carbide, DuPont, Stepan Chemical, and others, that had been found to be discharging hazardous chemicals into the air and nearby waterways. When anencephaly began appearing in Brownsville, the Texas Department of Health launched an investigation to determine the cause and to see if a link could be made between birth defects and environmental pollution. Families of twenty-eight anencephalic children, meanwhile, didn't need a study to know who to blame. They filed a class-action suit against the Matamoros maquiladoras.

In the early 1990s, as debate over NAFTA focused attention on the border environment, the Mexican government stepped up its oversight of the maquiladoras. Some companies were fined or closed temporarily, and a few, such as General Motors, Mexico's largest foreign employer, announced tougher pollution control measures. But Mexico did not have the resources to police all of the more than two thousand foreign-owned firms operating on the border, and the few government inspectors who did oversee maquiladora operations tended to work closely with company officials. The inspector in Nogales, for example, had his office donated by a maquiladora. Violations and fines, if any, were not made public, and independent observers were not allowed access to companies or their records. Jimmy and others remained convinced that, regardless of the Mexican government's claims, poverty and corruption prevented meaningful enforcement of the country's environmental laws. "When I worked over there as a produce broker," Jimmy often said, "I never had a problem I couldn't solve with a hundred-dollar bill."

Maquiladora managers in Nogales, Sonora, were outraged at the suggestion that they were responsible for cancer and lupus across the border. "Why would I dump something in the ground that's going to run to where I live in Rio Rico?" asked Lewis Mitchell, chairman of the environmental committee of the Nogales Maquiladora Association. Mitchell said that his company, Alcatel—a French-owned firm that made telephone transmission equipment—accounted for all hazardous materials, returned to the United States everything that originated in the United States, sampled its air and water discharges twice a year, and was subject to surprise inspections. He said all the other maquiladoras in Nogales did the same, adding, "We don't have anything to hide here."

Mitchell had his own ideas about what was causing the diseases in Nogales. As he pointed out, there were many other potential pollution sources in town besides the maquiladoras, including paint shops, print shops, beauty shops, dry cleaners, and gas stations that had sprung up over the years along the wash on both sides of the border. Some of these businesses operated with little or no environmental concern. In May 1991, workers at one of the gas stations on the Mexican side dumped hundreds of gallons of oil into the wash, which caught fire, requiring the evacuation of several blocks of downtown Nogales, Sonora. The railroad, whose tracks and switching yards had run right along the wash since before Nogales was built, was almost certainly a major suspect. By the early 1990s, several hundred train cars a day passed through town, many of which carried hazardous materials. Leaks and spills were common. In 1993, five serious incidents occurred on the U.S. side alone, including one in November when tankers leaking ammonium sulfide sickened several railroad workers and forced a two-day evacuation of downtown schools and stores. A derailment on the Mexican side in early 1994 also forced an evacuation.

Serious problems were also coming to light on the U.S. side of the border, specifically at the UMI factory in Potrero Hills. Susan Thomas Ramirez told me about a revealing horseback-riding excursion in 1987, the same year her daughter was diagnosed with leukemia. As she came over a hill, she looked down and was surprised to see a large, fluorescent green pond in the area behind UMI. Company officials later admitted they had been dumping metals and solvents for decades. "When we dumped it out the back door, we didn't know any better," one said. The Arizona Department of Environmental Quality (ADEQ) investigated and found an underground plume of TCE-tainted water moving from beneath the factory toward a public water well in Potrero Hills.

After listing the many suspects he felt could be the causes of illness in Nogales, Lewis Mitchell told me he personally believed Camp Little was the source of the cancer cluster on Carrillo Street. Rumors had persisted over the years that the camp had been used as a chemical and munitions dump, and that military canisters and materials had been unearthed during the building of new subdivisions. According to Jimmy's mom, when she and Jimmy's father built their house in the 1950s, the rumors were of buried treasure, not munitions. "We looked for it when we dug holes for trees and bushes," Anita Teyechea said. "Of course, we never found anything." Tests of dirt on Carrillo Street and other nearby sites showed no contamination, and Jimmy and other

LIFE members pointed out that diseases had been found all over town, not just on the former Camp Little grounds.

Still, Jimmy was disturbed by the revelations about UMI and Camp Little, and he recognized that toxic dumping was not confined to the maquiladoras or to Mexico. He had read about industrial contamination in Love Canal, New York, and in Woburn, Massachusetts; also, he and other LIFE members had met with cancer victims from the south side of Tucson whose drinking water had been poisoned by TCE dumped by Hughes Aircraft and the U.S. Air Force, among others. Jimmy believed that the situation in Nogales was a harbinger of things to come. "We have maquiladoras all over the place," he said. "We call them Ford and General Motors. In five, ten years, this will be all over the nation. People who right now are able to say, 'It's not my problem,' well, it will be tomorrow."

As 1993 began, Jimmy received some bad news. The bone marrow transplant had failed, and the cancer was back. This time, it had spread throughout his body. Jimmy kept visiting people, and he tried to keep his spirits up. But as the year went on and his energy ebbed, his enthusiasm and optimism turned increasingly to anger.

In the spring, LIFE recruited and trained about fifty volunteers to conduct a health survey in Nogales. The work had barely begun when the group had a falling out with the scientists. Doctors Joel Meister and Larry Clark had written a grant proposal calling for a multimillion-dollar, five-year, binational study, and when Jimmy saw it, he blew his stack. He was angry that LIFE had not been asked to help prepare the proposal, and he felt that the study's scope and time frame were too ambitious. The scientists maintained it would take at least five years to do a complete study and that it was crucial to get Mexican cooperation not only to look for possible disease clusters on the other side, but to get the support necessary to identify and clean up pollution sources. "We run grave political risks if Mexico is blamed prematurely," Meister said.

The question of Mexican involvement was a difficult one for LIFE. On one hand, the group had anecdotal evidence of high rates of cancer, lupus, anencephaly, and other serious health problems across the line. On the other, Jimmy and Anna were afraid that involving Mexican public officials would politicize the investigation and turn it into a cover-up. In their experience, Mexico was unlikely to admit a problem existed, even if there was one. Mexican health officials had denied that there were excessive rates of cancer and lupus in Nogales, Sonora, despite the fact that lack of infrastructure and rapid population growth made accurate studies impossible. They were also defensive about the accusation that pollution from Nogales, Sonora, was harming people in Nogales, Arizona. "If it weren't for all the commerce on our side, maybe Nogales, Arizona, wouldn't be here," said Dr. Ernesto Rivera-Claisse, the Sonoran secretary of public health, at one meeting. Susan ruefully agreed: "The maquiladoras are probably what kept this town alive to be killed."

Given the difficulties posed by working binationally, LIFE members decided it would be a waste of time, effort, and resources to attempt to include Nogales, Sonora, in the study. "We're not interested in the contextual and sociopolitical issues," Jimmy wrote in a letter to Meister. "We want to attack the problem. We want to stop our kids from dying." He believed that the scientists "were only asking for a whole lot of money so they could attend meetings and conferences for the next five years." He accused Meister and Clark of being "grant pimps" who were exploiting the suffering of people in Nogales for their own advancements. Meister responded to Jimmy's personal attack by suspending the survey and closing his office to the LIFE group. He called it "the worst experience I ever had in my professional life." Jimmy disagreed with Anna and Susan about what to do next. The two women shared his reservations about the proposed study, but they also felt that LIFE couldn't afford to alienate the few academics who took their concerns seriously. They decided to try to keep working with Meister and Clark; Jimmy, citing his failing health, resigned as president of LIFE.

Despite or because of his resignation, Jimmy became more outspoken than ever. As 1993 went on, his attacks on the scientists, politicians, and maquiladoras began appearing in newspapers and on television in Phoenix and Tucson. He also spoke out against NAFTA, a particularly unpopular position with local civic leaders, given the almost complete dependence of Nogales on binational trade. Most business people in town and all along the border supported NAFTA, arguing that as well as encouraging cross-border commerce, the agreement would bring resources and attention to the region's problems. "We who breathe the air and drink the water along the border are the first to say we support free trade, yet we also want a long-term plan for the environment," said William Joffroy Jr., scion of a prominent local family of customs brokers.

Dismayed by the favorable publicity Jimmy and LIFE were receiving, some Nogales businessmen struck back. The *Nogales Herald,* a conservative weekly, attacked LIFE for making people in Tucson and Phoenix think the town was a toxic waste dump. "The Nogales City Council should protest to Tucson newspapers on continued coverage of slime, dirty air, steel drums, [and] lead in water," one editorial said. "The fact is that Nogales is no better or worse than Tucson itself." The paper also quoted two industrial recruiters warning that "continued talk of Nogales as a 'cancer center' makes the rest of the nation think residents here are mutations." The backlash only fueled Jimmy's anger. "What they're saying is, it's okay for me to die, but it's not okay to hurt business in Nogales."

In his frustration, Jimmy attacked not just the business community, but everyone else in town. "If we fail, it will be because this town doesn't care. People here accept the status quo. It's a prevalent attitude among Hispanics." Jimmy had no patience with the *fatalismo* he perceived among his neighbors. He said folks in Nogales would rather eat a burned steak, complaining about every bite, than send it back to the kitchen. Too many of them, he believed, used their faith as an excuse to do nothing. "They think, 'God gave me cancer, who am I to argue with

Him?' If it's really the water, then we can get mad about it, but if it's God . . . "

Jimmy also became embroiled in the controversy over whether Nogales should support the proposed construction of a steel wall downtown. The year 1993 had seen record numbers of undocumented immigrants being arrested in southern Arizona, and the U.S. government was contemplating how best to stem the tide. Jimmy felt a wall would be preferable to vast increases in the size of the Border Patrol. (As it turned out, Nogales got both.) In April, after a Border Patrol agent stopped him and asked for his citizenship while he was driving to Sylvia's house in Rio Rico, Jimmy sat down and wrote a letter to the *Nogales International.* "A steel fence doesn't chase kids onto school grounds to try to arrest them. A steel fence doesn't abuse anyone's civil or constitutional rights and then arrogantly say, 'Have a nice day.' A steel fence doesn't put bullets from an automatic weapon into anyone's back and then drag the body and make burial plans," he wrote, referring to the 1992 killing of Dario Miranda Valenzuela by Border Patrol agent Michael Elmer. He then went on to call Border Patrol agents "pigs." Jimmy's father, a retired highway patrolman and former Santa Cruz County sheriff, begged him not to send the letter, as did Anna and Susan. "I feared we would not be taken seriously if Jimmy shot his mouth off in another area," Anna said. "I told him, 'Damn it, Jimmy, you're going to die and leave us with this mess you created.'" Jimmy sent the letter anyway.

With the scientific inquiry at a standstill, LIFE beset by infighting, and the backlash against the group mounting, the fall of 1993 could have been a low point for Jimmy. Yet it was around this time that the national media became interested in Nogales. A reporter and photographer from *USA Today* came to do an extensive story, and when the front-page article was published on October 27, it caused a sensation. Anna said that someone went around that morning to every newspaper box in town and removed all copies of *USA Today.* Titled "Nightmare on the Border," the story asked, "What's killing the people of

Nogales, Arizona?" Soon, reporters began calling from all over the world, and television crews from the Discovery Channel, *A Current Affair,* and Gary Collins's *Home* show came to do follow-up stories. In some of the articles that appeared, Carrillo Street was dubbed "Cancer Street" and Nogales "Cancer Town, U.S.A." Jimmy was disgusted. "This is not Cancer Street. This is where I grew up." He was pleased, however, that the nation's attention was turning to Nogales. Maybe now something would be done.

The media attention forced Arizona's state leaders to take action finally. In early December 1993, Governor Fife Symington and Senator John McCain visited Jimmy on Carrillo Street—a meeting Jimmy had long anticipated. On the morning they arrived, however, he was so sick he could barely get out of bed. He was in the bathroom when the governor, senator, their entourages, security men, and a small army of reporters arrived, filling the living room and spilling out into the front yard. As Jimmy emerged from the bathroom, the cameras followed his slow movements toward the governor. He was hunched behind a walker, wearing a blue-and-white track suit and a cap that said "LIFE—Living Is For Everyone." As he reached Symington, he stuck out his hand and said, "Are you here to help, or is this a political parade?"

"I'm here to do whatever I can," Symington said.

The politicians stayed for about an hour, expressing regret for not doing something sooner and promising that the battle had now been joined. Symington told Jimmy that a $100,000 study would begin immediately to confirm the apparently high rates of multiple myeloma, leukemia, and lupus in Nogales. He also said he was forming a binational health task force and pledged to provide more staff and funding for the Arizona cancer registry. He said a preliminary report on the health study would be ready within three months. "This is going to be a new era, believe me."

"I'll believe it when I see it," responded Jimmy.

When Symington and McCain left to visit Jimmy's neighbors and tour the Nogales Wash, Jimmy talked with the reporters who remained.

"I'm mad," he said as tears welled in his eyes. "We've had our lives demeaned and devalued. We've been ignored." He considered the politicians' visit to be "major, big-time grandstanding."

"Toxic contamination is one of the most terrible things I've ever found myself up against. It's actually worse than the cancer. It's not like Hurricane Andrew or the Mississippi River flooding. It's man's inhumanity to man. It's something that shouldn't be."

The long-awaited acknowledgment by the state that the situation was serious did nothing to lessen Jimmy's anger. If anything, it made it worse because the money was going to be used to confirm what he already knew—that Nogales had unusually high numbers of cancer and lupus cases. He, Susan, and Anna believed that the studies were little more than an excuse for the government to do nothing. "They're just throwing money at us to make us shut up," Susan said. "We've been studied to death. We want action."

After NAFTA went into effect in 1994, the U.S. and Mexican governments did begin to take action to clean up the border. The environmental protection agencies of both nations set up binational committees to better coordinate efforts, and several communities, including Ambos Nogales, received grant money to educate people about pollution and health. The Mexican government also tackled some of the most urgent situations, including the burning dump in Nogales, Sonora. In early 1995, the dump was closed, and a new landfill opened far south of town. On the U.S. side, the biggest improvement came when a German firm bought UMI and worked out a deal with the state to clean up the TCE plume. The company also instituted a closed-loop system for the chemicals used in manufacturing.

Although NAFTA did not deal directly with the environmental practices of the maquiladoras, it made some improvements in that area as well. Some of the worst offenders—including the UMI maquila in Nogales, Sonora—were closed, and others took steps to improve their waste-management procedures. Health and safety engineers at a number of factories in Sonora formed a professional association and began holding training sessions; also, several Nogales maquiladoras started working with authorities in Arizona to institute pollution prevention programs and to reduce their use of toxins in manufacturing. Borderwide, U.S. Customs and the U.S. Environmental Protection Agency set up a program to track by computer any hazardous waste shipments going to and coming from the maquiladoras. Many local governments, including that of Nogales, Sonora, began licensing waste haulers. Still, NAFTA made no provisions for cleaning up existing pollution or for cracking down on polluters, and it had only limited authority to investigate charges of lax enforcement. Most oversight of maquiladoras remained on the level of self-reporting. The Customs tracking program, for example, relied on paperwork that maquiladoras and waste haulers filled out themselves. Customs itself only rarely checked the actual number and contents of barrels.

Although action to clean up the border environment was slowly beginning, health and environmental studies launched in the wake of Governor Symington's visit resulted only in frustration. The findings of the $100,000 cancer and lupus study, announced in December 1994, were as Jimmy had predicted. "Ninety-nine percent of reported cancer clusters turn out to be nonconfirmable," Dr. Clark told a gathering of about seventy-five people in the Nogales High School auditorium. "This is an exception." Clark studied five hundred people in Nogales and found twelve cases of multiple myeloma between 1989 and 1993, about two and a half times the expected number. He also found nineteen cases of lupus, almost twice the highest rate of the disease ever recorded. Nogales had ninety-four cases per one hundred thousand; the previous highest documented rate had been fifty-one per one hundred thousand. Clark did not find elevated leukemia rates, although Susan said she heard that leukemia was dropped from the study after problems arose with the data. The study also concluded that although the findings were consistent with exposure to environmental risk factors, no causal connection could be made between the diseases and pollution in Nogales. Interestingly, however, Clark noted that both multiple myeloma and lupus affect the same cell in the blood, and this study was the first to find a "concordance" of the two diseases.

Anna, Susan, and other LIFE members at the meeting were relieved, at least, to know their suspicions had been accurate. Yet their victory felt hollow. "This is the first time in my life I hate saying, 'I told you so,'" Anna said. Then Clarise Pierson, a young woman whose once-vibrant body had been ravaged by lupus, struggled to her feet and practically shouted at Dr. Clark, "We didn't do this, and we don't deserve the consequences. What's going to happen to us?"

In hopes of getting more money and attention for border health, Arizona state officials sent Dr. Clark's work to the federal Centers for Disease Control and Prevention (CDC) in Atlanta. Predictably, the CDC had problems with the study. Experts there said the sample was too small, the conclusions were questionable, and the whole thing needed to be redone. In early 1995, the CDC sent a Spanish-speaking doctor to Phoenix to begin conducting a broader, multiyear survey that compared health problems in several Arizona border towns to those in other communities throughout the state. His work was not expected to be completed until after the turn of the century.

Air and water studies in Ambos Nogales progressed at an equally agonizing pace, vindicating what Jimmy and other LIFE members had said about the perils of working binationally. The ADEQ took air samples in a number of locations in 1994 and 1995, including on Carrillo Street, although three years passed before the results were made public. Researchers said they needed to correlate the data with studies of air pollution sources on the Mexican side, which they could not release without the Mexican government's approval. When the figures were finally released in the summer of 1998, they showed that the air quality had not improved since the dump had been closed. Levels of car and truck exhaust, dust, and smoke from the squatters' camps were as high as ever. The scientists also noted that the air on Carrillo Street was the cleanest they sampled. At the same time, the International

Boundary and Water Commission studied the Nogales Wash and the groundwater beneath it, but also refused to release the results until the Mexican government completed its own study. Under the terms of the 1983 La Paz Agreement, the results of binational studies could not be released unless both governments agreed to do so. Although intended to promote cooperation on the border environment, the agreement essentially allowed government officials to stall the release of scientific data indefinitely, frustrating researchers and local residents who wanted answers. When partial results of the water study were at last revealed, also in the summer of 1998, they only confirmed what three previous studies had shown: that groundwater beneath the Nogales Wash on both sides of the border was contaminated with bacterial and industrial pollutants and not safe to drink.

After years of inquiry and many hundreds of thousands of dollars, the people of Nogales were no closer to knowing what was making them sick. Health experts said the delayed and inconclusive outcome of the studies was not surprising. "I don't think we'll ever know what caused the diseases," Dr. Comerci said. "We think it's a combination of an environmental hit on a genetically susceptible cell. It could have been something that happened many years ago. There are just too many possibilities." The studies were not totally in vain; the scientists and experts did learn from their experience in Nogales. When researchers from the CDC went to the southeast Arizona border town of Douglas to conduct a follow-up lupus study in 1997, they held a number of public meetings before beginning their work. They also agreed to use a portion of the grant money to help pay for their subjects' health care. As one environmentalist said, "Everyone wanted to make sure that what happened in Nogales didn't happen here."

On February 17, 1994, two and a half months after the politicians' visit to Carrillo Street, thousands of gallons of gasoline and diesel fuel spilled into the sewer in Nogales, Sonora. The spill was far more dangerous than previous spills into the Nogales Wash because the sewer system was enclosed, trapping vapors and making an explosion likely. In 1992, a similar spill in the sewer system of Mexico's second-largest city, Guadalajara, had caused an explosion that killed some two hundred people and injured six hundred more. In Nogales, the spill was not detected until the first traces of fuel reached the wastewater treatment plant, eight miles north of the border. By then, miles of sewer line running through Ambos Nogales were filled with petroleum vapors. About five thousand residents on both sides of the line were evacuated, and schools and businesses downtown closed for the day. Mexican authorities conducted an extensive investigation, but the source of the spill was never publicly identified.

As the evacuation was proceeding, Jimmy sat down to write a letter to Governor Symington. He noted that the three-month deadline Symington had announced was almost up and then attacked Dr. Flood, Dr. Clark, and other "burro-craps," as he called them, for squabbling over the $100,000 and for wasting the money on searching for more victims rather than using it to look for an environmental link. After mentioning the spill in the sewer line and another in the Southern Pacific train yard in Rio Rico, Jimmy wrote, "What are we, a damn dumping ground for anyone who wants to? When is something going to be done to stop this travesty? I'll tell you when! When 20 or 30 people are killed, and someone finally initiates a billion dollar lawsuit. That is when it is going to stop. Because here in Nogales, NAFTA opportunities, corporate profits, and plain greed are more important than human life." A week later, when I came to interview him for the *Arizona Republic,* Jimmy showed me the letter to Symington and said he had yet to receive a response.

Jimmy was intrigued by the possibility of suing the Nogales maquiladoras, and he and other LIFE members explored the idea with lawyers who represented families of the anencephalic babies in Brownsville. The lawyers told LIFE that without direct evidence of illegal dumping by specific companies, they had no case. In 1995, these same lawyers won a landmark victory when the maquiladoras in

Matamoros settled out of court for a reported $17 million, despite the fact that the Texas health department study had been unable to establish a link between anencephaly in Brownsville and environmental pollution. It was the first time any U.S. corporation had been made accountable for cross-border pollution, an outcome that thrilled environmentalists and worried maquiladora managers all along the border. "They should not have settled because they didn't do anything wrong, and this makes it look like they did," said Lewis Mitchell of the Nogales Maquiladora Association. As for LIFE's threats to sue the Nogales maquiladoras, Mitchell said he thought that LIFE itself should be sued for slander and defamation.

As March came and the mild Nogales winter turned to spring, Jimmy grew weaker. He could no longer walk, and his ribs became so brittle that he could barely move without one breaking. That month, Anna Acuña had arranged for Jimmy's daughter, Liana, to receive an invitation to a televised "youth conference" with President Clinton in Washington, D.C. Although his family begged him not to, Jimmy was determined to go with her. Sweating and delirious and confined to a wheelchair, he flew to Washington with Sylvia and Liana. When it came time for the conference, Jimmy was too sick to get out of bed, so Sylvia stayed with him in the hotel while Liana went by herself. She wasn't called on while the cameras were rolling, but afterward, during a picture-taking session with Clinton, she spoke up.

"Mr. President, my father is dying of cancer," Liana said. "He was too sick to come here with me today. Lots of other people in Nogales are sick, too. What are you going to do about pollution on the border?"

"That's what NAFTA is for," Clinton replied.

It was late on Sunday night when Jimmy, Sylvia, and Liana returned to Nogales. "As soon as we saw him," said Jimmy's mom, "we knew this was it." His clothes were disheveled, his eyes were glazed, and he could barely speak. His father carried him to bed, where he lay for three days, refusing to go to the hospital. On Wednesday he relented, and his family wrapped him in a blanket, put him in an ambulance, and took him to Holy Cross. Three more days passed during which Jimmy slipped in and out of consciousness. He developed pneumonia, and his breathing grew raspy. Sylvia and other friends came to say goodbye. Jimmy never spoke again, except once. He was restless, and his parents had been holding his hands to keep him from pulling out his catheter. "Let go my goddamn hands!" he cried. Around one in the morning on Saturday, March 26, 1994, Jimmy turned his head and looked into Liana's eyes. A few moments later, as his mother held him in her arms, he died.

At the wake, Jimmy lay in his coffin dressed in his best white suit. His LIFE cap was on his chest, along with some small silk flowers made by Clarise Pierson, each with a tag reading, "Jimmy Found Life." Hundreds of people turned out for the funeral mass at Sacred Heart the next morning, a warm, beautiful Wednesday before Easter. Liana sang "Be Not Afraid" without a single waver in her voice because she knew her father would have wanted her to be brave. Governor Symington gave the eulogy.

"Jimmy Teyechea came to us in a time when the world is struggling. His cause was a sober one, but he knew that each of us is given a different work, and he never asked to be excused from his. He was so affected by his suffering that for him the struggle was transcendent. For him, the answer lay far beyond this or any place on Earth. He lost his life to cancer, but he gained his life in fighting that cancer and fighting to find out what caused it. In a world that is said to have lost its heroes, we were sent one in this little border town, on Carrillo Street, U.S.A."

Jimmy was buried next to his uncle and grandparents in the Teyechea family plot in the Nogales City Cemetery just a few blocks from Carrillo Street. The rose granite tombstone says simply, "Jaime C. Teyechea Jr., July 2, 1949–Mar. 26, 1994," and "Beloved Jimmy." It does not say, as Jimmy once joked he wanted it to, "Here lies another victim of the contamination."

Four years later, I went to see Susan Thomas Ramirez in her new house in Amado, some thirty miles north of Nogales. She had just returned from a benefit barbecue in town for a thirty-eight-year-old produce broker with a brain tumor. Susan believed the man, the father of two young children, lived in one of the neighborhoods that had been served by a contaminated well, but she didn't say anything to him. "I've already said too much. People don't want to hear it." Even before Jimmy's death, Susan had withdrawn from an active role in LIFE. She was worn out from fighting with the local authorities, with the scientists, and with Jimmy himself, and she wanted to concentrate on her family and her job as a bilingual schoolteacher. Since 1993, Anna Acuña had been leading the LIFE group by herself. For a few years, the city gave her an office next to the border on International Street, and she continued to hold a support group for lupus sufferers. But with Jimmy gone and Clarise Pierson soon to follow, LIFE lost its combative fire, and membership dwindled.

Still, there was reason to hope. Susan's daughter Michelle, now twelve, had apparently beaten leukemia, and Fernie Espinoza was alive and doing well. Dr. Comerci said that the number of new cases of myeloma and lupus being diagnosed in Nogales had gone down, and people were more aware of health and pollution issues than in the days before LIFE. Most importantly, young people in town were becoming interested in the environment. In 1995, a drama class at the high school put on a play called "Now Is the Time" about the founding of LIFE. In the play, teenagers from a despoiled future go back in time to Nogales in the 1990s, when it is still not too late to do something about environmental destruction. They meet Anna and other LIFE members, their visit changes the course of history, and Nogales is saved. The play, which was partially funded by the Arizona Department of Health Services, drew large audiences in Nogales and was given a standing ovation when performed before a medical convention in Tucson. The drama teacher who wrote and directed it went on to found an environmental theater troupe at the new Rio Rico High School, which put on a sequel to "Now Is the Time" after a hazardous-waste explosion at the

Rio Rico dump in 1997. Science students also began to take an interest in the environment, holding health fairs to educate other teenagers about the issues. Students from Rio Rico formed an exchange program with students from Magdalena, Sonora, to monitor the condition of the Santa Cruz River and the Rio Magdalena, and to share the information over the Internet.

Liana Teyechea spoke to her classmates about the environment and wrote two essays about her father's legacy and her love for him. A straight-A student who wanted to be a doctor, Liana was awarded a full scholarship to attend the University of Arizona when she graduated from high school in 1998. Worried about the environment and convinced there weren't enough opportunities for her, she told me she planned to leave Nogales for good then. "There's nothing here," she said. Then, after a pause, she added, "Except family."

"My father died trying to make Nogales safer for his children," Liana wrote in one of her essays. "I cannot imagine not doing the same thing for my children, but it becomes almost impossible without support and cooperation. I can still hear my father saying, 'Shorty, the battle is not between living and dying. The battle is to give meaning to life.' It's very hard to try and give meaning to life when one is constantly wondering how long life will really be. I agree that praying, hoping, and having faith are very effective and soul-soothing methods, but sometimes it's not enough to wish for something to get better. Ambos Nogales is getting worse. People are dying, and time is running out."

CHAPTER 3

Rodney King of the Border

June is usually the hottest month in southern Arizona, and June 1992 was no exception. By noon on Friday, June 12, when U.S. Border Patrol agent Michael Andrew Elmer started his shift, the temperature was nearly ninety degrees, with a warm breeze blowing. Elmer and several other agents spent the afternoon cutting sign—following tracks—through the rolling, grass-covered hills east of downtown Nogales. They encountered no one, and the work was peaceful and pleasant, despite the heat. Only the sound of their own voices and footsteps and the occasional bird call or buzzing insect broke the stillness. Elmer, dark-haired, boyish-looking, and twenty-nine years old, was especially quiet. He had much on his mind that day. He and his pregnant fiancée were in the midst of planning their wedding, which would be his third.

At five, with the sun still blazing hot, the agents met back at the station to get ready for the evening's work. For several weeks, the Border Patrol had been hearing from local ranchers that smugglers were using an isolated canyon west of town to bring in large amounts of cocaine. They'd heard scouts were coming over before dark to make sure the coast was clear, and then ten or twelve mules—people carrying drugs—would follow. The sensors would go off, and the next day the agents would find tracks, but they hadn't been able to catch anyone. They hoped that tonight would be the night. Elmer was looking forward to it. He liked working drug stakeouts, which were much more satisfying and exciting than rounding up undocumented immigrants.

Over dinner, he and several other agents talked about what to do. They decided on what they call a "lay in," a maneuver in which they'd get out to the canyon before dark, hide from the scouts, wait until the mules crossed the border, and then jump the load from behind, cutting off the escape route to Mexico.

Elmer and four other agents collected their gear and climbed into four-wheel-drive vehicles for the half-hour trek over the hills to Mariposa Canyon. As Elmer and his partner pulled out of the parking lot, Agent Tom Watson called out to them. Tall, blond, and athletic, Watson was a former fur trapper and hunter, and Elmer looked up to him. He was thirty-five and had been a Border Patrol agent for five years, a year longer than Elmer. During that time, he had won several commendations for good service, including the Justice Department's highest award for risking his life to save two border-crossers from drowning in a raging wash.

Watson, for his part, thought Elmer was a hard worker—unlike many other agents, whom he considered lazy. But he also thought Elmer was full of crap. Elmer, who'd spent seven and a half years in the army before joining the Border Patrol, had gone around telling everyone about his exploits in Grenada and Desert Storm, when in truth he had never been in Grenada and had spent the Persian Gulf War refueling tanks in Kuwait. Elmer had also once bragged to Watson that he'd killed a Mexican in the Morley Avenue tunnel. He said he'd shot the man in the face and then weighed the body down with rocks in the water so it wouldn't be discovered. Watson had shrugged off the story as another one of Elmer's tales.

"You got a long arm?" Watson asked, meaning a rifle. All the agents carried pistols, but most also took rifles with them when they worked at night in the canyons outside town.

"No." Elmer glanced at his watch. "It'll take too long to get one."

"You want to try my AR-15?" Watson went to his truck and pulled out a short-barreled, semiautomatic carbine rifle. He had been wanting to sell it, and he thought maybe Elmer might try it, like it, and buy it. Elmer accepted the offer, and the agents set off for Mariposa Canyon.

On this same afternoon, a few miles away, a twenty-six-year-old resident of Nogales, Sonora, named Dario Miranda Valenzuela stopped by his mother's house to tell her he was going across the border to work in the United States. The father of two preschoolers, Miranda needed money, and a cousin with a drywall business in Tucson was offering him a job. Like many locals, Miranda had crossed back and forth illegally for most of his life, without incident. A couple of times, Nogales Border Patrol agents had picked him up and given him a ride back to the border without even bothering to do the paperwork. But on this day, his mother told him not to go. *"Hay algo mal,"* Luz Castro said—"Something's wrong." In recent years, it had become more difficult to cross in town, and people were going farther and farther out to avoid getting caught, which made them more likely to fall victim to crime or to the elements. Miranda reassured her he was traveling with his brother-in-law and another cousin, and they would get across before dark. He promised to call from Tucson. He filled his canteen with water, strapped it to his belt, and kissed his mother goodbye.

Elmer and four other agents arrived at Mariposa Canyon about an hour before sundown. As they climbed the last hill, they drove slowly to avoid raising clouds of dust that might tip off their prey. They parked under some mesquite trees, put on their bulletproof vests, sprayed themselves with bug repellant, loaded their weapons, and checked their radios. Elmer looked in his bag and realized he had forgotten his vest.

The agents—one woman, four men, and a drug dog—started off. Agent Enrique Yerena went first, climbing a steep hillside to get a view of the canyon. As he came over the top, he was surprised to see three men sitting on a ridge to the east. He ducked down, but they'd seen him. Scouts. What were they doing here so early? Yerena saw the men look over to where he was, and then he saw one raise his hand to his face, like he was looking through binoculars. Yerena radioed the other agents. They decided to split up, with Yerena and two others staying on the ridge to distract the scouts while Elmer and Watson snuck around to catch the men from behind.

Elmer and Watson set off, Elmer carrying the rifle Watson had loaned him and Watson carrying a Border Patrol–issued M-16. The two men moved forward like soldiers under fire, taking turns running to the next tree and then motioning the other up. Watson was out in the open when one of the scouts suddenly stood up on the ridge about fifty yards away. Watson froze. If the scout had looked down and to the left, he would have seen him. Instead, the man scanned the horizon through his binoculars, glanced south, and sat down again. Watson ran in a half-crouch up to where Elmer was hiding. Whispering and using hand signals, they agreed that Watson would continue up the hill while Elmer circled around and tried to catch the mule train coming up from the border. Watson didn't have much hope of that. He figured the load had already been blown, and the best the agents would be able to do was arrest the scouts. He was heading up the hill when suddenly one of the scouts ran across the trail in front of him.

"Párate, la migra! Párate, la migra!"—"Stop, Immigration! Stop, Immigration!"—Watson shouted and fired a burst of shots into the air. Border Patrol agents are forbidden to fire warning shots, but Watson and Elmer did it often. Usually, it made even dozens of men drop their loads and scatter like quail. Not this time. The scout turned and started running straight toward Watson, who was blocking the trail south. Watson pointed his weapon at the man, then raised the barrel, and fired again into the sky, six or eight shots. The scout turned off the trail and vanished.

Watson radioed Elmer. "Go south, go south, he's headed your way!"

Elmer, on the other side of the ridge, heard Watson's gunfire just as he saw someone running through the ravine below. He yelled "Stop!"

but the man kept running, turning south about forty yards away. Elmer fell to his knees, raised his gun, and squeezed off at least ten shots. The man dropped from view.

For a few moments, the sound of gunfire ricocheted off the hillsides. Then there was silence. Watson's radio crackled. "Are you guys okay?" It was Yerena. "Yeah," Watson responded, not wanting to admit he'd fired warning shots. "We were just playing around." Elmer headed toward Watson, his heart pounding and his face shiny with sweat. Watson said later that Elmer came up the hill with the look of a man who'd just bagged his first deer.

"What happened? I heard yelling," Watson said.

"That was my guy. I got one."

"You shot one? Did you kill him?"

"I don't know." Elmer pointed into the ravine. "He's down there somewhere."

The two agents started along the ridge. As they did, Elmer saw another one of the scouts running south over the next hill. Barely breaking stride, he raised his rifle and fired at that man, too, but missed.

Elmer and Watson headed down into the canyon. About halfway down the hillside, amid a tangle of leaves, twigs, and rocks, they found a man lying face up with his arms flung straight out. They didn't know it yet, but the man was Dario Miranda. His head was turned to the side, his eyes half-closed. His chest was soaked in blood, and a piece of gut oozed out through a hole in his shirt. Elmer and Watson pointed their guns at him and yelled in Spanish, "Don't move, don't move." Miranda didn't move. Elmer checked his pulse. "He's gone," he said.

Watson was silent for a moment, then he glanced around. "Mike, where's the gun? If this is going to be a good shooting, there's got to be a gun."

Elmer grabbed Miranda's belt and pulled up the limp torso, but there was nothing underneath.

"Well," Elmer said, gesturing toward Miranda's belt, "maybe I thought his canteen was a holster."

Elmer's mind began to race. He considered putting the canteen in Miranda's hand, but decided not to because it didn't look enough like a gun. He asked Watson if he could use his Glock pistol as a throw-down, but Watson refused. Everyone would know that it was his.

"Can't we say it was an accident?" Watson said.

"No. I shot a bunch of times, and I hit him in the back."

"We can't just leave him here," Watson said.

Rifle cradled in his arm, Elmer turned toward Watson. "I'm going to bury the body. Do you have a problem with that?"

Watson shook his head, and as he did, he remembered Elmer bragging that he had killed a man in the Morley Avenue tunnel. He hadn't believed it then, but now he wasn't so sure. He told Elmer he was going to keep looking for a gun, and as he started cutting back and forth up the hill, staring at the rocky ground, he heard a scraping sound. He turned, and there was Elmer, dragging Miranda by the feet down into the canyon. Watson kept going, and a minute later Elmer ran up beside him. "It's too heavy," Elmer said. "I think we should come back tomorrow, take the body into Mexico and bury it there."

"Nah, I don't want to do that. You take care of it yourself. Then I won't know where it is."

As the two headed back, Elmer said, "After we get off this hill, we're not going to talk about it anymore, right?"

Watson nodded.

"What the fuck happened?" cried Yerena, as Elmer and Watson came up. "Boy, we just lost the mother of all loads out there. We heard shooting. Are you guys okay?" They waved him off, and Yerena let it drop. Just a few weeks before, Yerena had told Elmer and Watson that he wanted them to cut out the warning shots. He'd said he wouldn't lie for them if anyone found out. Elmer had called him a wimp.

Back at the station, neither Elmer nor Watson nor any of the agents with them reported that there had been gunfire. Watson avoided questions by reloading his weapon before turning it in, and Elmer, having used Watson's rifle, didn't even have to do that. He went into the office, called his fiancée, and leaned back with his feet on the desk while they chatted about wedding rings. He and Watson then joined the Friday afternoon "choir practice"—agent's slang for a beer-drinking session—in the parking lot across the street from the station. Watson talked about having to sell some of his guns to make a truck payment, and Elmer said he was interested in buying the rifle he'd borrowed. Watson didn't answer. He finished his beer and left.

When Miranda's cousin reached home that night, he felt so sick he threw up. He told his family that he'd been walking about fifteen feet in front of Miranda when a Border Patrol agent had jumped up and yelled, "I'm going to kill you!" He'd started running and hadn't looked back; he didn't see what happened to Miranda. The next morning, when Miranda still had not shown up, his mother went to see his young wife, Margarita Tello de Miranda, and the two women sat together all day, crying and praying and waiting for Miranda to call.

Watson, meanwhile, spent a sleepless night before deciding to report the killing. The next morning he called his lawyer and his boss, then led sheriff's deputies out to Mariposa Canyon and showed them where Elmer had stashed Miranda's body. It was in a crevice behind an oak tree about a hundred feet from where they had found him. At noon, Elmer showed up for work as usual. His supervisors gave him a chance to report the shooting, but when he said nothing and was about to head out for the day, they arrested him. He was charged with murder, the first and only Border Patrol agent ever accused of this crime for killing a man while on duty.

It wasn't until Sunday that word began to get around Nogales that a Border Patrol agent had been arrested for killing someone. Miranda's family heard a description of the unidentified victim on Radio XENY, and when they told Luz Castro, she collapsed, crying, "My son, my son." U.S. authorities did not return Miranda's body—already starting to rot, with maggots in the nose and eyes—until five days later. He was quickly buried in the Pantheon of the Cypresses, a Nogales, Sonora, cemetery that lies in a ravine just south of the Mariposa port of entry.

At the wake, Miranda's two-year-old son looked in the coffin and asked, "Who is that man? He looks like my daddy."

Almost five years to the day later, on June 4, 1997, a young Border Patrol supervisor named Joe Pankoke took me to the place where Dario Miranda had been killed. I wanted to see Mariposa Canyon and what the light would be like at sunset. I also wanted to experience at least some of the daily routine of Border Patrol agents in Nogales. Joe and I spent several hours together on this afternoon, driving around town and talking about how things had changed in Nogales since the Border Patrol crackdown had begun here in 1994. Although Joe was only thirty, he had worked in Nogales during his entire eight-year career and considered it his home. He was married to a local woman, a Mexican immigrant from southern Sonora. "When I first started, Nogales was a lot quieter, smaller town," he said. "On a Saturday back then, to get 150 aliens was considered a good day. We didn't see anything like the numbers we're getting now."

Nogales didn't become a major corridor for border-crossers until 1993, the year the Border Patrol launched major crackdowns in the two traditionally favored crossing spots, San Diego and El Paso. Word got around that the passage was easier through southern Arizona. The Tucson sector, which covers 281 miles of border from the New Mexico state line to Yuma, soon surpassed San Diego as the busiest crossing point on the border. "We were catching ten thousand a month here, more," Joe said. "You could never get enough guys." Operation Safeguard, the Arizona portion of the crackdown, was launched the following year. The number of Border Patrol agents in the Tucson sector tripled to more than one thousand. "Used to be, most agents were from the Southwest," Joe said. "Now we're getting guys from Massachusetts, Florida, New York, Louisiana, you name it." In 1995, the U.S. government declared southern Arizona to be a "high-intensity drug trafficking zone," and with that declaration came hundreds of millions of additional dollars. The number of inspectors from the Immigration and

Naturalization Service (INS), U.S. Customs, the Drug Enforcement Administration (DEA), and other federal agencies increased sharply, as did the number of state and local forces assigned to the war on drugs. The U.S. military, which until the 1980s was banned from civilian law enforcement, took on an expanded role in drug interdiction there and elsewhere on the border. Besides conducting ground and air surveillance, troops were assigned to build roads and walls, and to help train Border Patrol agents. The National Guard, for example, built both the steel wall and the tunnel doors in Nogales. The Border Patrol also received an extensive array of high-tech equipment, including helicopters, radar balloons, surveillance cameras, infrared scopes, stadium lights, motion sensors, radios, trucks, vans, and weapons. It seemed as if everywhere one looked in Nogales, there were Border Patrol agents riding their bikes and sitting at pull-outs along the freeway or on overlooks in their new, white four-by-fours.

Joe and I headed east from downtown up into the steep, hilly neighborhood that lies just across the wall from the infamous Nogales, Sonora, neighborhood known as Buenos Aires. The streets on this side were quiet and shady, and the old houses for the most part well-kept, although the burglar bars and high fences around most of them were reminders of this area's secret underground life as a safe place for drug stashes and a haven for border-crossers. Joe pointed out the spots where locals threw bundles over the wall, mentioning that behind the quiet facades, many of the houses and garages were crammed with contraband.

"We tried doing what they're doing in El Paso, with Operation Hold the Line," Joe said. The Border Patrol had essentially stopped illegal crossings there by stationing an agent every few hundred yards along the river bank. In Texas, the Rio Grande served as a natural buffer between agents and Mexico. In Nogales, however, people threw rocks and bottles over the fence at agents and broke the windows of their vehicles; snipers regularly took potshots at them. "We were getting eaten alive." Joe had had his share of rocks thrown at him, but he tried not to take it personally. "You don't last very long in this job if you do." The Border Patrol was forced to draw back a little, away from the fence, and to concentrate on stopping people after they'd crossed. That meant they had to determine whom to stop and question based on appearance alone, a far from exact process that caused friction with local residents.

Joe watched some kids walking by and decided that they were locals. I asked how he could tell who belonged and who didn't, considering that almost everyone in Nogales was of Mexican ancestry. "It's hard to articulate, but they're just not American looking. Things like shaggy hair, dirty clothes, beat-up old dress shoes—those are all signs of a fresh *ewey* [entry without inspection]. It's just something you learn from experience. Usually, newer agents have a harder time telling who's an alien and who's not."

We headed out to the unpopulated area east of town, a land of rolling hills, dried grass, and cow pies. The road became a dirt track paralleling the fence. Bouncing along over these rugged, rocky roads was making me carsick, so I was relieved when Joe came to a stop. We were in Smuggler's Gulch, a popular illegal crossing spot where Attorney General Janet Reno had been pelted with rocks during her first visit to Nogales three years before. Today, no one was around, and Joe and I got out to look. "The hills, the terrain we have here is smuggling terrain. You can see people when they crest the ridge, and that's it. In the ravines and valleys, there's lots of blind spots where our cameras don't do any good."

Out here in the open, with the twin cities spread below us, I began to get a sense of the Border Patrol agent's job around Nogales. Much of the work involved hiking for hours through these quiet canyons, following tracks or "cutting sign," as they called it. When they did encounter border-crossers, agents were almost always able to round up even dozens of people without incident. Acts of bravery and compassion could be found on both sides; the Border Patrol frequently rescued people who were dying in the desert, and one time near Nogales, a group of immigrants stayed to help a female agent who had fallen and hit her head, even though they could easily have run away. An agent's job was routine, even boring, yet it contained the ever-present risk of real danger. "The drugs are a whole different world than alien traffic," Joe told me. "They play for keeps. They all are armed to protect themselves and the load. A guy who's just coming across to work—he can cross any day. But they have to get that load through." Joe said he'd had to draw his gun a few times, but never fired it at anyone. "You just hope you never have to." Most of the time, low-level drug mules—even armed ones—surrendered peacefully.

The rise in the drug trade around Nogales aggravated tensions between U.S. and Mexican law enforcement, who had never gotten along that well to begin with. In one notorious incident in the summer of 1995, a Border Patrol agent was nearly paralyzed after being shot by a Mexican policeman in Smuggler's Gulch. Agent Art Lopez and his partner had been called to a potential crime scene, and as they approached, they saw two uniformed cops beating up two men on the Mexican side. Without warning, one of the Mexican cops stepped through the fence into the United States and started firing at the agents. "Shoot 'em in the head!" yelled the cop's partner. Lopez, who was wearing a bulletproof vest, dived for cover and was struck in the rear. The bullet lodged next to his spine, and he had to undergo several surgeries before he eventually returned to work. The Mexican cops claimed that the border bandits had shot Lopez, or, alternatively, that Lopez had accidently shot himself. Lopez said he was "absolutely positive" the shooter was one of the Mexican police officers. Border Patrol officials were outraged by the incident. "Many of these individuals wearing uniforms are doing nothing more than providing protection for drug smugglers," Tucson Border Patrol Sector Chief Ron Sanders said. Inquiries were launched in both Mexico City and Washington, D.C., but the investigation was dropped three months later when the cop accused of shooting Lopez was himself shot and killed in Smuggler's

Gulch. According to his partner, the cop had been playing Russian roulette with some bandits, saying, "You think you are macho? I will show you who is more macho," before shooting himself in the head.

While on the east side of town, Joe and I stopped by the old Border Patrol station—a dark, cavernous, former car dealership that had been home to the Nogales Border Patrol from the early 1980s until 1996. It featured a row of dusty saddles captured from smugglers over the years, hanging like trophies on the wall. Joe said agents were planning to use the horses and tack they'd confiscated to start a mounted patrol, just like the old days. We watched as a half-dozen excited agents brought in a load of pot they had just captured from a man driving a beat-up pickup truck on Ruby Road. There were sixteen packages total, about seven pounds each. The bales had been crushed in a trash compactor, shrink-wrapped in plastic, numbered and weighed down to the fraction of a kilo, and then bundled in burlap potato sacks. I was surprised at the professionalism of the packaging, which the agents assured me was standard. "They do it to keep the mules from taking any." One of the bundles had been torn into and about an ounce removed, apparently by the driver of the truck. Using real mules was no guarantee that the load was safe either; a few days after this capture, the Border Patrol stopped a truck pulling a horse trailer on Ruby Road. The driver escaped, but inside the trailer, agents found a horse and 1,306 pounds of marijuana. The horse had been chewing on the burlap-wrapped packages, trying to eat the dope.

Joe and I went back downtown, drove west along the fence for a while, and then went down into a ravine beside the highway and parked beside a large cottonwood tree and an old livestock watering tank. Joe pointed out the culvert that cut under the highway through which the migrants would come. I asked if he ever felt frustrated by the apparent futility of his job. "When I was new, it bothered me. You learn that you just do the best job you can. I tell the new agents, 'It doesn't matter if you see the same guy four times a day; it's an administrative violation, and you treat it as such.' You don't want to shoot somebody."

"I believe in what I'm doing. I'm not for tearing down the fence or electrifying it. What I do prevents the U.S. from becoming a third world country. We can't take on all of Latin America."

As dusk approached, we headed back to the new Border Patrol station that sits among the *maquiladora* warehouses, customs brokerages, and produce companies that line Mariposa Road west of the freeway. Joe showed me around the huge complex, with its offices, classrooms, holding cells, and rows of brand-new, white Ford Explorers parked outside. We set off on the dirt track leading from behind the station up into Mariposa Canyon. The four-wheel drive bounced along over the hills and valleys, and I stupidly continued to try to write down what Joe was saying. After about twenty minutes, when we reached the border fence, I was really carsick. I apologized, got out, and threw up. "You sure have a weak stomach," Joe said.

So this was the place. Here or perhaps the next ravine over—Joe couldn't say for sure—was where Elmer had killed Miranda. We were about seven miles from downtown Nogales, far from any people or houses. The only evidence of human presence was a five-strand, barbed-wire cattle fence marking the international line. The sun was low in the sky, casting the western face of the ravine into deep shadow and bathing the eastern face in a warm orange glow. Mesquite and scrub oak trees, yucca, and barrel and prickly pear cactus stood out like stage props against a hillside that had been stripped by cattle of most other vegetation. To the southwest, in Mexico, the blue-green Pajarito Mountains filled the lower half of the horizon. The canyon was quiet except for the wind and a few flies buzzing. At 7:15, about fifteen or twenty minutes after the time Elmer had shot Miranda, the sun sank from view. Joe and I stood for a few moments in the silence. "As you can see, we don't have swarms of people crossing here," he said. "If someone does come out here, it's either a rancher, a dope smuggler, or us."

Word of the death of Miranda spread quickly. In Nogales, where Miranda was known as one of the best players on the Curios, a top amateur soccer club, people reacted angrily. Radio XENY was inundated with callers, and when Elmer came up for a bond-reduction hearing in July, local people held three days of demonstrations downtown, one of which briefly closed the port of entry. A taco vendor working the port hung from his cart a large sign reading "Elmer—Assassin," and shops in the tourist district displayed similar banners. To the relief of many, Elmer's bond was kept at one million dollars. "It makes me believe there may be justice in the United States justice system after all," one man said.

In the United States, immigrant-rights activists dubbed Miranda the "Rodney King of the Border." They hoped his case would expose racism and brutality in the Border Patrol the way the videotape of four white cops beating a black man named Rodney King had exposed racism and brutality in the Los Angeles Police Department. Since the mid-1980s, groups such as Human Rights Watch, Amnesty International, and the American Friends Service Committee (AFSC) had documented hundreds of Border Patrol agents' and other immigration authorities' acts of violence against Mexicans, including kickings, beatings, vehicle run-downs, and shootings. These groups had also found that agents accused of wrongdoing were often allowed to be reassigned or even promoted after being cleared by a secret internal review process. But this time, they said, the evidence, like the Rodney King tape, was too damning to be explained away. "If we can't get justice in this case, we can't get it in any case," proclaimed Tucson attorney and immigrant-rights activist Jesús Romo Véjar.

In the six months leading up to Elmer's trial, comparisons with the Rodney King case began to prove all to apt. Like King, Miranda turned out to be a flawed martyr. The autopsy found he had marijuana and cocaine in his system and cocaine residue in his nose, meaning he'd snorted it within twelve hours of his death. Miranda also had been carrying a little marijuana folded in a piece of paper in his pocket. Outraged by this information, his family insisted the drugs must have been planted; they wouldn't put anything past Elmer and other law enforcement agents, including planting evidence and doctoring the autopsy report.

More damaging than Miranda's drug use was evidence that he had been out in Mariposa Canyon serving as a scout for smugglers and not merely crossing the border to work. All the agents on the scene claimed that Miranda and his companions had been hanging around and scanning the border with binoculars, not walking north. Miranda also had been suspiciously dressed in dark green pants, black T-shirt, and army boots. His family said he just liked the military look, and Luz Castro angrily denied to reporters that Miranda was a smuggler. "If my son had sold drugs, do you think we would be living like this?" she said, looking around the two-room, cinder-block house with no indoor plumbing where she had raised her seven children. "The boy didn't even have a roof to put over his head."

At the time of his death, Miranda, his wife, Margarita, and their two children, Hetzel, four, and Rubén, two, were living with Margarita's widowed mother while they saved to build a home of their own. Miranda was by all accounts a hard worker. His mother, a divorcée from Carbo, Sonora, had not remarried, and from the time he was little, he had helped support the family. He shined shoes, sold bread and popsicles, picked garbanzo beans, and washed police cars. He left school at the age of fifteen and thereafter held jobs as a mechanic, a cook in a maquila, and a construction worker. When work ran short in Nogales, he jumped the fence and headed to Tucson or Phoenix, where friends or family members gave him jobs and a place to stay for a while.

Michael Elmer, meanwhile, turned out to be no choirboy either. In 1991, the Tucson Office of Inspector General (OIG), the internal investigative arm of the Justice Department, received a tip that Elmer had stolen five kilos of cocaine from a bust he'd made the previous year. The OIG investigated, but turned up no additional evidence and closed the case. As his murder trial approached, however, Elmer's ex-wife told investigators he had shown her the cocaine, and they had snorted some of it together; another man claimed he had helped Elmer bury the drugs.

Stories of Elmer's trigger-happiness also surfaced. In March 1992, less than three months before Miranda's death, Elmer and other agents had been working with the National Guard, scanning the hills east of Nogales with an infrared scope. Around 10:00 P.M., Elmer learned that a group of about thirty people, some carrying bundles, were headed northeast along the Yerba Buena Wash. A woman named Aurelia Serrano said she had been walking for almost four hours when suddenly she heard someone scream, "Drop the pot, you fucking mules! Immigration!" Bullets started whizzing by, striking the dirt around her. One of the people with her was hit in the leg and stomach. When the man later showed his wounds to agents at the station, they gave him some salve and told him not to worry about it. Elmer's ex-wife later said he'd bragged to her that he'd "shot a guy's leg off at the knee."

Both Serrano and the man who was wounded remember something else about Mike Elmer, a strange illustration of the contradictions that exist along the line. Minutes after shooting at them, Elmer was chatting and joking with his captives as if they were old friends. He asked if they wanted to see the high-tech equipment that had led to their arrest. He had been using a machine gun with an infrared sighting system that shoots out a dot of red light visible only through night-vision goggles, and he let the immigrants take turns trying on the goggles. "It was like daylight," marveled Serrano.

Elmer's trial took place in Tucson in late November 1992. Aurelia Serrano and the man Elmer had shot in March, who still had the bullet fragment in his stomach, were brought from Mexico to testify. Although Elmer was not on trial for that incident, they were called to show his propensity for violence and perhaps to put a face on his victims because, besides the coroner, every other person to testify was either a Border Patrol agent, sheriff's deputy, or National Guardsman. A string of agents testified that the border at the time was a "war zone" where the smugglers outmanned and outgunned law enforcers, even though armed encounters between agents and smugglers were rare. Several long-time agents said they had never had to fire their weapons in all their years on the line. Agents also testified that Mariposa Canyon was used only by drug smugglers, never by undocumented immigrants, although they also said the same thing about Yerba Buena Wash, where Elmer had shot at Aurelia Serrano and the others in March.

Because the evidence pointed to Miranda's being a drug scout, the prosecutor seemed to think that the less said about him, the better. Miranda's cousin and the other man who was with him that day denied they were scouts, but prosecutors found them unconvincing, and they were never called to testify. Not a single person who knew Miranda took the stand. The jury heard about his drug use and the pot in his pocket, but never learned that he was a good son, a loving husband, and a devoted father who played with his kids for hours on end. They never heard he was a local soccer star. He was anonymous, barely human. Even the prosecutor referred to him as "the scout" or "the deceased."

Elmer, in contrast, was "Mike" to his lawyer and the other agents who testified. The trial testimony brought out his childhood in the eastern Arizona mining towns of San Manuel and Kearny, his service in the army during Desert Storm, his two children and the third on the way, and his new Mexican American bride (the judge had married them after a pretrial hearing in November). But the jury heard nothing about his alleged drug use and the accusation that he had stolen cocaine.

Elmer made a tearful spectacle on the stand. He described the confusion and terror he'd felt that day, surrounded by what he thought were armed smugglers. He said he thought the canteen on Miranda's belt was a holster, even though he could clearly see and describe the rest of Miranda's clothes down to his black-and-green army boots. Feeling exposed and vulnerable without his bulletproof vest, he thought Miranda was going to turn and fire. Everything happened so fast. He described the moment he had shot Miranda as an out-of-body experience: "I felt like I was looking down on this like a third person." He said Watson had convinced him not to report the shooting by insisting they had to find a gun, and he was afraid he'd get fired for using an unauthorized weapon. "I just began to panic, and things started going through my head. I saw my whole life going down the tubes."

The jury knew this incident was not the first time Elmer had shot at people. They knew he was an expert marksman who'd been trained not to panic under fire. They knew he shot Miranda before sunset and should have seen that Miranda had no gun. They knew Border Patrol agents are not allowed to shoot fleeing suspects, even armed ones. They knew that, after the killing, Elmer had behaved like a guilty man by hiding the body and keeping quiet. None of that mattered, however. In the end, the case came down to the word of Elmer, an American, a veteran, and a law enforcement officer, against the silence of a dead, drug-using Mexican who'd been skulking around in the bushes on the U.S. side of the border. It wasn't even a close contest. The jury of eleven whites and one Hispanic took only about three hours to reach a verdict of not guilty on all counts.

When the all-white jury in Simi Valley acquitted the four cops who'd beaten Rodney King, a riot ensued. When Elmer was acquitted, there were small demonstrations in Tucson and Phoenix, but no widespread protests. "It was as if they had killed a dog, not a man," said Luz Castro, who had attended the trial every day. "I would like to congratulate Michael Andrew Elmer's mother," she added bitterly, after watching Elmer's mother cry with relief when the verdict was announced. "Her son is alive. I have one who is forever dead and I will always be crying for." Miranda's widow, Margarita, said she felt "impotent rage" as the verdict was read. "What am I going to tell my child? That his father could not get justice? [Elmer] gets to enjoy and see his children alive, but my husband is dead." "Maybe they should give him a medal for killing Mexicans," said one of Miranda's cousins, who lived in Tucson. "If a Mexican had killed a Border Patrol agent, where would that Mexican be today? You tell me."

In contrast to the muted reaction of the American public, the verdict provoked deep anger in Mexico, where it was seen as further proof that Americans view Mexicans as less than human. People in Nogales, Sonora, threatened an economic boycott of the U.S. side; politicians called for demilitarization of the border; and the Mexican consul general filed a formal protest. "People in Mexico are offended because they feel the judicial system is biased in the U.S.," said Irasema Coronado, a researcher at the Colegio de la Frontera Norte in Nogales. "You have all of this, and it doesn't mean anything because the Border Patrol is always right."

Activists seized on the verdict to renew their calls for a binational human rights commission and a civilian oversight board for the Border Patrol. The trial had brought out numerous instances of agents misbehaving and breaking the rules, which confirmed what many critics had charged was a longstanding pattern of abuses. Arizona Senator Dennis DeConcini, hardly a tough critic of the Border Patrol or the INS, joined some of his House colleagues in backing legislation to create an oversight board. At the same time, Miranda's family, represented by Jesús Romo and other attorneys in Tucson, filed a $25 million civil suit against Elmer and the Border Patrol. Activists also launched a petition drive, demanding that the U.S. Justice Department file federal charges against Elmer for violating Miranda's civil rights.

When the Border Patrol and the National Guard put up the wall in 1994 and 1995, it quickly became the most visible and controversial symbol of the law enforcement crackdown in Ambos Nogales. Two and a half miles long, ten to fourteen feet high, and made of rusted, corrugated steel landing mats left over from the Vietnam War, it cut through the middle of downtown like a jagged scar. Locals denounced it as hideous and insulting. "Before, we had a beautiful view toward a friendly country on the other side," said the owner of Elvira's, a restaurant on the Mexican side where customers used to be able to sit and watch people cross back and forth through gaping holes in the chain-

Border Patrol agents repair holes in the fence between Ambos Nogales while a Mexican man steps into the United States. The photo was taken just before the present wall was built.

link fence. "Now they put up this terrible sight that doesn't go with the times we live in." People in Nogales, Sonora, said it made them feel like they were in prison, and dozens of would-be immigrants injured themselves trying to climb over it.

Just as the wall physically divided Nogales, locals were divided over the crackdown. Many residents, tired of crime and vandalism, welcomed it. "I have neighbors who've been broken into nine times," one man who lived on the U.S. side told me. "A friend of mine came home, found his glass door broken, and then saw two feet sticking out from under the drapes. The guy had been trying to steal some underwear, socks, and a warm coat. A few months ago, I saw a head pop up over the edge of my balcony, and I felt three strong emotions in the space of a minute: scared, then pissed off, then pity. Another time I woke up at 3:00 A.M. and heard a noise in my kitchen. A woman and a fourteen-year-old girl were in my house, telling me they needed to use my phone."

Such incidents did decrease after the wall went up. Determined, long-distance travelers were diverted away from town, and local, casual crossers found it increasingly difficult to go back and forth. Crime in Nogales, Arizona, dropped to a ten-year low. But the wall and crackdown coincided with the most severe economic crisis Mexico had experienced in thirty years, and between these two events, the retail economy of downtown Nogales, Arizona, collapsed. Nogales businessmen blamed the tightened border for driving away their customers and demanded that the INS speed up the six-month wait for Nogales, Sonora, residents to obtain border-crossing cards. They also insisted that something be done about the wall's hostile appearance. After much debate over how to construct a barrier that was both aesthetically pleasing and impenetrable, the U.S. government agreed to spend $750,000 to replace a quarter-mile of the wall as it passed through the main shopping district with a "decorator" structure made of pink concrete and see-through steel mesh. This new section of the wall, a first of its kind on the border, was completed in 1998.

The law enforcement crackdown in Nogales also increased tensions at the port of entry, where complaints about long lines and rude inspectors were common even prior to the crackdown. People reported being detained and strip-searched, and having their documents confiscated. Wealthy, well-dressed Mexicans in nice cars said they were treated like criminals. "Well, the question is, how did they get that fancy car? The wealthiest persons in Mexico probably are involved in narcotics smuggling," the deputy port director for immigration told me. In one case in 1996, a group of government officials on an official state visit were denied entry for fifteen hours and missed a reception in their honor in Phoenix. "I don't understand the Clinton administration," Nogales businessman Harlan Capin said. "They fought to get NAFTA signed, but then everything they do is against free trade and against the spirit of the agreement."

Controversy also erupted over increasingly intrusive Border Patrol vehicle stops and checkpoints. Civil libertarians charged the border was becoming a "deconstitutionalized zone" where people's rights were routinely infringed upon in the name of stopping illegal immigration and drugs. Several lawsuits were filed charging that Hispanics were singled out for scrutiny, including one suit by a nineteen-year veteran Border Patrol agent who said he had been stopped and searched numerous times while off duty simply because he looked Mexican. Southern Arizona locals were also up in arms over the Border Patrol checkpoint on the main highway between Nogales and Tucson. For years, the patrol had operated a temporary checkpoint at Peck Canyon Road in Rio Rico, twelve miles north of the border, where they set cones on the highway to divert traffic up onto an overpass. As the population grew, the line of cars often backed up onto the freeway, creating a serious traffic hazard. In 1996, the Border Patrol announced plans to build a large, permanent facility at a safer location some thirty miles north of the border, but that idea ran into furious opposition from people in Tubac, an artist and retiree haven just south of the proposed site. Arguing that the checkpoint would "militarize" their community and turn it into a drop-off and pickup point for undocumented immigrants, opponents gathered hundreds of signatures and successfully lobbied Representative Jim Kolbe, Senator John McCain, and other Arizona politicians to cancel the construction. The cancellation, a rare defeat for the Border Patrol, left Tucson as the only sector on the Mexican border without at least one fixed checkpoint. Concerns also began to be raised about the temporary checkpoint at Peck Canyon after a new elementary school opened nearby. Parents worried about shoot-outs or high-speed chases endangering their children.

These concerns were hardly theoretical. As the crackdown tightened the screws on undocumented immigrants, they resorted to increasingly desperate measures to evade the Border Patrol. Many were forced into the hands of smugglers who would stop at nothing to get their loads through, including risking lives. In the first few years after the crackdown, the number of border-crossers killed in accidents rose sharply as smugglers raced around checkpoints and tried to outrun

The Border Patrol catches a group of border-crossers trying to enter the United States through the hills on the east side of Nogales.

pursuing agents. In southern Arizona alone, four crashes took the lives of nine people, including a woman and child, between December 1996 and September 1997. Most of these deaths were blamed on the smugglers. In one case, a U.S. Customs agent chased and rammed a car carrying four undocumented immigrants on the Tohono O'odham Indian Reservation southwest of Tucson. The car rolled over, killing a passenger who had been on his way to Phoenix to sell homemade crafts. The Customs agent responsible for the crash retired, although he was later cleared of wrongdoing.

Some experts argued that the crackdown had not slowed illegal immigration at all, just moved it to more remote and risky areas of the border. A 1997 study by the University of Houston's Center for Immigration Research found that some twelve hundred people had died trying to cross the border between 1993 and 1996. The vast majority had drowned; others had been run over, killed in wrecks, or died of exposure. "It's the equivalent of a large plane load of people crashing every year," said Nestor Rodriguez, one of the study's authors. "But they do not all die at once, so these are like invisible, silent deaths." And this number represented only the deaths the study was able to confirm; no doubt hundreds more died and were never found. The study also revealed that the numbers of deaths appeared to have risen sharply since the crackdown. In the summer of 1996, at least fifteen people were found dead of dehydration in the Arizona desert, including six near Nogales. In August 1997, a flash flood near Douglas trapped a group crossing through a drainage pipe, killing eight, and in the spring of 1999, another ten froze to death in a sudden snowstorm in the mountains east of San Diego. It seemed that, no matter the risks, people were going to keep coming. As one man standing by the Nogales wall observed, "They can bring all the army of the United States if they want, but they will not stop us from working to feed our families." Shrugged another, "They can't kill us all."

Michael Elmer had been acquitted of murder, but, as with the acquitted cops in the Rodney King case, the system was not yet through with him. Eight months after his first trial, he was indicted again, this time on federal civil rights charges. The hope was that a jury that balked at convicting Elmer of murder might be willing to convict him of violating Miranda's civil rights and obstructing justice. In the Rodney King case, the strategy had worked; the second trial resulted in convictions and jail time for two of the four cops who beat King. For Miranda, such a result was not to be.

The government did send lawyers and investigators from the Justice Department to present a better case than before, but Elmer's second trial, which took place in Phoenix in January 1994, was in most respects a replay of the first. Only Border Patrol and other law enforcement agents testified; Miranda was assumed to be a scout; Elmer made a sympathetic case for self-defense; and again the verdict was the same. After four and a half hours of deliberation, the jury of eleven whites and one black acquitted Elmer on all counts, including using excessive force, wrongfully firing his weapon, and obstructing justice by moving the body and failing to report the shooting, all actions he had explicitly admitted to taking.

The second acquittal passed with even less public reaction than the first. At a press conference in Tucson, Luz Castro, still dressed in mourning clothes, hung her head and spoke quietly to Dario. "I'm sorry, my son. We did all we could." Jesús Romo, the attorney representing Miranda's family in their civil case, seemed mystified. "To shoot someone in the back, drag him down a hill, and intend to bury him, that a jury could find that a reasonable act for a police officer is incredible." Romo blamed the outcome on prejudice against Mexicans. "There was a huge gulf between the jurors and the victim in this case that could not be crossed. The jury identified with a murderer."

Wallace Kleindienst, one of the prosecutors in Elmer's second trial, was also shocked at the acquittal. Years later, he said it still bothered him. The government had done everything it could to convict Elmer of something, but jurors just wouldn't do it. A clue to the reason why came in a message that the jurors sent to the judge after the case was over. The judge called Kleindienst and the other prosecutors into his office and told them that in the jury's opinion, "Something ought to be done about the Border Patrol in Nogales." Kleindienst was aghast. Wasn't that what they had been trying to do? The jurors, however, apparently thought the government was scapegoating Elmer for widespread misbehavior among Border Patrol agents in Nogales—misbehavior that had contributed to the killing and the cover-up.

Especially troubling were the actions of Watson, Elmer's chief accuser. He'd loaned Elmer an unauthorized weapon; his warning shots may have given Elmer cause to believe a gun battle was going on; and his reason for waiting twelve hours to report the killing—that he was afraid of Elmer—seemed weak. Watson could have reported the shooting as soon as he and Elmer rejoined the other agents at the scene. Instead, he lied to Yerena about the gunfire, hid evidence by reloading his weapon before turning it in, attended "choir practice," and then went home without saying a word. Watson's behavior cast doubt on his testimony about one of the most crucial aspects of the case, the issue of whether Miranda was really dead when they found him. Like Elmer, Watson always insisted he was dead, but some wondered if Watson wasn't just saying that to cover up his own failure to get help. All the coroner could say was that Miranda lived between five and thirty minutes after being shot twice in the lower back. Miranda's family will always believe that had Elmer and Watson tried to save him, Miranda would still be alive.

Despite his failings, Watson did come forward, which is more than can be said for Elmer and the other agents who heard gunfire that day. He paid a high price for doing so. He was placed on leave and ultimately fired for using warning shots and for failing to report the killing sooner, among other infractions. During his long, unsuccessful effort to get his job back, his wife left him, and he was reduced to making a living as a bounty hunter. "It's a big cover-up," Watson told the *Los Angeles Times*. "I broke the code of silence, and they want to get back at me. I knew I was doing the right thing by turning him in for murder, even though I embarrassed them." Watson did receive some support from the Mexican consulate, who congratulated him for coming forward, and from Miranda's family. "If it hadn't been for him, we never would have known what happened," Luz Castro said.

Elmer, who was allowed to resign from the Border Patrol, eventually pled guilty to the separate charge of endangerment for shooting at Aurelia Serrano and the others that night in March 1992. He was given sixteen months in jail, received credit for time served while awaiting trial on the murder charge, and was paroled after ninety days. All told, he spent nine months behind bars. After he was released, he moved to Phoenix with his third wife and their two children, and went to work as a landscaper. Miranda's family told me he never made any attempt to apologize.

The impact of the Elmer case rippled through the Nogales Border Patrol station for years afterward. Nearly every high-ranking officer at the time of the shooting was transferred or reassigned, and in 1995, three lower-ranking agents were fired for lying to investigators in connection with the case. Two of them were accused of covering up the fact that warning shots had been fired in both the March and June 1992 situations, and that a man had been hit in the former incident. The third, the one female agent who was in Mariposa Canyon with Elmer and the others on June 12, was fired for denying that she heard gunshots that day, a claim prosecutors found incredible. Although the three fought to get their jobs back and eventually were reinstated, many Nogales agents remained angry over the firings, which they felt were payback for Elmer's sins and for the government's failure to convict him. "That case really brought the scrutiny down on the whole station," Joe Pankoke told me. "It really divided everyone. Watson's remarks were so inflammatory—that it was the norm in Nogales to fire warning shots. I've never been with anyone who fired a warning shot. It takes away all the good work everybody does because one guy is trying to save his hide."

Nevertheless, this case wasn't the only one that gave the Nogales Border Patrol its renegade reputation. At the time of the shooting, at least two other agents in the Tucson sector were being charged with drug smuggling, and other agents and support staff were found to have committed perjury, stolen from immigrants in the jail, and defrauded the government. Nor was Elmer the only Tucson-sector agent accused of a violent crime. In late 1993, Larry Dean Selders, a thirty-one-year-old married father of six and an eight-year veteran in Nogales, was arrested and charged with raping a woman while on duty. His accuser, a twenty-two-year-old mother of two from Nogales, Sonora, said Selders had picked her and another woman up downtown and offered them their freedom in exchange for sex. When they refused, Selders ordered the friend out of the car, drove her to an isolated spot east of town, and raped her. Selders' lawyer claimed she was a prostitute, but after several other women came forward to say he'd harassed them as well, he pleaded guilty to sexual assault. He was given a year in jail and kicked out of the Border Patrol. Over the next few years, two more Tucson-sector agents stationed in Douglas were investigated for murder, and one, Jorge Mancha, was convicted of cocaine smuggling and sentenced to thirty years in jail.

Border Patrol officials in Tucson denied that the Elmer case revealed widespread or systematic problems. "Had the agents followed policy, this probably would not have happened," one said. Despite their denials, pressure from activists and politicians over this case and others led to some changes in the INS. The agency began issuing more beanbag guns, batons, pepper spray, and other nonlethal weapons. In 1994, after years of foot-dragging, it also established a citizens' advisory panel, which called for improvement in complaint procedures, for agents to receive more instruction in cultural sensitivity and civil rights, and for supervisors, whose ranks were rapidly expanding, to undergo additional training. The advisory panel was weakened by having no investigative or enforcement authority and was disbanded after issuing a final report in 1997. Nevertheless, immigrant and civil rights groups hailed it as a step forward and pushed for its mandate to be extended.

Given the unprecedented increase in the size of the Border Patrol and of the INS during these years, the need for adequate training and supervision of agents was critical. In the past, the Border Patrol had been found to be lax in its hiring standards, at times putting convicted felons and people with mental problems on the line, and now the pressure was on to recruit and train new agents as quickly as possible. As U.S. Representative Jim Kolbe told me in reference to Border Patrol funding, "We've given them all they've asked for and more. It's like stuffing foie gras down a duck." Plans called for expanding the size of the Border Patrol nationwide by a thousand new agents per year through 2001, for a total of more than ten thousand on the southwest border. The push to beef up border law enforcement at all costs has meant that confrontations and abuses were bound to continue, despite local citizens' and activists' best efforts.

Even Mike Piccarreta, Elmer's lawyer, said as much. "The country has decided it wants a war on drugs. We're sending people down to the border, armed to the teeth, and the traffickers are armed to the teeth. This is not going to be the last time something like this happens."

Indeed, it was not. By 1998, the U.S. Border Patrol had grown so fast that almost 40 percent of the four thousand agents nationwide had spent less than two years on the job. Large numbers of relatively inexperienced agents confronting mostly nonviolent border-crossers, with a few armed drug smugglers thrown in, was a potent mix. In the summer of that year, such a combination led, as Elmer's lawyer had predicted, to another tragic death in the canyons west of Nogales.

Around 1:00 A.M. on June 3—almost six years to the day after the killing of Dario Miranda Valenzuela—a young Border Patrol agent named Alex Kirpnick and his partner surprised a group of marijuana backpackers in Potrero Canyon. Kirpnick's partner chased after two of the fleeing backpackers while Kirpnick ordered two others to get down on their knees and put their hands behind their heads. One of the men tried to escape. As Kirpnick grabbed him, the other smuggler apparently reached for a handgun hidden in his pocket. The man raised the gun and fired, striking Kirpnick in the head. The twenty-seven-year-old agent, who had been on the force only a year and a half, was airlifted to a hospital in Tucson, but died a few hours later.

Kirpnick was the first Border Patrol agent killed in the line of duty in Nogales since 1926, and his death prompted an outpouring of concern. More than two thousand people, including Attorney General Janet Reno and Border Patrol agents from twenty-one different sectors, attended a memorial service for him at Tucson's new baseball stadium. The service featured such military honors as a fife and drum corps, a riderless horse, and a six-helicopter flyby in the "missing man" formation. Reno eulogized Kirpnick as a "model of what it means to be an American" and as a man who died "protecting his newfound freedom." Kirpnick, ironically enough, had been an immigrant, an Orthodox Jew who had come as a teenager to Los Angeles with his family from Ukraine. He spoke six languages and often served as translator when the Border Patrol captured undocumented immigrants from Eastern Europe. His alleged killer, a twenty-five-year-old Nogales, Sonora, man with a string of drug arrests, was caught by police in Nogales a few days later. After the Mexican government received assurance that the accused man would not be given the death penalty, he was extradited to the United States for trial.

In the wake of the Kirpnick shooting, another wave of violence both directed at and by Border Patrol agents engulfed the border. Agents were pelted with rocks and bottles and had laser beams and potshots fired in their direction; and at least six times between June and September 1998, they responded to the attacks with gunfire. Several immigrants were injured, and one, twenty-three-year-old Antonio Rentería Martínez, was shot dead after allegedly threatening an agent with a rock near Yuma, Arizona, on September 9. Although Rentería and the agent were about fifty yards apart when the shooting occurred, the agent claimed he feared for his life. He was cleared of wrongdoing, as was another agent who shot and killed a rock thrower south of San Diego later that month.

The Border Patrol attributed the increase in violence to the immigrants' growing anger that it was becoming so difficult for them to cross. No doubt, the crackdown was heightening tensions by pushing people into areas where they had not been before. The buildup in Nogales shifted the flow eastward to the Douglas–Agua Prieta area, prompting staggering numbers of arrests there, some one thousand per day in the spring of 1999. The Border Patrol reported that hundreds were massing on the Mexican side and running across in groups, just as they had done years earlier in southern California. Some rural residents, angry that border-crossers were tearing down fences, breaking water pipes, and leaving trash, took the law into their own hands. A wheelchair-bound Santa Cruz County man shot at and almost blew the arm off an immigrant who was walking across his property, and ranchers near Douglas began rounding up dozens at gunpoint. The ranchers and others demanded that the military be deployed on the border.

The prospect of military patrols raised alarm bells on both sides of the line. Not only was the border prime smuggling territory, it was home to a growing population of several million law-abiding U.S. and Mexican citizens. Even the Border Patrol, which was trained in civilian law enforcement, had trouble distinguishing between who belonged and who did not. "The last thing we want is untrained people patrolling the border with weapons against people with babies in their arms," said Douglas Mayor Ray Borane, expressing a view that was widely shared. Either not understanding or not caring about the implications for local residents, the U.S. House twice voted in the late 1990s to deploy up to ten thousand troops on the border. It took yet another tragedy to demonstrate how misguided the policy was.

On May 20, 1997, a teenager from the remote West Texas border town of Redford came home from school and, as he often did, took his family's goats down to the river to pasture. Esequiel Hernandez Jr., eighteen, had lived his whole life in Redford, population one hundred. He was known as a polite and respectful kid, the son of a schoolteacher who had founded the local library. On this May afternoon, he was carrying a turn-of-the-century .22 rifle that he used to protect the herd from coyotes and rattlesnakes. As he came up over a ridge, he was spotted by four young Marines camped out on a nearby hilltop. Unbeknownst to Hernandez or anyone else in Redford, the Marines has been there for three days, waiting for drug smugglers to come across the sandy, shallow Rio Grande. The Marines say Hernandez took a shot at them. They were hidden and dressed in full camouflage, so Hernandez probably didn't even know they were there. He may have thought he was shooting at an animal. The Marines reported they were under fire and then followed Hernandez for about twenty minutes from across a ridge about seventy-five yards away. At that point, they say, he turned to shoot at them again. Marine Corporal Clemente Banuelos, twenty-two, responded with a single shot from his M-16. The bullet hit Hernandez squarely in the chest and sent him sprawling into a feed trough. The Marines went to where he lay and stood over him for almost half an hour without rendering aid, even though one of them was trained as a medic. Like Dario Miranda, he bled to death.

Hernandez's death, the first killing of a civilian by the military on U.S. soil since Kent State, galvanized opposition to border militarization. He was, after all, no drug smuggler, not even an undocumented immigrant—just an innocent, small-town American boy shot less than a half-mile from his home. After a grand jury failed to indict Corporal Banuelos, the people of Redford, angry and heartbroken, formed a committee to go to Washington, D.C., and demand that the military be withdrawn from the border. One man from Redford showed lawmakers a picture of Esequiel's mom being given a "Point of Light" award by President Bush, the same president who first ordered troops to the border in 1989. Local residents' pleas, plus both the military's and the Border Patrol's reluctance to continue the policy, led to a suspension of ground patrols. The military continued to be strongly involved in border law enforcement, however, including surveillance, road and wall building, and other support operations.

The ominous trend of military involvement on the border had tragic consequences in Mexico as well. As in the United States, the Mexican military had taken on a major role in the war on drugs in the 1990s, including setting up checkpoints on northbound highways and patrolling rural areas known to be smuggling corridors. In December 1997, one of these army patrols encountered a group of eleven men who were planning to cross the border illegally through the canyons west of Nogales. The men were about three miles from the border when, they said, soldiers started shooting at them without provocation. Juan Pedro Lopez Saldate, a twenty-eight-year-old maquiladora worker and father of two from Nogales, Sonora, was killed, and his brother was injured.

The army claimed the men were suspected drug couriers and had fired on them first, but no drugs or weapons were found. Gunpowder tests showed that although none of the eleven men had residue on their hands, seventeen of twenty-three soldiers in the platoon did.

Border Patrol officials claimed that if only they could hire enough agents, sixteen thousand or more, they could handle the situation themselves. Perhaps, although the Border Patrol was already straining at the seams after doubling in size within the space of five years. Hiring problems that had plagued the agency in the past were beginning to resurface. One new agent in Nogales was found to have sold cocaine and murdered another drug dealer in New York before joining the Border Patrol, and another was accused of helping plan a murder in south Texas. Concerned that new hires were not being adequately screened and that their inexperience posed a danger to more seasoned agents, the Border Patrol union called for a slowdown to give the force time to adjust. By 1999, the INS was having trouble finding enough qualified people to fill the ranks, and the Justice Department asked Congress for a one-year moratorium on hiring. Border Patrol officials and border state lawmakers howled that the administration was abandoning its commitment to stop illegal immigration.

About a year after Elmer's second acquittal, Miranda's widow, Margarita, reluctantly settled her civil suit against Elmer and the Border Patrol for about half a million dollars in annuities. She will receive nine hundred dollars a month for the rest of her life, and when Hetzel and Rubén turn eighteen, Hetzel will receive seven hundred dollars and Rubén eight hundred dollars a month for the rest of their lives. "It made me really sad when I got the money," Margarita said. "It would have been so much better for the children to have had their father." Miranda's mother was awarded a few thousand dollars, most of which she spent on an elaborate tomb for Dario. The settlement was a far cry from the two million dollars later paid to the family of Esequiel

Hernandez, but considering what happened in Elmer's two trials, Miranda's family was lucky to get anything. Mike Piccarreta, Elmer's lawyer, said he considered the settlement "a gift" from the U.S. government. "Legally, they aren't entitled to anything."

The money did nothing to lessen the bitterness of Miranda's family, and Luz Castro didn't want to accept it. "Elmer got away with murder. My son is dead, and no one was ever punished for it." Miranda's sister said she had fantasies about killing Elmer and that people she knew in Phoenix had come to her and offered to do the job themselves. Miranda's little boy Rubén told his mother that when he grew up, he was going to kill the man who killed his daddy.

Yet, as the years passed, Rubén began to forget about his father. When he turned seven, Margarita sent him to live with her sister in Nogales, Arizona, so he could attend school in the United States. He did very well and developed a passion for soccer. "I was hoping he might want to be a doctor, like my father, but he wants to be an athlete, like his father." Margarita's daughter, Hetzel, still missed Dario, a pain Margarita understood because she, too, had lost her father as a child. Margarita and Hetzel continued to live with Margarita's elderly mother, and Margarita became friends with another widowed young mother who lived nearby. Margarita didn't go out much. "The border is such a lost place. I see junkies on the corner, injecting themselves. There's so much violence and drugs and gangs. People steal children, take out their hearts, and sell them. I worry about my kids. I want to set a good example, so they'll turn out okay."

On June 12, 1997, the fifth anniversary of Dario Miranda's death, I went to visit Luz Castro in her home overlooking the highway. In previous years, this date had been the occasion for memorial services and protest rallies in Nogales, but today nothing was planned. "I thought you'd forgotten about us," she said as she sat in her small, bare kitchen peeling potatoes. In the afternoon, Luz Castro, one of Miranda's sisters, a couple of neighbors, and I—all women and a few children—

went to the Pantheon of the Cypresses to pray over Miranda's grave. The tomb Luz had bought with her settlement money was a large slab of blue granite with a headstone shaped like an open book at one end and two stone globes, painted to look like soccer balls, at the other. It was surrounded by a locked cage with a tin roof to keep people from stealing the artificial flowers the family brought on the Day of the Dead and on Miranda's birthday. We stood on a little square of AstroTurf beside the tomb while one of the neighbor women said the rosary. The children paid attention at first but soon wandered off to play on nearby graves. After the prayers were finished, we walked slowly back to the car. Miranda's mother, crippled by arthritis and leaning on a cane, began to cry. I put my arm around her; I didn't know what to say.

Margarita didn't go with us to the cemetery that day. When I had gone to visit her the week before, she'd told me she and Miranda's family had had a falling out, and she was ashamed to visit his grave when they were there. The argument had started over the money—Miranda's family was unhappy with the settlement she'd made—and then had become worse when, four years after Miranda's death, she had had a child out of wedlock. The birth was difficult; the child, Ramses, was entangled in his umbilical cord. Margarita had almost bled to death and had required emergency surgery. The doctors told her she probably shouldn't have any more children. Despite her pain and shame, she was thrilled to have another baby. "He's been a blessing to me." She was hurt that Miranda's mother wouldn't accept Ramses as a grandchild, but for the sake of her other children, she wanted to stay on good terms with her in-laws.

At twenty-eight, Margarita still seemed fragile and childlike. She said she was thinking of starting a little grocery store in a front room of her house, which would give her something to do while allowing her to stay home with her kids. The settlement money didn't seem to have changed her life at all. Like Luz Castro's house, Margarita's looked the same as it had years before: bare floors and walls, a few worn pieces of furniture and a small stereo. She had bought a car, then sold it again.

"I'm saving the money in case my kids get sick, in case something happens. It's their patrimony." She told me she could remarry without losing her settlement, but hadn't met anyone worth marrying. Ramses' father was out of the picture and she wasn't seeing anyone else. "I would like to get married again someday, if that's what God wants for me."

I wondered about a large bruise on her cheek, which had been there the last two times I'd visited her. She assured me no one was hitting her. "It's nerves. I've gotten them all over my body since I was a child." She said she still suffered from anxiety attacks and was seeing a psychologist. Even though she had a crossing card, she was afraid to go across the border. A couple of times she'd had to let friends go across without her while she sat on a bench to calm herself because the thought of being interrogated by men in uniform caused her to panic. "When I'm over there and I see the Border Patrol, at McDonald's or someplace, I get the shakes. I see Elmer's face in all of them. I can't forget it." Still, she no longer had the revenge fantasies. "It's not up to me to punish Elmer. God knows where he is, and I have faith and confidence that God knows what his punishment will be."

Even five years after Miranda's death, Margarita could not talk about her husband without tears coming to her eyes. "I try to think about the good things, the happy times, but it's so difficult." She and Dario had gone to parties together. A fan of romantic ballads and of the *norteño* style of music popular in northern Mexico and the U.S. Southwest, he had loved to dance and sing. He probably would have appreciated the *corrido* written about him a few years after his death. In the song "Cañon Mariposa," the singer recounts Miranda's grim tale while an accordion, drums, and keyboard beat out a rollicking, almost joyful accompaniment. A subsequent music video added such satiric touches as a brass section in the jury box playing the theme from *Perry Mason* while the singer looks at the American flag and shakes his head. Both the song and video enjoyed a run of popularity on Spanish radio and television stations across the United States.

Fue en el Cañon Mariposa
No me quiero ni acordar
Mataron a un inocente
Dicen que era un ilegal.

It was in Mariposa Canyon,
I don't even wish to recall.
They killed an innocent man;
They say he was an illegal.

His name was Dario Miranda,
The year was 1992.
It happened in Nogales, Arizona,
Watson was the one who told the tale.

They shot Dario in the back,
Two bullets to the heart.
Michael Elmer the patrolman
Shot him with his AR-15.

Elmer was an agent of the *migra*
And a filthy dog he was.
He threw Dario in a ditch
To cover up what he did.

Watson saw the murder
and had a guilty conscience.
Fifteen hours later
He turned the assassin in.

Ay Dario, my brother,
God keep him at Your side.
Little Virgin of Guadalupe
Pray for him.

Elmer was arrested
and tried on fifteen federal charges,
And though I can't explain it,
He got off scot-free.

What a joke to absolve a murder.
Jurors, please be more objective;
You know killing a poor wetback
Is still considered homicide.

Friends, don't cross anymore,
Don't jump the fence,
Learn from this tragedy,
It could cost you your life.

Fly vulture, away from me,
You belong with the sheriffs
and the *migra* in Nogales, Arizona.
This is where I draw the line.

CHAPTER 4

"Down There No One Is Boss"

A secret world lies beneath the streets of Ambos Nogales, a maze of tunnels and passageways invisible to the casual observer yet well known to the *coyotes* (people smugglers) and drug smugglers and bandits who prey on undocumented immigrants. The tunnel system consists of two main passageways as big as streets that run for three miles underground on either side of the railroad tracks, roughly parallel to Morley and Grand Avenues, plus a number of smaller connecting and tributary passages, for a total of almost five miles of binational storm channels beneath the valley floor. Their many entrances and exits through drains and manholes both official and clandestine make them almost impossible to police. They are so dangerous that even though they offer easy passage under the border, they did not come into wide use until the early 1990s, when safer above-ground routes were sealed off by the wall and the Border Patrol. After that, the coyotes and drug smugglers moved underground, where they encountered another sad consequence of the *maquiladora* boom: a gang of homeless children.

The tunnel children called themselves Barrio Libre Sur (Free Neighborhood of the South), a small, southern outpost of a Latino street gang with branches in several U.S. cities, including Los Angeles, Phoenix, and Tucson. During its heyday in the early 1990s, this gang controlled the tunnels. Armed with rocks, sticks, screwdrivers, knives, and guns, as many as a hundred young people, ranging in age from four and five to eighteen and nineteen, roamed the dark passageways. No one, not the border-crossers or their guides or even drug smugglers, passed through without paying them off. Depending on their mood or their relationship with the smugglers, the kids let some go for only fifty dollars. Others who lacked proper credentials or respect were beaten senseless and robbed of everything they had. It was a brutal business. "The coyotes catch us and beat us up," said Cristina, a veteran tunnel kid who went by the name La Fanta. "We fight with other gangs, too, like Pleito con Oro [Battle with Gold] from Monte Carlo," a neighborhood in Nogales, Arizona. "We have to fight them, or they'll kill us."

Within the gang, Barrio Libre Sur had a caring side. Older kids looked after younger ones and boys after girls. "Some of the boys were really bad criminals, but others protected us and wouldn't let them touch us," Cristina told me. Certain kids developed a following as they grew in age and experience, although there was no strict hierarchy. "Down there no one is boss. The tough ones survive, that's all." Among the boys, one of the leaders was a kid named Manuel from Guadalajara. He was well traveled and even knew some English, having lived for a while with his father, a former cop, and his stepmother in Washington State. Among the girls, the leader was Cristina's best friend, a dark-skinned girl known as La Negra. La Negra's mother had died when she was two, and her alcoholic father had left her and her brother to the streets. Most of the other *bajadores*—undergrounders—had similar stories.

Cristina insisted she wasn't thrown out of her house or abandoned like so many of the others. "A lot of times, when the police catch you, you say, 'My mother hit me' or 'I was mistreated.' But in my case, I have to say that's not true. My mother always was looking for me." A baby-faced girl with freckles and long black hair, Cristina had grown up shuttling between her mother in Nogales and her father in Guaymas; she had managed to complete only four years of school before dropping out. When she was ten years old, she started living in the tunnels full-time. Cristina preferred life underground to the one-room cardboard shack in Colonia Solidaridad she shared with her mother, stepfather, and six younger siblings. "I like being a vagrant," she said with a shy smile.

Cristina showed off her tattoos, more than a half-dozen in all. A crudely done, black-ink heart with a ribbon reading "Gracielda" adorned her upper arm. "That's my mother's name. On my other arm is 'Maria'; that's my grandmother. And I've got my name on my leg. I'm going to get some roses too." On her hands, three dots between thumb and forefinger signified Mi Vida Loca—My Crazy Life—the universal symbol of Latino gang membership. "If anyone asks, I'm from Barrio Libre Sur. We're like brothers." Cristina said she felt safe with her *plebes,* her pals, but life in the tunnel was dangerous for a boy, let alone a girl. "Sometimes I carry a knife. It's the style. I don't look for trouble, but if they come after me, I'll fight. You have to defend yourself." She was sturdy and strong, not a skinny waif like some of the other girls, and she considered herself a good fighter. She had gotten a few black eyes and bruises, and once, another girl stabbed her in the stomach. "She stuck me, and I started bleeding. About a week later I started to feel bad, so I went to the doctor, and they took my appendix out."

Cristina claimed to be "noble and sensitive," yet acknowledged she had a temper. "Anything pisses me off." She once had a job at a maquila but lost it after less than a month for fighting with another girl. She would have quit anyway because it took her a week of factory work to earn what she could make in less than an hour in the tunnel. "Sometimes we make a thousand dollars in one night." Besides robbing immigrants, the kids used the tunnels to go over to the U.S. side, commit crimes, and come back. They hopped freight trains in Nogales, rode the rails to Tucson and Phoenix, and stayed in abandoned houses or with fellow gang members while they broke into people's homes to steal TVs, VCRs, and stereos. Some were caught and sent to prison. Cristina herself was picked up by the cops and the Border Patrol several times, although she usually was just sent back to Mexico. Once she had spent two months in the Santa Cruz County Jail in Nogales, Arizona, and had done time in Consejo Tutelar para Menores (COTUME), the youth prison in Nogales, Sonora, which made her somewhat of an expert on the difference between the two country's juvenile justice systems. "On the other side, they just catch us and throw us on the floor. The jail is a lot cleaner, and they take us out to play basketball, eat in the lunchroom, and watch TV. Here, they kick us and beat us, and you're in the cell all day long. There's no heat, and the beds are made of cement."

Still, cops and jail weren't the worst of it. "One time, I almost died. It was in '93 or '94. Three or four of us were crossing with some illegals, and we came across three coyotes at the entrance to the tunnel. One of them asked me where were the pills I was supposed to get him so he could get high. A few days before I had told him I could get him some, but I hadn't gotten any yet. It was my first crossing of the day, so he took out a knife and held it to my throat and said if I didn't get him the pills, he'd kill me. Then another guy yelled that more people were coming, and he let me go. He said if he saw me again, he'd kill me."

Despite constant fear, Cristina insisted no one in the tunnels had ever raped her or forced her to do anything against her will. "I didn't do drugs or have sex until I was thirteen, and then it was because I wanted to." With all the drugs passing through, pretty much everything was available: pot, coke, speed, downers, heroin. Cristina tried them all, except heroin—she was afraid of becoming a junkie—but her favorite, like a lot of the kids, was inhalants. "It makes me feel really good, real *suave*." The kids poured a little paint thinner in a soda can and carried it around with them all day long, taking sniffs from time to time to dull the pangs of hunger and sickness and the winter cold.

Cristina also found her first boyfriend when she was thirteen—another tunnel kid about her age, originally from Sinaloa—and they went together for about a year and a half. "I had sex with him only twice, and I got pregnant. I thought you couldn't get pregnant the first or second time! We separated, and then I started vomiting—that's how

I knew. I didn't tell him I was pregnant until I was four months along. When he found out, he didn't want to have anything to do with me. He said the kid I had in my belly was a gringo because we'd been up there around the time I got pregnant." Cristina left the tunnel and went home to her mother for the rest of her pregnancy. "I knew the drugs were bad for my baby, and it was too much of a temptation for me to stay down there." In the summer of 1995, she gave birth to her daughter, Sayra, and a stillborn twin. The dead twin was perfectly formed, but very small. "I fell three times while I was pregnant. Maybe that's why it died." Cristina stayed home to breast-feed her daughter, but the lure of the tunnel soon proved to be too strong. Within a year, she had left Sayra with her mother and gone back underground.

Cristina's story piqued my curiosity, but I was too afraid to go below with just her and the other kids. I knew reporters who'd been robbed and had knives pulled on them in the tunnels, so I arranged instead in February 1998 to go along with the kids' mortal enemy, Grupo Beta, the elite Mexican police unit that swept through the tunnels and chased the kids from their lairs several times a day. Grupo Beta was founded in Tijuana in the early 1990s to combat border bandits, coyotes, and other criminals who preyed on migrants. After gaining a reputation for being incorruptible, this "border police" unit was expanded to several other cities on Mexico's northern and southern frontiers, including Nogales and Agua Prieta. Hand-selected from federal, state, and local forces, Grupo Beta's officers received special training and were paid much better than ordinary policemen—all in order to encourage loyalty and professionalism.

Adán Leal, the twenty-five-year-old supervisor of the Beta force who took me into the tunnels, wouldn't disclose how much he made, but claimed it was at least three times the average policeman's salary of $230 a month. Born and raised in Nogales, Adán had attended military college in Mexico City and spent several years on the Nogales police force before being recruited for Beta. A small, thin, light-skinned man with a silver lining surrounding one of his front teeth, he obviously reveled in his work. In black boots and a black leather vest over a polyester print shirt, he even looked the part of an urban cowboy.

Two nights before I went underground with Grupo Beta, a smuggler had been shot and killed at the entrance to one of the tunnels. We were going below at midmorning, a relatively safe time of day, but the four young officers were nervous about the killing, and they insisted I put on a bulletproof vest. Three of them carried Glock pistols, and Adán wore an additional Smith and Wesson .44 strapped to his leg. The fourth man, big and silent and sporting mirror sunglasses like a Mexican movie star, cradled an AK-47 assault rifle in his arm. Adán did most of the talking. "This is the first killing in the tunnel since we started patrolling here in '94. The tunnel kids accuse us of doing it, but we all took paraffin tests and passed. They always accuse us of everything. They'll say, 'I'll give you a hundred dollars if you let me go.' 'I'll tell them you beat us up.' They're a bunch of lowlifes."

Adán explained that it was a crime just to be in the tunnel, so he and his men arrested everyone they encountered. "A lot of the time the kids just run over to the U.S. side and wait until we leave." Once in a while, Grupo Beta held joint, pincer-type sweeps with the U.S. Border Patrol, but as a rule the two didn't work together. "We don't stop people from migrating. That's their job." Adán called the Border Patrol his "good friends," and he attended the funeral of Agent Alex Kirpnick in Tucson later that year, but he also thought some agents were a little soft. "They're afraid to go in the tunnel, and when they do, they put on masks." He laughed.

Adán drove us downtown and parked his brand-new white Dodge Ram pickup beside the border fence a few blocks west of the port of entry. It had been a rainy, El Niño–soaked winter, and construction crews were busy reinforcing a concrete-lined drainage channel that ran parallel to the fence. We jumped down onto the wet sandy floor of the arroyo and headed east into the tunnel, which was maybe ten feet across and five feet high at the entrance. The channel sloped downhill so that

Grupo Beta officers watch a suspected smuggler from within one of the tunnels that runs under the border between Ambos Nogales.

all the men soon could walk standing up. Two of them, the studious-looking one in wire-rimmed glasses and the sharp-featured one wearing a brand-new Boston Celtics cap, went far ahead to make sure there were no surprises. Adán stayed right behind or in front of us, and the silent one with the assault gun brought up the rear.

A small but steady stream of water ran down the middle of the floor of the tunnel, the remnants of what had been a torrent the week before that had washed the place clean. It was a chilly February morning, and the air in the tunnel smelled fresh. We could hear street noises overhead and our way was lit by sun pouring in through storm drains and gaps in the concrete. At one opening, a clear curtain of water cascaded like a fountain through a broad band of daylight. After a hundred yards or so, the channel dipped deeper underground and merged with the Grand Avenue tunnel, an airy cavern perhaps fifteen feet across. Yellow police tape had been strung across the main passageway south, no doubt for my benefit. "You can't go down there," Adán said. "That's where the shooting took place, and we're still investigating."

Climbing over a large, black-plastic sewer pipe that bisected our path, we continued up the tunnel. After another fifty feet or so, we came to the steel doors that the National Guard had installed in 1994 to deter illegal entrants. The massive doors were designed to push open during heavy rains—otherwise catastrophic flooding would result—but that left them vulnerable to pressure from tunnel kids and smugglers. ("They close them; we open them. It's no big deal," Cristina later told me.) The day we were there, the doors stood open a couple of feet, enough to let through a narrow waterfall and, of course, any determined human being. The Beta officers made no attempt to close the doors. That was the Border Patrol's job. We turned back.

Our next stop was a street corner just east of the port of entry, at the entrance to the Buenos Aires neighborhood that overlooks the plaza. After ducking through a three-foot gap between the street and the curb, we climbed another six feet down onto a large stone ramp that descended into Morley Avenue tunnel. This tunnel was huge—maybe twenty feet across and twenty feet high—old and deep underground. It was the granddaddy of them all, made of stones embedded in concrete in the 1930s by the Works Progress Administration. At the bottom of the ramp, the air was warm and humid and filled with the roar of rushing water. It was pitch black. We turned on our flashlights and looked at the water coursing over the rocks, a raging natural stream unnaturally confined in this dungeon. We turned north and walked along a narrow ledge beside the streambed. No one spoke. Concentrating on my steps, listening to the water, and breathing the damp air, I felt the lure of this place myself. The water looked and smelled clean, and it was a kick to be somewhere secret and forbidden, close to the everyday world and yet so hidden. We reached the steel doors, which were standing wide open. As in the other tunnel, we saw no one.

We headed back up the ramp, and Adán pointed out something we'd missed on the way down. A pocket-size, maroon, plastic photo album lay face down in the mud. We picked it up and looked at the pictures: children, a wedding couple, and people at a party, all well dressed and smiling. A few photos had been torn from the album and lay scattered on the ground, soaking wet and streaked with mud. "Must have belonged to an illegal," Adán observed. We left the photos where we found them and climbed out onto the sunny street.

Back at the Grupo Beta office, Adán showed me his own album of Polaroids and mug shots of various tunnel kids. He knew them all by name. "Here's one they call 'El Enano' [the Dwarf]," he said, showing me a blurry photo of a small teenage boy, apparently taken in the tunnel. "He's only fifteen, but he's one of the ringleaders. And here's his girlfriend, La Güina [the Louse]. Here's Manuel." He turned the page. "These two, El Morgan and El Gato, have been arrested."

Later, I told Cristina, Manuel, and some of the other tunnel kids about my visit with Grupo Beta. They wanted a full report. "What did they say?" "Did they mention me?" "Did they have my picture?" The kids told me Grupo Beta was *muy malo,* just as Adán said they would. "They beat us up and hold our faces down in the tunnel water and make us drink it." The kids knew the smuggler who'd been shot, and they blamed Grupo Beta for his death and for a couple of others along the fence. They laughed when I told them I'd heard Beta officers were incorruptible. "They take bribes just like any other cop." (I later learned the entire Nogales unit had been fired in 1996 after federal investigators discovered that they were taking bribes and committing crimes.) One time, the tunnel kids said, Beta caught a kid who had been accused of raping a girl in the tunnel. The officers took the boy back to the station, where, to teach him a lesson, they made him put on a dress and took pictures while another street kid raped him.

The kids' faces lit up when I brought out some newspaper and magazine articles about them that I'd collected. They smirked at photos of themselves making gang signs and looking tough, and Cristina laughed out loud when she saw one of herself, taken three years before, when she was fourteen. Her bangs hung over heavily made-up, half-closed eyes; a cigarette dangled from bright red lips; and her right arm was thrust forward with thumb and forefinger held in the shape of the letter *L.* "I can't believe I looked like that! Do I look older now?" We talked about the different kids in the photos. Some were still around, some had moved on, some were in jail. One boy was dead. He had fallen from a moving train the previous summer. Somber for a moment, the kids contemplated his fate; then one cracked a joke, and they all were laughing again.

By 1993, businesses near the entrance to the tunnels on the U.S. side had become fed up with Barrio Libre Sur. The kids were completely out of control—breaking into pay telephones, stealing cans of spray paint and gasoline additives from the hardware store, smashing windows on cars being worked on at Joe's Garage, accosting customers at Church's Fried Chicken, and stabbing one man in the stomach with a screwdriver when he refused to share his meal. "They throw rocks at customers who won't give them food," the Church's manager said. "They busted out the windows on a Saturday afternoon when there were a lot of people inside eating." Employees at the Nogales Public Library were threatened as they walked to their cars, and one time when they forgot to set the alarm, the kids broke into the library and ransacked it. Crime and vandalism reached record levels. Of the 578 burglaries committed in Nogales, Arizona, that year, at least a third were estimated to be committed by the tunnel kids.

Authorities on the U.S. side didn't know what to do. The Border Patrol would arrest the kids and return them to Mexico, but within hours they'd be back hanging out in front of Church's again. The Santa Cruz County juvenile detention center was full of them, so much so that local youths were being turned away. "We talked to the Nogales, Sonora, authorities, and they said, 'We don't have a problem; you do,'" recalled Santa Cruz County Attorney Jan Smith Florez. In desperation, the Nogales city council declared a state of emergency, and Florez arranged for copies of a video that showed rival gang members inhaling paint thinner and throwing rocks at each other to be sent to politicians and news outlets in Phoenix and Tucson. The shocking pictures soon appeared on television in both the United States and Mexico.

Some of the stories after that dubbed the kids "vampires" and "tunnel rats," names Cristina found insulting. "We're human beings just like everyone else," she told me.

Although yet another black eye for Nogales, the publicity did shame the U.S. and Mexican governments into doing something about the tunnels. Patrols were stepped up on the U.S. side, and the doors were constructed; most of all, Grupo Beta put the tunnel kids on the run and succeeded at keeping most of them in Mexico. But there was another side to this story. Florez, Santa Cruz County Manager Dennis Miller, and other longtime Nogales, Arizona, residents were disturbed by the situation and felt it needed more than just a law enforcement response. "If they were adults, I'd feel differently, but they're children," Florez said. "They were put in our face, and we must act responsibly, even if they are criminals." In 1994, Florez helped obtain a fifty-thousand-dollar grant from the Arizona Supreme Court Juvenile Crime Reduction Fund to create a drop-in center for the kids in Nogales, Sonora. The center, called Mi Nueva Casa (My New House), was a private, binational effort to reach kids whom everyone else had long since given up on. It was not going to be easy.

Mi Nueva Casa opened in November on a downtown side street only yards from the international fence. One side of the small, narrow duplex served as the living room, dining room, and kitchen; the other side had the office, schoolroom (for basic literacy classes), and game room; and a small back courtyard connecting the two sides served as a laundry and outdoor shower. The house was set up as a place where kids could get off the street, have something to eat, watch TV or play games on the computers, and maybe learn something.

The board hired a local community activist named Teresa Leal to be the first director. This single mother of eight set the tone: care for the kids, have certain rules and expectations, yet don't be so strict as to drive them away. "All we can do is make it available to them," said Jan Smith Florez. "We can't force ourselves on them." The rules were fairly

14-year-old Salvador visits Mi Nueva Casa one morning after spending the night in the tunnels.

simple: no swearing, no fighting, no drugs, and the kids had to show up by 9:00 A.M. to have breakfast before attending class.

A core group of about twenty responded enthusiastically. During the first few months, they helped to paint the place inside and out, adding colorful figures of Yaqui deer dancers on the front, along with the words *Mi Nueva Casa*. Some kids took the opportunity to go to the doctor, dentist, or barber, take classes or enroll in trade school, enter drug treatment, and reconcile with their families. "If you want help, they'll help you," one boy told me.

The house attracted much favorable attention on the U.S. side, including visits by politicians such as Attorney General Janet Reno and Arizona Senator John McCain, as well as support from big-name donors such as musician Carlos Santana. When MTV came to Nogales to hold a benefit for the Casa, Santana, who was raised in Tijuana, donated more than ten thousand dollars and gave the tunnel kids free tickets to one of his concerts, where they were also allowed to set up a fund-raising booth. The kids were thrilled.

The house had been open a little more than a year when lifelong Nogales, Sonora, resident Cecilia Guzmán was hired to serve as schoolteacher. Cecilia had been a church volunteer during the sanctuary movement, and she had heard Central American refugees' horrific stories of death squads and massacres, yet nothing had prepared her for the reality of the tunnel kids' lives. "It was a very powerful experience. I saw a side of life I'd never seen before." At the Casa, Cecilia met Inez, an angelic-looking girl who had been abandoned by her mother when she was three or four. By the time she was thirteen, Inez had already been drinking, taking drugs, and prostituting herself for several years. "She had a bad case of syphilis. One day she came into the Casa barely able to walk. She'd been used by a lot of guys—she'd have sex with them for a joint, whatever." A lively and outgoing girl who loved to sing along with her favorite romantic ballads playing on her Walkman, Inez was also an excellent student who dreamed of graduating from high school and becoming a secretary.

Another one of Cecilia's brightest and most dedicated students was a fifteen-year-old girl named Alma. "When I started at Mi Nueva Casa, Alma had just gotten back from Tijuana," Cecilia recalled. "The year before, she had had a child who died shortly after birth. She said she thought she was pregnant again, so I took her to the clinic, and it turned out she was, but she also had a very advanced case of syphilis. There's a lot of venereal disease among the kids—herpes, gonorrhea, syphilis. Also tuberculosis. Thank God none of them have tested positive for AIDS." Cecilia took Alma to a specialist, who, like most of the doctors and labs used by the Casa, treated her for free. In spite of the scars, Alma gave birth to a healthy baby boy. "The day before she had him, she was in the tunnel, taking drugs. When she started to have labor pains, she left the tunnel to go to the hospital." The Mexican child-welfare authorities found out about Alma, and when the baby was about six months old, they took him away and gave him to her sister to raise. Alma went back underground.

Cristina, for her part, avoided Mi Nueva Casa for almost two years after it opened. "I thought they were going to arrest us or something. I didn't want to go, but some kids I knew were going and said it was okay. One morning, I went there to look for them and have breakfast." Wary and distant at first, she blossomed under Cecilia's tutelage. She learned she was good at math, even though she had forgotten many things, and began coming to class almost every day. She also started hanging around with Manuel, the tunnel kid leader who had become another Casa regular. "Manuel really wanted to get out of that life," Cecilia said, "but he had a lot of resentment from being abandoned by his mother." He came to class in the mornings and got a job selling tacos in the street in the afternoons. Cecilia always had at least ten or twelve kids in her class. "On days when I had fewer, I'd go out and look for them in the street." She taught some to read and write, and helped others to finish primary school. The kids called her *profe* (short for *profesora*), and when Cecilia quit working at the Casa in 1997, they brought silk flowers and candy, and wrote her thank-you notes in their careful, newly learned letters.

One day in early 1998, Cecilia and I went to COTUME, the juvenile prison, to visit Alma, who had been caught in the tunnel the previous weekend. On the way, Cecilia told me more of Alma's story. Her father, a bricklayer, had done his best to raise Alma and her brothers and sisters when their mother had run off with another man. When Alma was seven, her mother reappeared and took her to live with her new stepfather in Caborca. Alma had been there for only a few months when the stepfather raped her. He was arrested and jailed for the crime, and Alma went back to Nogales to live with her real father. "But after that, she started to rebel against everything and everyone," Cecilia told me. She quit going to school in fifth grade and went into the tunnels. A few years later, her mother showed up at Mi Nueva Casa to ask Alma to help her get the stepfather released from jail. "I'll never forget that day. We were so angry. How could a mother ask for something like that? Very probably, Alma got syphilis from him."

We arrived at COTUME, a small L-shaped building fronted by a fenced-in courtyard on a narrow, sloping side street in downtown Nogales. Cecilia called to a woman working in the kitchen, who came out and unlocked the gate. We waited in the courtyard while she went to get Alma. From the doorway, I could see down the hall to the dark cells where kids were kept, boys in one and girls in the other. Small hands reached through the bars while children's voices called out to Cecilia, "Profe, profe." When Alma emerged, the COTUME staffers, unfailingly polite, brought chairs for the three of us to sit on. Alma was a tall, thin girl with long dark hair and a damaged right eye that wandered as she talked. (Cecilia later told me the injury was from birth.) "Grupo Beta caught me on Saturday night," she said. "I told them I was pregnant so they wouldn't beat me up. It worked." She smiled. This was Alma's third arrest, which made her eligible to be sent to Hermosillo to do hard time because COTUME was supposed to be only a temporary jail, for a month's stay at most. But, Alma claimed, "One of the girls in the cell with me has been here two months already, and nobody's come to visit her. She's from Navajoa. She knows La Negra. The other one, she's from Imuris. She cried all night and wet her pants." Alma, who apparently had not bathed, changed clothes, or brushed her hair in days, was nonchalant about her fate. She asked if we could come back tomorrow with some candy for her. Cecilia promised to bring both candy and shampoo.

Licenciado Alejandro Guzmán, the director of COTUME, an earnest and serious young man wearing a mustache and oversize glasses, invited me into his cramped office beside the jail. It was an early spring day and through the open window we could hear birds chirping and children's voices drifting over from the cells, including Alma and the other girls singing their favorite songs. Guzmán (no relation to Cecilia) explained the jail had space for thirty-five, and currently twenty-two were incarcerated. "We're getting many more girls than ever before, for the same crimes as the boys, and also prostitution, even girls thirteen years old," he said softly, shaking his head. "We really weren't prepared for this." He described a big increase in gangs, vandalism, drug use, and other antisocial behavior by young people in Nogales in the 1990s. "We haven't reached the extremes of Juárez or Tijuana yet, but we've identified at least one gang in every barrio in the city." He blamed the large "floating" population that had been attracted by *maquila* jobs or by the prospect of immigrating illegally to the United States. "Parents are split up, with the father on one side and the mother on the other. There's a feeling of impotence or disappointment for the parents that they can't reach their dreams. Without a house, without a stable job, without the possibility of social or economic advancement, the family falls apart. The kids end up in the street."

The crackdown in the tunnel and along the fence had produced a paradoxical effect on Ambos Nogales. Burglaries, assaults, and other crimes had dropped by more than half on the U.S. side, whereas in Nogales, Sonora, crime had gone up. Juvenile arrests jumped by almost a third between 1995 and 1996—from 1,120 to 1,475—and remained high. The tunnel kids were only part of the increase, but the figures made clear that much more prevention and rehabilitation of young criminals needed to be done on the Mexican side. "Up until now, we haven't had the resources," Guzmán said. "We have to protect these kids from themselves, even if it means putting them in jail. We have to work at the level of the family because if the family doesn't change, the kid won't. Some parents drop their responsibilities on us. They think it's a joke that we've arrested their kid."

To Guzmán, the problem of young people going astray reflected a loss of social, moral, and spiritual values. The situation was especially bad on the border, where maquiladoras had caused widespread social dislocation and the temptations of U.S. consumer culture were strong. "The border is the door to the rest of the country, and so many problems manifest themselves here first. People from the south bring their ideas and their customs with them at the beginning, but after they stay a while, they pick up the ways of the border: the manner of dress, the way of thinking, even eating flour tortillas." He was quiet for a moment. "The basic problem goes beyond working mothers. It's that people aren't prepared for a technological society. They don't know how to cope. It seems as we become more technological, we lose our humanity. I see people on the street here selling stuff from Taiwan." He smiled at the absurdity of impoverished Mexicans hawking cheap goods made on the other side of world.

Yet, the modernity of the border—through its exposure to the United States—had its advantages, Guzmán felt. "In the United States, people have been working on these problems for a long time and have a lot of experience with programs that work. We are twenty years behind in terms of prevention. We need to go beyond the outmoded ways we have of dealing with youth, such as paternalism. We as parents, citizens, members of society have to come together to find a way to be more human without losing the values of the past. We have to show respect for the rights of youths, while still preserving Mexico's traditional values of respect for family, culture, nation, and religion."

At the time we talked, Guzmán and other community leaders in Nogales had recently announced the formation of a coalition focusing on youth. The coalition, led by the new mayor of Nogales, Wenceslao Cota, a former teacher and juvenile probation officer, would have both law enforcement and social service components and would involve the private sector as well as community groups in creating new social, artistic, and recreational outlets for young people. As its first priority, the coalition planned to launch a program called Rescate (Rescue), in which teams of police and social workers would go into schools and neighborhoods, identify kids at risk, and educate both parents and children in how to prevent delinquency.

"I have hope that, with these programs, the problems of antisocial conduct will be reduced," Mayor Cota later told me. If Rescate were to succeed, it would have to start in primary school because most kids dropped out before eighth grade, the legal minimum for leaving school in Mexico. It also would have to go to where the majority of teenagers were: the maquiladoras. "The maquilas have an obligation with

Nogales, if not formal, then moral," Cota said. "Most of them are aware of this. The big firms, like Chamberlain, want to help us and are looking for ways to be present in the community. Some have basketball teams. We would like them to be greater contributors and participants in channeling energy in positive ways."

Guzmán walked me out to the fenced courtyard, where two boys, inmates in the jail, were painting a stack of old tires blue and white. "They're doing community service," Guzmán explained. "Those tires are going to be used to make a playground in a new park." We stood there for a moment and watched the boys work. I asked if I could see the cells where the kids were kept, but Guzmán refused. I think he was embarrassed.

After the initial bloom of success wore off, cracks began to appear in Mi Nueva Casa. The same qualities that made the place attractive to kids—the fact that they weren't required to be there, the sympathetic adults, the lack of strict rules and expectations—also limited how much good it could do. "The kids' lives are a vicious circle. For two, three months, they come to the Casa, get off drugs, keep clean," Cecilia said. "But the alternatives are too few and too hard, and the kids are too weak. Someone offers them drugs, and they're back in the tunnel."

Two of Cecilia's students, both boys in their early teens, quit using, left the tunnels, and got jobs in maquilas. For the others, progress came slowly, if at all. After graduating from eighth grade, Inez went on a bender and ended up in detox. The Casa then paid for her to enroll in beauty school, which she attended only a few months before dropping out and resuming her street life. Manuel took off to Tijuana or Juárez or no one knew where whenever he felt like it, often disappearing for days or weeks at a time. Alma went back to the tunnels after serving a month in COTUME, and Cristina, despite having received a shot of Norplant, ended up pregnant again, this time by Manuel. "These kids don't see beyond tomorrow," Jan Smith Florez said. "They think life is a series of random acts."

The Casa's most obvious limitation was that it was open only during the day. "They have a place to keep the youths busy for a few hours, but not a place where they can stay," said Guzmán of COTUME. When the doors closed in the evening, the kids went back to the street or down into the tunnels again, where they inhaled paint thinner and promptly forgot all they had learned. Florez and other board members talked about building a twenty-four-hour facility, and Habitat for Humanity in Nogales offered to help with construction. Yet, without a steady source of funds to build, staff, and maintain it, an overnight shelter remained a distant dream. Even if such a place could be built, it would hardly be a cure-all because many street kids wanted nothing to do with the very structure and discipline the shelter was intended to provide.

Another difficulty centered on staff turnover. The house mothers remained constant, but numerous directors, teachers, and counselors came and went during the Casa's first five years. Conflicts and power struggles sprang up between the U.S.-based board and the Mexico-based staff. Cecilia Guzmán quit after less than a year, although she stayed in touch with the kids and invited some to her house. Teresa Leal didn't last long as director, either, and her successor, a young Mexican American from El Paso who was part of the Border Volunteer Corps, had to leave after just a few months when he learned corps members weren't allowed to work in Mexico. (The short-lived Border Volunteer Corps, one of President Clinton's AmeriCorps programs, was itself soon axed amid charges of poor performance and financial mismanagement.)

The next director, a Spanish-speaking social worker from Tucson named Ron Rosenberg, was instrumental in obtaining a $300,000 grant for the Casa from the Kellogg Foundation, but that money also turned out to be restricted to use on the U.S. side. Rosenberg ended up taking his grant to the Boys and Girls Club in Nogales, Arizona, and Mi Nueva Casa was again left leaderless. The situation illustrated the headaches that arose from working binationally. On the premise that "we should be helping our own first," many U.S.-based volunteer and funding agencies were forbidden to do cross-border work. Yet, as Jan Smith Florez pointed out, "These kids are 'our own.' If we don't help them over there, they'll be over here causing trouble." The Casa also received scant support from authorities and charities in Nogales, Sonora. Some local residents even went on Radio XENY to denounce the place for enabling the kids to lead lives of crime. "They were leading very good lives of crime before we got there," retorted Florez.

Although the Arizona Supreme Court Juvenile Crime Reduction Fund reduced funding for the Casa each year after its inception and eliminated it entirely in 1998, Florez was confident the house would survive. She told me the board was soliciting donations from other sources and had registered Mi Nueva Casa as a nonprofit organization with the Mexican government, which should make it easier to bring donations across and perhaps to obtain more funding. She rejected the claim that the Casa was ineffectual. "Prior to Mi Nueva Casa, nobody had been there consistently for the kids—not their family, school, society, nothing. We've been there five years." As she pointed out, success with these kids was relative. "Success is not being syphilitic. It's not having lice. There are children who are alive today and relatively healthy and who still have a future because of Mi Nueva Casa. They've been shown a different way. That's success."

In the summer of 1998, just a few months after Grupo Beta's Adán Leal took me into the tunnels, he was arrested for murder. According to Adán, he and his girlfriend were eating a taco late one night in Colonia Solidaridad, a poor neighborhood on the city's southeast side, when some kids came up and told them two Nogales city policemen had been shot nearby. Adán went to see if the officers were alive, but they were not; he then radioed for help. Considering his story a little too coincidental, Nogales police arrested him the next day. "Now I know why people don't report crimes," a dejected Adán said from his jail cell. News of his arrest raced through town, vindicating what the tun-

A house in Colonia Solidaridad made of discarded cardboard, wooden pallets, and tin is home to two boys washing their hands in barrels once used to store industrial chemicals.

nel kids had said about Grupo Beta. "I hope he rots" was Cristina's reaction.

The murders and the accusation against Adán caused shake-ups in both the local police and Beta. The police chief and the head of Beta promptly resigned, and the new head of Beta lasted less than six weeks before he too resigned, reportedly to take a job in the private sector. Murder charges against Adán were soon dropped because of lack of evidence, but he continued to be held for several months on charges that he had shot a border-crosser in the buttocks the previous February. After he finally was released, Grupo Beta fired him, and he moved to Phoenix. The killings of the police officers remained unsolved.

The murders, Adán's arrest, and subsequent shake-ups in local law enforcement revealed a major flaw in programs such as Rescate, which relied on police exhorting children to stay away from gangs and drugs. Even if not all the Nogales, Sonora, cops were on the take and involved with drug and people smuggling, the public perception was that they were. "With role models like these, how do we expect the children to act any better?" asked Cecilia Guzmán. The Rescate program had other problems, too, according to local artist Alberto Morackis. "Each new administration that comes in wants to create its own programs, so there's no continuity beyond three years, at most." A year after Rescate was formed, Morackis, who often worked with young people on art projects, told me he had never heard of it.

Throughout the 1990s, Alberto Morackis's brightly hued, politically themed murals began appearing on walls and public buildings all over Nogales. The work was so well done that the city paid Morackis and his young assistants to paint several of the most visible spaces in town. His large mural at the downtown Plaza Miguel Hidalgo featured red, green, and yellow anatomical drawings of human and mythical figures, Yaqui deer dancers, and Aztec gods with hearts, muscles, and bones revealed, superimposed over olive drab vertical lines representing the border wall. "It's called 'The Horizon Is Hurt by a Fence,' and it's meant to show the diverse social culture of this city and the triumph of human solidarity." Morackis and I also visited a mural he and his assistants had painted on the wall of the public basketball court next to COTUME. This work was another colorful celebration of the faces of Nogales—Indian, Mexican, Anglo, Asian, and African—gathered to play the city's favorite game. "Nogales has a big basketball tradition. There's been lots of championships won here. Every barrio has a corner where the kids put up a hoop." Morackis said kids in Nogales, no matter how tough, appreciated art. "Murals are a Mexican tradition. None of the ones we've done has been vandalized. Even the *cholos* [gang kids] like them. Some have asked me to paint a Virgin of Guadalupe in their neighborhood."

Other than the family, the church is probably the one institution in Mexico that still commands enough respect to make a difference in kids' lives. Many people who worked with youth in Nogales told me they believed faith-based programs were the best, if not the only, way to combat delinquency. One of the city's most respected youth advocates, businessman Marco Antonio Martínez, was a firm believer in this approach. A cultured, English-speaking Nogales native in his midforties and a member of the prominent Dabdoub family, Martínez served on the board of Casa Hogar, a home for abandoned and abused kids that was run by Italian nuns from the Little Sisters of St. Teresa of Jesus. Since Martínez's tenure had begun in the mid-1980s, the orphanage had grown from caring for six kids to housing more than twenty and had also begun offering counseling and other services. Yet Martínez had become increasingly concerned about the number of troubled kids in the city. "After a while, we felt we weren't really making an impact on the problem."

One afternoon I went to visit Martínez in his small office, which overlooked the floor of one of the stores of the local supermarket chain he ran, EconoMax. Plaques honoring his civic accomplishments and photos of his model-beautiful wife and their five children decorated the walls. As we talked about social conditions in Mexico, Martínez referred frequently to books and papers piled high around his desk. The statistics were frightening. Mexico is one of the five poorest countries in Latin America, despite its position next to the booming United States. Martínez told me one confidential government study found that people in the poorest state, Chiapas, actually ate better than people in one of the richest, Sinaloa. "And on the border, I'm sure it's worse." Education was at its lowest level in fifty years, with elementary teachers paid so little they had to make tortillas or sell produce to make a living. Of every one hundred kids who started elementary school, only three went on to *preparatoria* (the equivalent of high school in the United States).

In 1996, Martínez heard about the work of the Salecinian Society, a Catholic organization that ran more than two dozen youth centers in fifteen cities in northern Mexico. He went to Juárez to see what they were doing and was very impressed. The centers operated on a four-part model: sports and cultural activities, schooling, vocational training, and religion. "They take kids from ages eight to sixteen, mostly dropout boys, but girls as well. There's not a lot of requirements to get in. You just show up and register. Everything's free. They try to empower the kids as fast as they can, in two- or three-month classes. They get them back in school, or if not school, they teach them to read and write. They develop skills, like carpentry and farming. They do music and art. They also try to influence the kids' home life, to educate fathers and mothers how to handle money and help the husband, who in many cases is a drunk. The secret is to influence kids when they're eight or nine, so they can make it through the teen years. Ages ten, eleven, and twelve are the most dangerous. If the kids learn values and a skill by then, the chances they will get involved in drugs are minimal."

Martínez acknowledged the Salecinians weren't set up to help youths like the tunnel kids. "We're more looking at prevention. When you prevent, you can take care of a thousand kids in a week," far more than at Mi Nueva Casa or Casa Hogar. "We don't work with kids already in trouble with the law. We need to promote other groups to work with them." Victory Outreach, a Christian drug-treatment program, had some success with a few gang members. Martínez also knew of an effort to establish a ranch for troubled youth near Magdalena, where they would be able to undergo drug rehabilitation while they studied, did chores, and learned a trade. The tunnel kids probably needed this kind of structured, rural setting to turn their lives around. Martínez told me he'd formed a board to establish a Salecinian Center in Nogales, and they'd already secured a 60,000-square-foot *terreno,* or plot of land, in Colonia Bella Vista, a far southeast-side neighborhood next to the old dump. Now all he had to do was raise the money.

In October 1997, when seventeen-year-old Cristina was seven months pregnant with Manuel's baby, Grupo Beta arrested her in the tunnel. "I wasn't using drugs," she protested. "I was just down there to make money crossing people." It didn't matter. The officers gave her a stern warning: if they caught her down there again, she would lose her kids, just like Alma. The threat scared her, and she tried to go straight again. When we met at Cecilia Guzmán's house the following February, she was neatly dressed in a black pantsuit and light makeup, and her two daughters, the oldest two years and the other two months old, appeared well cared for and adorable as dolls in frilly clothes. Still carrying the weight of pregnancy, Cristina breast-fed the baby while we talked. She and her children were living with her mother, and Mi Nueva Casa had enrolled her in beauty school and was paying her bus fare. "They're helping a little, but it's up to me to change. I want to work hard for my kids and for me." She sounded like she didn't believe she could do it. "I want to go down in the tunnel, but I'm scared they'll catch me." She told me she hung around with the gang above ground instead, especially Manuel. "We're more or less in love. I don't think about marriage, though. We're okay like this." She watched her older daughter Sayra playing on the floor. "Look at how fast she's growing. What's she going to think of me when she gets older?"

Despite good intentions, Cristina had a tough year. Manuel took off again not long after our visit. He went to Tijuana, where his father lived, and then to Juárez. Cristina later discovered he had gotten another girl from the tunnel pregnant, and they were now living together in the port city of Empalme. She wasn't sad, though. "We didn't fight or anything. He just went crazy and took off. I don't love him anymore, and I wouldn't take him back. I can't trust him. He comes to see the little girl, and that's it." She didn't have much use for men at all. "What for? All they want to do is get you naked." She said she had an IUD. "I definitely don't want any more kids. Kids are God's punishment for having sex! I don't have a boyfriend right now, either. I'm fine as I am. I want to dedicate myself to my kids, and I'll come out better in the end."

Cristina tried perhaps too hard to go straight. She not only went to beauty school during the day, but got a night job at Sumex, the Xerox maquila, refilling ink cartridges for copiers from 7:00 P.M. to 7:00 A.M.

She took home less than $3.50 a day after deductions. "It was really hard. I almost didn't sleep." She was also having problems at home. She had to leave her children with her aunt during the day because her mother, with six other kids of her own, refused to take care of them. Her stepfather, whom Cristina disliked, was back in the house after serving four months in a U.S. prison for alien smuggling. "Neither one of them helps me at all. They basically don't want me there." After one argument, the stepfather kicked Cristina out for several weeks, and she and her children had to sleep in a broken-down car in front of the shack.

The tension and lack of sleep built up. In August, Cristina got into a fight with Alma because Alma told people at Mi Nueva Casa that Cristina was a whore. "She said I'd had sex with all the guys. That's the way she is, not me." Cristina and Alma went at it on the street, flinging punches and pulling each other's hair. "She didn't lay a glove on me." By October, Cristina couldn't take the long hours and lack of sleep anymore. She left Sayra with the girl's paternal grandparents, her younger daughter in the care of her aunt, and took off.

"One night, I crossed through the tunnel with a couple of other kids from Barrio Libre. We climbed out near the courthouse and walked a little to wait for the train. It was about midnight. The *migra* [Border Patrol] checks it sometimes, but we hid between the wheels. I wasn't afraid for myself, but for my kids. I kept wondering what would happen to them if I fell. I know lots of people who've lost feet or legs or died." In Tucson, Cristina stayed with members of Barrio Libre. "We were ripping off houses during the day. I don't know what part of town we were in—Broadway, Speedway. I went where they said." After a couple weeks of this, the kids were caught inside a house, and several of them were charged with burglary and held in the Pima County Jail. Cristina, now eighteen and eligible for adult prison, once again escaped with only deportation to Nogales.

When I next saw her, she seemed subdued. She was back at home and in beauty school, and Sayra was still living with relatives in another part of town. "I can see her anytime I want, and it's fine. I miss her, though, and I want to get her back. I want to get a terreno for my-self and my kids. Since my mom won't help me take care of them, I'm better off on my own." Cristina insisted she didn't want to go down in the tunnel anymore. "It's not the same. I'm still a member of the gang, but they're friends, *no mas*. La Negra is the only one I really hang with. She just got out of jail in Hermosillo. I don't do thinner anymore ei-ther, not even when I was in Tucson. I don't want to have anything to do with drugs. Only cigarettes. I almost don't forget anything now. I want to go back and finish primary school." She was quiet for a minute.

"What I'd really like is to go to Tucson again, but not to rob. I want to take my kids up there and work. I don't want to rob anymore; they might catch me. I am afraid of being locked up and my kids being left alone and me not knowing what's going on with them—where they are, how they are, what they're doing, if they're sick, if they need some-thing. It's not the same as when I was alone. Now I have my kids, and nothing else is important. Not even me. Thank God I have them. If I didn't, who knows where I would be—dead, in jail, on the road to no-where? I don't want them to have the same experiences as I did. You suffer a lot in the street."

CHAPTER 5

Faith, Hope, and Charity

On a windswept hill overlooking one of the poorest neighborhoods in Nogales, Sonora, stood the Casa de la Misericordia, or House of Mercy. The house occupied four, neatly whitewashed buildings scattered over a slope, surrounded by a wall and barbed-wire fence, and crowned by a chapel with praying hands and the words *Servir es Amar* ("to serve is to love") painted in scrolling letters on the side. Like Mi Nueva Casa, which was set up to aid the tunnel kids in the area, the House of Mercy was a private effort to care for some of the city's worst off. Every weekday throughout the school year, hundreds of neighborhood children and a handful of adults who worked as trash pickers at the nearby dump received a free hot lunch here—for most, their only substantial meal of the day. "Feeding these kids a good, healthy meal, that is my priority," said House of Mercy founder and president José Torres. "Everything else comes second."

The House of Mercy, a labor of love for José and his wife, Hope, stood as a unique symbol of the conscience of the *maquiladora* industry in Nogales. When the Torreses first came down from Phoenix to take over the place in the late 1980s, they realized the factories were an untapped resource. "I knew they had money, but nobody had ever asked them," José said. Starting with Hope's boss at Walbro, Roscoe Combs, the couple approached managers at several large companies, and those at Walbro, Wilson-Jones, Chamberlain, General Instrument (GI), and the Nogales Maquiladora Association agreed to help. With between fifty and two hundred dollars a month in money and store credits from each company, plus other contributions from churches, civic groups, and individuals on both sides of the border, José never had to close the house a day from lack of food. "If my wife and I and the people behind us can do this," he told me, "think of what more could be done."

I joined José on his morning rounds on a sunny, breezy day in January 1997. Starting from the House of Mercy, we drove his old pickup with a camper shell down a steep hill and through the confusing maze of washboard streets that made up Colonia Bella Vista in southeast Nogales. We passed small, ramshackle homes behind fences made from old tires and car hoods and rusted box springs until we reached pavement and turned north, toward the border. José was quiet and polite, a short, trim man in his midfifties, wearing jeans, a cowboy shirt, and a black baseball cap. He spoke English softly, with an accent. He told me he had grown up working in the fields since the age of four, picking tomatoes, cotton, bell peppers, and carrots from dawn until dusk for twenty cents an hour. "I know what it's like to go to bed cold and hungry." His family lived illegally in the Rio Grande Valley until the mid-1950s, when, threatened with deportation by Operation Wetback, they applied for and received their residency papers. "Everyone in my family became a U.S. citizen except me. I never knew why until I got the chance to take over the House of Mercy. If I'd been a U.S. citizen, the Mexican government wouldn't have let me do it. Now I know the Man Upstairs had this planned for me."

We crossed over to the U.S. side, where José kept a mailbox and a storage locker full of used clothes and toys donated by Paz de Cristo, a charity based in Mesa, Arizona. José sold the clothes for a few pesos at a rummage sale every Saturday to raise money to pay the House of Mercy's utility bills. We got out of the truck, stuffed a few clothes in bags, and threw them in the back. A few years before, the Mexican government had banned the importation of used clothes, supposedly at the request of businessmen who were being hurt by the practice. José and Hope, as well as many others, had found that if you brought over a few bags at a time or, better yet, carried the clothes in suitcases, you could claim them as your own and avoid paying fines or having them confiscated.

The next stop on our journey was Hope's office in an industrial park on Mariposa Road across from the Nogales, Arizona, high school. Hope was the purchasing manager at Walbro, a maquiladora that made miniature carburetors and other parts for chain saw and weed-eater engines. Splitting her time between the factory on the Sonora side and the shipping office on the Arizona side, she bought all the company's supplies except those used in manufacturing. José told me she was a workaholic who often put in twelve- and fifteen-hour days, but he didn't seem to mind. In fact, he was obviously proud of her. He said she was the highest paid executive at Walbro and that both Chamberlain and Prestolite had tried to hire her away. "She supports me. I couldn't do this without her." When I met Hope, she was as José described—a no-nonsense woman wearing short hair, glasses, and a business suit—yet she treated her husband and his work with as much kindness and respect as he did hers. The depth of love I saw between this couple was remarkable.

After leaving Hope's office, José and I drove up to the Mariposa port of entry, got the green light, and carried our forbidden cargo into Mexico without even a glance from the guards. We headed south on the *periferico* (truck bypass) and then cut down into the valley along a winding, tree-lined street that eventually brought us to the Centro Comercial downtown. Chamberlain had set up a $200 per month account for the House of Mercy at this hardware-type store, and José needed a half-dozen old-fashioned, corn straw brooms. "The companies are doing a good thing helping us," he said as we watched a stock boy load the brooms into the back of the truck. Our last stop was a *tortilleria* not far from the House of Mercy, where several stacks of warm corn tortillas were waiting to be picked up, again free of charge. José had two paid helpers, a woman named Ester and an older man named Don Fito, each of whom made about fifty dollars a week. The rest of the staff, a half-dozen grandmothers from the neighborhood who served as cooks and lunch ladies, were volunteers whose only pay was the leftover food. All of them had been working for José for many years.

When we got back to the House of Mercy, the cooks had been busy for hours, and it was almost time to open the doors. Dozens of children had already washed their hands at the water faucet and lined up in separate boy-girl lines outside the lunchroom. José put on an apron and took his place at the door next to Don Fito, who had been keeping order while José was gone. Some of the children in line were dressed in school uniforms and carried book bags; others wore dirty sweatshirts and ripped pants. There were older siblings caring for younger ones, teenagers with babies, and a few with mental and physical disabilities. When twelve o'clock arrived, José called one girl forward to lead the others in the Lord's Prayer, which they all knew by heart. She was allowed to enter the lunchroom first. José then let the others go in a few at a time, greeting some with their real names, others with the physical nicknames so common in Mexico. "Go on in, shorty." "Hey, blondie, how's it going?" Kids who acted up or got too pushy were held back until they quieted down. "Take it easy, no running," José told them as he noted on a clipboard the number of kids he let in—on this day, more than two hundred.

Inside, the sunny and spotless lunchroom was decorated with pictures of the pope, Jesus, and the Virgin of Guadalupe, plus framed newspaper articles and photos taken during the House of Mercy's annual Christmas parties. Two long tables with folding chairs faced a kitchen counter where three middle-aged ladies in hairnets stood ready to serve each child a dollop of beans, a scoop of Ramen noodle soup, a soy hot dog, and a tortilla directly into the partitions of their hard plastic trays. The menu, posted in the kitchen, varied from day to day. Often, they had some kind of beef, donated by the son of a wealthy local rancher, and always tuna salad on Fridays. The kids also drank Koolaid or soda pop served in styrofoam cups with airline logos on them. They ate quickly and quietly, and brought their trays up to the counter, where two women moving like clockwork scraped, washed, rinsed, and dried the trays as well as the plastic silverware and styrofoam cups. The women let me help a little, although I think they were both amused and annoyed at how slow I was. By one o'clock, most of the children had eaten, and volunteers, adults and children alike, had wiped off the tables, put up the chairs, and swept and mopped the bare cement floors. The ladies in the kitchen washed all the pans and divided up the rest of the food. José told them to give me ten of the leftover flour tortillas. I felt awkward about taking this gift, but he insisted.

With the work done for the day, José gave me a tour. Above the dining hall were a number of rooms furnished with beds, examining tables, and an old dentist's chair. José explained that in the late 1970s, his mother, an Assembly of God follower, had bought the land and built the place, which was then called the Templo Manuel. She used these rooms to bring in American doctors and dentists to see local people for free. "We had babies born here." The authorities found out about the free clinic and closed it down because the doctors weren't licensed to practice in Mexico. José didn't have much good to say about local government, which, as far as he was concerned, was failing in its basic obligations. "They know I'm doing what they're supposed to be doing." The city did run four public kitchens, including one in Los Encinos and one in Buenos Aires, where they charged two pesos a meal for children and three for adults. José was adamant that he didn't want the city involved in running the House of Mercy. "Everything they touch goes down."

Although devoutly Catholic, José also didn't think much of organized religion. After his mother had died, it had taken him two years and most of his and Hope's savings to wrest control of the property from an Assembly of God preacher claiming squatter's rights, and the experience had left him suspicious of supposedly religious people. "You can go to church every morning and every afternoon, but here's the work," he said, gesturing toward the lunchroom. "Ladies come here from churches with rings on every finger, have their pictures taken with the kids, and then never show up again." He wanted the House of Mercy to be open to all children, regardless of faith. "It's not their fault their parents are Jehovah's Witnesses or Mormons or whatever they are." He also enjoyed having U.S. student and church groups, like those from Borderlinks, come and stay for a few days, help feed the kids, and do work projects. Some of these groups continued to support the House of Mercy with fundraisers, and one of them, a Quaker college in Wilmington, Ohio, invited Hope to come for a week each fall to teach about conditions on the border.

I was impressed by the smooth, almost military precision of José's operation, though I wondered if the barbed-wire perimeter fence was really necessary. He assured me it was. "The old fence people tore down and walked right through." The neighborhood was dominated by gangs and had one of the highest crime rates in the city, and José had reinforced the doors and windows of the office and storage shed with metal frames and burglar bars. His and Hope's modest block home, built into the base of the hill on which the House of Mercy stood, was as impenetrable as a fortress. Yet the danger and squalor surrounding the place merely convinced José even more that this hill was where he belonged. "Since I've been doing this, I haven't been sick a day. They tell me I'm going to go to heaven with my boots on."

After the tour, José and I sat on the porch in front of his office and soaked up some of the afternoon sun. We watched as the latest arrivals to Nogales staked out *terrenos* (plots of land) amid the grass and scrub oak and mesquite bushes on the next hillside. A stoop-shouldered woman carried two pails of water up the path to her cardboard home. "Every time I look down the hill, I see another shack going up," José said. "It hasn't changed for the poor people who came here ten, fifteen years ago, and it's not going to. The people in the middle class down south are now here, working in the factories. When they first arrive, they have the American dream. They try three, four times to get across, and when they can't, they end up here. They can't go back where they came from. You see it in their faces, on the street. They're lost. They

Tom Higgins, president of the S.L. Waber maquiladora in Nogales, Sonora, talks with an industrial engineer on the plant floor.

don't know where to go. It was hard in '44, when I was coming up. I don't know why anyone expected the maquiladoras to change things."

If Tom Higgins had anything to say about it, the maquiladoras *would* change things. When I first met Higgins, he was in his second-floor office at S. L. Waber, a maquiladora that made surge suppressors and voltage regulators. From his desk, he could look out the window across the valley and see two rows of new tin roofs shining on a hilltop. "I'm so pleased," he said, "that in all the crap and corruption of this world, the little guys got something good."

An affable, self-described "gringo with a Mexican soul," Higgins had reason to be pleased. As a longtime maquiladora manager in Nogales, he helped pioneer a unique collaboration between his industry and the Mexican government to build homes for low-income maquiladora workers. Since its inception in Nogales in the early 1990s, the program had enabled tens of thousands of workers in northern

Mexico to buy their own homes. Thousands more were planned. It was the most ambitious public-works program ever undertaken by the *maquilas,* demonstrating a new level of commitment to the border on the part of both industry and the Mexican government. "We all feel shame about the deplorable living conditions that still exist for newcomers," said Marco Antonio Valenzuela, head of the Mexico City-based National Council of the Maquiladora Industry and former director of the Nogales Maquiladora Association. "Hopefully, this program will have a long-term effect toward eliminating the housing shortage on the border."

The idea for the housing program was born in 1990, after Higgins's boss Douglas Chapman, the CEO of Chicago-based ACCO World Corporation, visited the company's maquila in Nogales for the first time. Under Higgins, ACCO Wilson-Jones, which made office supplies, had developed a reputation for being among the more progressive maquilas in town—one of the few to offer dormitory-style housing for unmarried workers and the first to provide day care. Nevertheless, Chapman was shocked at what he saw. "As Tom was driving me from the U.S. to Mexico, we went by these barrios and saw the houses. I was incredulous. I said, 'Tom, is this how our people live?' and he said, 'Probably so.' Then we got to the factory, and I saw how clean it was, how clean and bright-eyed everyone was, the esprit de corps, and I wondered, how could they come out of those houses and go to work in our factory? The image really stuck in my mind."

Around this same time, Chapman was reading the Sunday *New York Times* when an article in the magazine section caught his eye. It was Sandy Tolan's story "The Border Boom: Hope and Heartbreak" (July 1, 1990) that so angered maquila managers in Nogales. The article described a maquiladora worker family building a new home for themselves out of wood pallets and cardboard boxes. To Chapman's surprise and horror, the boxes they were using said "Wilson-Jones" on the side. "I'm not a liberal bleeding heart, but it was so poignant; it had a big impact on me. I had pangs of guilt. I felt that if we're profiting and benefiting down there, we had an obligation to try to do something about this."

After talking it over with his wife, Chapman decided to set up a charitable foundation to build homes for maquiladora workers. He put up several hundred thousand dollars of his own money, convinced other senior ACCO executives to do the same, and named it the Esperanza (Hope) Foundation. At first, Chapman thought of building houses only for his employees. But after learning that in order for the foundation to receive tax-exempt status, it would have to benefit all maquiladora workers in Nogales, he expanded his goal. Chapman and Higgins met with the board of the Nogales Maquiladora Association, which agreed to sponsor the project and to seek contributions from members. Tom Higgins figured that if every maquiladora in town put in five cents an hour per worker, more than two million dollars a year could be generated. "Can you imagine what we could do with that kind of money?" he said.

What Chapman and Higgins wanted went far beyond what the maquiladoras had ever done before. In Nogales and most other cities, companies were involved in charity work on an individual or small-scale basis, such as their contributions to the House of Mercy. The Nogales Maquiladora Association had a charitable arm called the Nogales Project, which had donated about thirty thousand dollars a year since 1988 to buy fire trucks and ambulances, build the community kitchen in Los Encinos, help 120 families build homes in Las Torres, provide sewer pipes, build basketball and volleyball courts, provide lights for the baseball stadium, and participate in other projects. Critics said this charity was a drop in the hat and primarily benefited the maquilas in any case. The fire station, for example, served the industrial park, but not the shacks that burned down with regularity in the nearby hills. "For thirty years, they didn't do anything," said Francisco Trujillo, head of the Nogales, Sonora, chamber of commerce and a former maquiladora supervisor. "But," he added quickly, "it's never too late."

The local elite was divided between those who believed the maquiladoras were benefiting Nogales just by being there and those who believed the maquiladoras were not doing enough for the community. Most of the former tended to be newcomers, the American managers and Mexican businessmen from out of town, and the latter were usually the local old guard. One of the most outspoken critics, perhaps because maquiladoras paid no local taxes, was the former mayor of Nogales, Sonora, Abraham Zaied. "The maquiladoras pay in one day here what they would pay on the other side in an hour," said Zaied, a member of the same Dabdoub family that had developed industrial parks and attracted some of the city's first maquilas. "They are like an aspirin for Mexico's economic sickness, nothing more. They keep people from dying of hunger, that's all." He pointed out that his city had a seven-million-dollar annual budget, whereas Nogales, Arizona, with a fraction of the population and by no means a wealthy town, had a budget of thirty million dollars.

Some cities, such as Juárez, had attempted to levy a local tax on the maquilas, but the maquilas fought the tax in Mexican court and won on grounds that it was discriminatory. Many managers feared that the cities would keep pushing the issue and saw their charitable contributions as a way to lessen pressure on local governments to tax them. The brochure listing the advantages of the charitable work of the Nogales Maquila Association stated flat out that "non-participant companies are more likely to be affected by a mandatory/unilateral charitable program enforced by the city authorities." In Nogales, at least, the city had not put much pressure on the maquilas. "Mayor Zaied complains about them a lot, but he doesn't do anything," said chamber of commerce director Trujillo. After Zaied left office, the new mayor, Wenceslao Cota, promised he was going to be a tough negotiator when the lease on the main industrial park came up for renewal in 1999, a prospect dreaded by maquila managers.

Most managers told me it wasn't a question of not caring. "A lot of managers wish they could do more, but their primary responsibility is to the parent company and to the stockholders," Roscoe Combs said. "The maquiladoras are not the Sisters of Charity," as Zaied pointed out. Chapman had a slightly different perspective, however. "Generally, American companies could do a better job of corporate community responsibility. Many companies do, but many don't. As an employer, I would have thought we have a bigger responsibility than that."

When José had told Hope he wanted to move to Nogales to take over the House of Mercy, her heart had sunk. That was the last thing she wanted to do. "It was like going back in time." Hope had been raised in a poor family, one of seven children of an Apache father and Mexican American mother in what was then rural Glendale, Arizona. When she was seventeen, she had dropped out of school to marry José, whom she'd met years before when he and his family had come through the area picking cotton. The couple settled in Phoenix and had three children. With only an eighth-grade education, José worked first as a detail man and then got a job loading trucks at Southwest Feed and Seed, where he eventually rose to become superintendent of the company. Hope went to work at a men's underwear factory in Phoenix, a "maquiladora," as she called it. For ten years, she sewed elastic bands on briefs before deciding she'd had enough. "I thought, 'Is this what I want for the rest of my life? My eyesight and back going?' I went to José and said, 'I have a brain.' He said, 'Go do your thing. I'll take care of the kids.'" Hope went back to school, got her GED, took a mechanic's course, and went to work for Valley National Bank. For several years, she was one of only a handful of people in Arizona who knew how to repair automatic teller machines. By the mid-1980s, she had risen to the rank of vice president.

Hope was understandably reluctant to leave her family, friends, and career to follow José to Nogales. For the first six months, she commuted back and forth, but José had encouraged and supported her to fulfill her dream, and she felt it was only fair that she do the same for him. "I knew he'd always wanted to go back to Mexico and help his people. My mother told me to go with him. 'He's a good man,' she said. Besides, I'd invested too much money in him." Hope swallowed her pride, quit her job, and moved into the house José built for them in Colonia Bella Vista. "The first year was hell. Everything was so dusty. You washed the clothes, hung them out, and you'd have to wash them all over again." The dirt roads, the outhouses, the kids playing baseball in the street—"It reminded me of when I was growing up, when we used kerosene lamps and took baths in an aluminum tub and played in the sugar beets and the chalk arroyo." In Mexico, Hope was an outsider. The locals ridiculed her use of Spanglish. "If I said something like 'wacha' [border slang for 'look'], they called me *pocha* and made me feel bad because I didn't know my own language." She was also a woman who didn't know her place. When she became involved in a local church and tried to organize a singing group, some of the women's husbands refused to let them participate, saying, " 'No woman is going to tell me when my wife can leave the house.' They told me I was a grandma, and I should be home rocking my grandkids. They said, 'In the U.S., women run the place. Here in Mexico, the men do.' "

When Hope first arrived on the border, the only job available to her was as a part-time teller at the Valley National Bank branch in Nogales, Arizona—quite a step down from vice president—but she worked hard, filled in for people on vacation, and was quickly promoted. One day, Walbro manager Roscoe Combs came in looking for a bookkeeper who knew English. Hope told him she could do it, and he hired her on the spot. She loved her new job. "In those days, Walbro was like a family." She invited Combs to the House of Mercy, and he became one of its biggest supporters, helping her to approach other maquila managers and loaning her a company van to carry donations of food and supplies.

Hope was just starting to feel at home in Nogales when she and José suffered a devastating loss. Their youngest son, who had been a star baseball player in high school and planned on going pro, was staying with them for a few months while he recovered from a fractured leg. One evening, he decided to go visit some friends. He had just stepped out the door when his leg snapped and he fell backward, hitting his head on the deadbolt lock. He died almost instantly. Although numb with grief, Hope and José somehow managed to carry on. They leaned on each other and buried themselves in work. "José always told me, 'Don't look back.'" Hope handled her pain by writing poems, playing the guitar, and singing spiritual songs. "I don't cry," she told me.

Her son's death left Hope with a lot of anger, which she began to direct at the young toughs in her neighborhood. "José was always telling me not to get so mad." A scrawny teenager had been terrorizing the *colonia,* knocking down old ladies and grabbing their purses, and one night he broke into José and Hope's laundry room. Hope heard the noise, grabbed one of José's guns, and ran outside. She saw the kid climbing over the fence with a box of detergent under his arm. She aimed the gun at his leg, shot, and missed, hitting the detergent instead. The kid ran away, leaving a trail of soap powder that Hope followed to his home three doors away. She banged on the door and yelled at the kid's mother that if he ever broke into her house again, she'd kill him. "They later caught him breaking into a money exchange, and he got sixty years in prison in Hermosillo." Another time, a young man who lived across the street called José a wimp for letting his wife support him. Hope stepped in front of José and challenged the man to a fight. When he picked up a rock, Hope reached down, picked up a much bigger rock, and heaved it over her head. The man dropped his rock and yelled at José, "Your old lady's crazy!" "I know," José replied. "You never know what she'll do."

Perhaps the most extreme example of Hope's ferocity took place a few years later, when her new black Dodge Ram pickup—a favorite of cops and drug dealers in Mexico—was stolen from near the Tucson airport. "I think I was set up by someone in the company because they were the only ones who knew I was going to be in Tucson that day."

The next morning, Hope heard that the Nogales, Sonora, police chief was driving her truck. She and José went down to the station and sure enough, her truck was parked right out front, with the steering column broken and the license plate still on it. "They said, 'Oh, we confiscated it from the guy that stole it.' They weren't going to let me have it. I saw there was a machine gun in the truck, so I got in and held it and said, 'This is my truck, and if you don't give it back, I'll blow it up.' They all turned white." The cops pulled their guns on Hope, she pointed the machine gun at them, and a tense standoff ensued. "Joe was telling the cops not to shoot and was trying to calm me down. I told him, 'I can kill two of them before they kill me.'" Finally, the cops let her take the truck.

As one of the few women maquila managers, Hope had to be almost as tough at work. "People don't respect you or listen to your opinions. I had one man who worked for me tell me that 'No goddamn woman was going to boss him around.'" Machismo and sexism were rampant in the maquilas. Although the companies created jobs for engineers and mechanics and helped some workers receive training and promotions, those who got ahead were almost always men. Women for the most part stayed stuck in low-level assembly line and secretarial jobs, their only avenue of escape being a love affair with an American manager. Hope knew several managers who had left their wives for one of these girls.

Still, the maquilas had given Hope back her career, and when it came to questions of corporate responsibility, she was a realist. Business was business. Her own sister had lost her job when the underwear factory where she worked—the same one where Hope had worked for ten years—moved to Honduras. Hope's sister even went to Central America to help set up the new factory. As for the maquiladoras, Hope did not believe they were exploiting people. "If it weren't for them, these people wouldn't have anything." Worker surveys bore out this perception; more than eight out of ten workers said they were better off now than before coming to the border. As a woman whose three daughters worked in the factories once told me, "At least they don't have to dig in garbage like I did." Yet Hope, like José, was disturbed by the persistent poverty among workers and their families. "Every once in a while I let things get to me. There are so many hungry people, so many problems. Our Band-Aids don't even begin to cover these deep wounds. I offer up to God what we do at the Casa de la Misericordia with the prayer that we're doing His will and that maybe we're not to see the significance of our actions. But sometimes even prayer seems elusive."

Despite Chapman's and Higgins's efforts, the maquiladora housing project got off to a slow start. A few companies—including Samsonite, Avent, Xerox, Delta, Alcatel, and Joffroy Customs Brokers—made one-time donations to the Esperanza Foundation, but not a single one joined ACCO's annual pledge of five cents per hour per employee. Managers had various objections to the plan. They pointed out that their companies contributed millions to the Mexican economy through salaries, taxes, and local suppliers, and that they already paid a 5 percent per worker housing tax, which, like the other taxes they paid, was sent off to Mexico City and never seen again. "The Mexican government's attitude has been, 'The gringos are rich, let them take care of the border,'" said Don Nibbe of the *Twin Plant News*. Managers also did not like the fact that the foundation was set up to benefit all maquiladora workers, not just workers for contributing companies. "If we're going to invest money, we want to make sure that it goes to our people," the Chamberlain personnel director told me.

Nevertheless, with the Esperanza Foundation leading the way, most of the maquiladoras in Nogales agreed to help qualified workers make a down payment on a home. "It doesn't matter how they do it, as long as they do it," Chapman said. Some did it through the Esperanza Foundation; others gave all or most of the money directly to their employees. After Chapman appealed personally to the CEO of Chamberlain in Chicago, that company pledged down payments for more than one

New homes in the San Carlos housing project overlook an industrial park of maquiladoras.

hundred of its workers, and GI soon followed with funding for thirty-six. Maquilas that went through the foundation were given a number of houses in proportion to the size of their workforces, with every company in the maquila association receiving at least one house. Because there were so many more qualified workers than houses, the first groups of homeowners were chosen by lottery.

Getting the support of the maquiladoras wasn't the only hurdle the foundation had to overcome. "What set us apart was that we weren't prepared to grease any palms," Chapman said. "Maybe we were naive, but we wanted them to be nice houses, with bedrooms, bathroom, water, sewer, electricity, paved streets, sidewalks, and street lights. They told us we were tilting at windmills, that it would never happen." Problems with the first developer cost the project two years and almost two hundred thousand dollars. "It turned out he didn't have title to the land," Higgins sighed, sounding like a maquiladora worker who had been tricked out of his terreno. He vowed to pursue the developer in court. After another false start, he finally found an honorable developer, but just as construction began, the 1994 peso devaluation hit. For a year after the devaluation, the Mexican federal agency backing the project suspended its bridge-loan financing nationwide, and construction was halted. "We've been through not only an industrial revolution in Mexico, but a revolution in the banking and housing industries as well," Higgins said.

Things finally came together in late 1995, when Infonavit, the Mexican government's low-income housing authority, agreed to finance the construction and to make the houses affordable by easing its requirements to qualify for a home loan. In the past, these loans had been out of reach for most maquiladora workers because of their youth and low wages. Moreover, Infonavit houses were in woefully short supply, especially in the wake of the devaluation, and workers who did qualify were placed at the bottom of years-long waiting lists. But in the case of the San Carlos project, as the new housing development was called, the contribution of the maquiladoras as well as agreements by state and federal government to build streets and infrastructure prompted Infonavit to back the idea. "We know it has been a hard time in this area," Infonavit director Alfredo del Mazo said later, acknowledging the Mexican government's failure to address the workers' housing crisis. Then he couldn't resist adding, "Let us not forget that the maquiladora entity is very broad and the one that is closest to the United States."

In the fall of 1997, just a few months after I first met José and Hope, their story took a sudden turn. The back gate of José's pickup had fallen and hit him in the chest that summer, leaving a nasty bruise that took a long time to fade. By October, he still wasn't feeling well. He was constantly battling colds, and the shots and treatments the doctor had given him hadn't helped. José was pale and sweating as he drove Hope to the airport for her annual trip to the Quaker college. He assured her he'd be all right, but after she boarded the plane, he doubled over in pain. "It hurt so bad I prayed, 'God, either let me live or take me right now.'"

When Hope returned, José met her with his bag packed, ready to go straight to the hospital in Green Valley. "The x-rays showed white stuff all over. We didn't know what it was." Hope put José back in her truck and drove like mad to St. Mary's Hospital in Tucson, where the diagnosis was made. "The doctor told me it was cancer. When Joe saw the look on my face, he said, 'Am I dying?' I said, 'Yes, you are.' We didn't cry. The doctor said that if it was spreading from the lung to the liver, he had three to six months to live. If it was from the liver to the lung, he'd be gone within six weeks." The doctors offered chemotherapy, which would require being at the hospital in Tucson three days a week. José refused. At best, the chemo could offer him only a few extra months of suffering. "If God wants me, he knows where I am." He insisted on going back to Nogales. "That was the only time he ever cried," Hope said. "He wanted to come home."

In the living room of their house in Nogales, Hope fixed a bed for José so he could lie down and look out the window at the House of Mercy on the hill above. His condition declined rapidly. When I visited in early December, his voice was little more than a whisper, and he could barely eat. He sat on the edge of the bed to greet me, dressed in pajamas and wearing an oxygen tube in his nose. With no chemo, his hair was still dark and full, his deep widow's peak contrasting starkly against his papery skin. "It's a hell of a thing," he whispered, shaking his head. He asked me how I was, what was new, but I could tell he didn't want to talk. I didn't stay long. José spent the next month in and out of the hospital in Tucson. Hope kept working, driving back and forth to Tucson in the evenings to see him in the hospital and relying on Ester to take care of him when he was at home. José was covered by Hope's U.S.-based insurance, which meant oxygen tanks and other equipment weren't supposed to go across the border and the home health people couldn't come visit. Nor could Hope find a hospital bed. I told her about the Living Is For Everyone group in Nogales, Arizona, established to aid the many cancer victims in the area, and with Anna Acuña's help, Hope borrowed a bed and was able to bring it over for

José. At Christmas, the House of Mercy had its annual party for four hundred kids, but José was too ill to attend.

It turned out José's cancer had started in his lung and spread to the liver. He had never smoked, and Hope and I wondered whether he could be another victim of environmental pollution in Nogales. After all, the House of Mercy stood just one hill over from the burning dump. But the wind tended to blow the smoke north, not south, and Hope and José had lived in Nogales only nine years. More likely, his twenty-five years at the grain company, inhaling fine particles that perhaps had been treated with pesticides, and his family history—his dad had died of spinal cancer, and one of his brothers had prostate cancer—were the causes. Whatever it was, José accepted it as God's will. "We're in good hands," he would say, cupping his hands like the Allstate Insurance commercial.

José wanted Hope to stay on in Nogales and continue to run the House of Mercy. "'You have to accept you will be alone,' he told her, 'but my spirit will be here, and a lot of people will be here to help you. Just don't get mad. Be calm.'" Hope promised she would keep the House of Mercy running for at least the next few years or until she could find someone else to do it. She told me she was mad at God and was searching for His purpose in taking her husband when he was still so young. She coped by singing and writing poems, including one for José called "Always Prepared" that went, in part,

When his children were young he was prepared
to join in the fun for he
never had a childhood when he was young.
He toiled and worked and had no fun.

He was prepared to return to his home
And to fight for his land
When tragedy struck
He was prepared to accept and go on
And never look back.

He was prepared when Jesus made him
the temple of his glory
Feeding and clothing
the children of his homeland.

He was prepared to fight
the demon within, when Jesus
whispered, "It is time to retreat,
I'm taking you home, for your
task is complete."

José died at Holy Cross Hospital in Nogales, Arizona, on February 2, 1998. He wanted to die at home, but on the night before, Hope had become scared and asked him to let her take him to the hospital. "Ester and I dressed him, and I carried him down the steps to the car. He was saying, 'Don't leave me. Don't turn off the light. I'm afraid. I don't want to die.' At the hospital, he was better. He said, 'I'm going on a trip. He's coming for me. I see the man; he's waiting for me.' I held him, and he was gone."

The wake took place in the chapel at the House of Mercy three nights later. Although it was bitter cold, with the wind whipping fistfuls of rain at the windows, José and Hope's large extended families came from Phoenix, New Mexico, and Texas to gather around the wood stove, and there was plenty of hot coffee and food. José lay in front of the altar in a black-and-copper casket with "praying hands" symbols on the handrails, which Hope had picked out especially. "As soon as I saw it, I knew it was the right one." José was dressed in a black shirt and trousers, and his best white straw cowboy hat was placed on top of the casket. The heavy doses of morphine he had taken near the end made his hair, eyelashes, and moustache more lush and full than ever, although the olive-toned pancake makeup and pinkish lipstick put on him at the funeral home gave him an unnatural look, not like himself at all. All evening long, curious children kept coming up to peer into the glass-covered coffin. As one little girl looked in, I asked if she was afraid. "Why should I be afraid of José?" she said.

The next morning, with Nogales blanketed by new-fallen snow, more than a hundred mourners filled the chapel to say goodbye. The priest, an old friend of José's, came from Agua Prieta to give the mass. A dozen large flower arrangements surrounded the casket, each decorated with a ribbon announcing the donor's name in gold glitter: the Chamberlain Group, the Sanchez family, the Pharisees (José's joking name for a group of his supporters), the cooks and their families. The service was quiet and solemn. The priest talked about José's devotion to the children, and Hope led the group in singing two a cappella hymns. Afterward, the pallbearers carried the casket out to the hearse, and we all climbed in our cars and trucks to head over to the cemetery. I took a load of kids in my car. They acted matter-of-fact about the occasion, one boy noting that it reminded him of his father's funeral. We followed the procession down the hill and through streets coursing with water, until we reached José's mother's plot in the Pantheon of the Cypresses. By the time we arrived, the sun was out, but it was still a cold, windy day. We stood on the frozen muddy ground of the hillside plot that overlooked a truck yard and struggled to hear the priest's words over the roar of semis going by on the periferico. When the final prayers were spoken, the men lowered José's casket into the tomb next to his mother and sealed it with cement. The inscription on the headstone read, "Let the little children come unto me and do not forbid them, for the Kingdom of God belongs to those who are like them."

By 1996, the $10 million San Carlos project, looking much like Chapman and Higgins had envisioned it, was well under construction on a massive hill above a new industrial park on the east side of Nogales. The first 500 of the 511-square-foot, two-bedroom homes were presented to their owners in a ceremony that fall, and another 250 were finished the following summer. Thousands more homes and an elementary school were planned for the future. At least one worker at each of the forty-one companies that belonged to the Nogales Maquiladora Association—employers of some 90 percent of the twenty-five thousand maquila workers in town—received a house.

I visited the San Carlos project in early 1997, when some of the homes were still under construction and others recently occupied. They all appeared much alike, with the same salmon color and gently peaked, corrugated metal roofs lined side by side up the hill. A few featured individual touches in the iron work on the windows and flower gardens out front. Some already had little commercial signs that said "Coca-Cola" or "Fanta," indicating residents were operating convenience stores out of their living rooms. Several people told me they liked the peace and quiet and cleanliness of the new neighborhood, but complained it was too far away from work. Chamberlain, where at least one-fifth of the first group of residents worked, was at least a half-hour away by bus. A few complained that the water came on only a couple of hours a day, a not uncommon problem all over Nogales. Others said their roofs leaked. Most, however, were delighted.

On one steep corner stood the home of Andres Espericueta, who told me he considered himself lucky to have gotten a house in San Carlos. "This is pretty nice, better than where we were before," he said as he held his two-year-old daughter in his arms. He and his wife, Karla, also had an eight-month-old girl. The family had lived before with Karla's relatives in another part of Nogales, in a house not much bigger than this one. They had been in their new home for several months, and even though the living room was still bare, Karla described it as "very comfortable." Espericueta worked for Tom Higgins at S. L. Waber. He had been there four years and made about sixty pesos (then, eight dollars) a day. He was the only one of Waber's 425 employees to get a new house. "Your income has to be in a certain range, not too low and not too high, to qualify," he said. The Esperanza Foundation paid his $2,100 down payment, and he owed Infonavit a mortgage of about $9,500, plus 6 percent annual interest, which he would pay back through payroll deductions of one-quarter of his weekly salary for the next twenty to thirty years. He could sell the house, but not rent it. "I think it's fair," he said, adding that he had friends at work who also could qualify if more houses became available.

Like the Espericuetas, most of the people living in San Carlos were in their twenties, married with children, and had worked in the maquiladoras for several years. They made $1.35 an hour including benefits—about a dollar an hour in take-home pay—or about three times the border minimum wage. The fact that only long-term employees received houses illustrated how the program benefited the maquiladoras as well. "One of the intentions of the program is to stabilize the labor force," said Marco Antonio Valenzuela of the National Council of the Maquiladora Industry. Espericueta said he didn't have to promise to stay at Waber in order to get the house, but he expected he would.

After Tom Higgins and others proved the maquiladora housing program could work in Nogales, Infonavit took it borderwide. In the summer of 1996, officials announced plans to offer similar loans and credits to low-income maquiladora workers in Ciudad Juárez, Chihuahua, Nuevo Laredo, Reynosa, and Matamoros. They expected to build eighteen thousand homes in the next three years. General Motors, whose Delphi Automotive Systems was the largest foreign employer in Mexico with seventy thousand workers, agreed to subsidize at least half the cost of a down payment for seven thousand homes. Its housing development in Juárez quickly grew to resemble a small city. The company also signed up as the first corporate sponsor of fifty Habitat for Humanity homes in Matamoros. Ford, Philips, and other companies moved to set up their own housing programs, and Marco Antonio Valenzuela said he was working to expand participation in his organization, which represented hundreds of maquiladoras in twenty-two cities across Mexico. He believed most companies would do it as long as they had to support only their own workers. Some maquilas agreed to pay the full down payment, others half. A few wanted to loan workers the money. At GM, workers had to repay the down payment if they left the company before five years.

Tom Higgins, meanwhile, was trying to figure out a way to systematize contributions to the Esperanza Foundation so that more homes could be built in Nogales. Only ACCO's maquiladora continued to make regular contributions, although both Chamberlain and GI pledged to spend up to two hundred thousand dollars a year to help their workers with down payments. "In spite of what we're doing, the job at hand is larger than we know, and in the future, we should be doing more," Higgins said. From his office window at Waber, he could see not only the rooftops of San Carlos, but also some of the shantytowns where most maquila workers still lived. The view put his efforts in perspective. "We haven't solved the problems of the two to three hundred thousand who live in this city," he told me. "But those houses weren't on that hill a year ago."

For the first few months after José died, Hope was in shock. She kept going to work and kept the House of Mercy running, yet she felt lost. She dreamed she was drowning, and no one came to save her. Tempted to sell the house to a Christian minister couple from Mesa who wanted to turn it into an orphanage, but afraid that would be the end of José's goal of providing free food for neighborhood children, she called all the volunteers together and told them, "If you don't help me, this place will close." Ester, Don Fito, and the others promised to help. Everything seemed to be going all right until, a few months after José died, someone broke into the storage shed and stole a bunch of food. Hope put the word around that whoever did it was stealing from the children, and if it happened again, the House of Mercy would close. "I was so angry. Then I felt a hand on my shoulder, telling me, 'It's not the children's fault.' It was José." News about the break-in went out over Radio XENY, and contributions doubled. "We had to give food away."

Hope began to feel better. At Walbro, she was busier than ever and would sometimes not come home from work until nine or ten at night. Now, however, the *marijuaneros* across the street were treating her with respect, opening and closing the garage door for her and telling her,

" 'If anyone bothers you, señora, you tell me.' I feel comfortable here, protected," she said to me then. "My life is here now." She installed a hot-water tank on the house, something José had never wanted to do, and spent time visiting her sister in Tucson and children in Phoenix. She was thinking of retiring at the end of 1998, after ten years at Walbro, and of running the House of Mercy full-time. That summer, she had the kitchen retiled and the whole place painted. It looked really good. José would have been proud.

But Hope was tested again. In late August, less than six months after José's death, she came home from work one night to find her house had been broken into. Thieves had pried the air conditioner out of the bedroom window and taken José's gun collection, some jewelry, Hope's cell phone, and anything else small enough to pass through the window. Hope called the police and told them who had done it—everyone in the neighborhood knew—but the police didn't do anything. "One of the kids lives right behind me. What kills me is these kids who broke into the eatery and our home are the same ones we've fed. A family across the street tried to sell me back José's pellet gun and my cell phone. Can you imagine? I'm not going to pay for my own goddamn stuff. I just said, 'The hell with it.'" Hope was so enraged that a few weeks later, when she heard that one of the kids who'd broken in was playing video games at the arcade, she went down and attacked him. She grabbed the kid, spun him around, socked him in the face, threw him on the ground, and kicked him several times. Although she didn't seriously hurt the boy, she scared herself. "I have to get out of here. I'm afraid I'm going to kill somebody."

Hope decided she had to give up the House of Mercy. "Joe could be here all the time to watch the place, but I have to work. It was Joe's thing, anyway. I came down here because I loved him, but I can't do this anymore. My family, my grandkids—everything's in Phoenix." Looking around for an organization that would keep the lunchroom open, the donations coming in, and the staff employed, she met with representatives of the Salecinian Society, who were planning to build a youth center on the next hill over, but they had different kinds of programs in mind. There was one other possibility. Borderlinks, the Tucson social service organization that had brought many American church and student groups to the House of Mercy for many years, was growing rapidly. Not only was it conducting more seminars for North Americans, but was also starting to sponsor meetings and exchanges between Latin American activists as well as undertaking development projects in the Nogales colonias, such as microcredit and environmental awareness training. Borderlinks was looking for a conference center and dormitory in Nogales, and in the spring of 1999, members of the group approached Hope about buying the House of Mercy. After receiving written assurances that the lunchroom would stay open and the staff employed, Hope agreed to sell. She retired from Walbro, moved back to Phoenix, and settled into life surrounded by her family.

José once told me that when the time came, God would decide who should run the House of Mercy. Perhaps Borderlinks was God's choice because this group offered the promise not only of continuing the work José and Hope had begun, but of expanding it. José and Hope had made the House of Mercy a place where the business and caring sides of Nogales came together. If Borderlinks built on this idea, the House of Mercy could become a place where all the faces of Nogales—maquila managers and workers, business and church people, rich and poor, American and Mexican—came together in a spirit of compassion and reconciliation.

CONCLUSION

San Ramón the Unborn

Before the first industrial park was built in Nogales, Sonora, a small wooden shrine to San Ramón Nonato stood on the east side of the road just south of town. The shrine was near a grove of walnut trees where the bus drivers had stopped, turned around, and sometimes taken a break to rest in the shade. Travelers on their way north and south had offered prayers as they drove by, and over the years, San Ramón had become a kind of unofficial patron saint of Nogales. Locals recalled that the shrine had been built in the 1920s or 1930s by a rancher wanting to give thanks after his wife survived a difficult childbirth. According to legend, the thirteenth-century Spanish saint was known as "the unborn" because he had to be cut from his mother's womb after she died giving birth to him. He was the patron of midwives and, some in Nogales believed, of the impossible.

In the early 1970s, to make way for construction of the industrial park, the shrine to San Ramón Nonato was demolished. A massive cement-block building went up in its place, but on the corner where the shrine had been, the factory wall refused to stand. It fell once and was rebuilt, fell again and was rebuilt again. After the second rebuilding, the story goes, the chief construction engineer came over to check on the site. As he was standing next to the wall, it collapsed a third time, killing him and two laborers. After that, the builders gave up and rebuilt the shrine into the outside corner of the factory. A simple, unadorned cement room facing the highway, the new shrine became a popular meeting spot for maquiladora workers who stopped in to light a candle and say a quick prayer at lunch or on their way home from work. The industrial park was christened—first jokingly, then officially—Park San Ramón.

Whether by design or not, San Ramón was the perfect metaphor for the new Nogales. As he had endured a brutal birth, this border town was enduring a painful transition into the modern world. San Ramón's mother had died so he could live, just as small-town Nogales— the Nogales of the Old West and of La Caverna restaurant—had had to die so an industrial city could be born in its place. Old-timers and locals lamented the passing of the old Nogales, yet they were often the ones who couldn't wait to leave the town and move to Tucson or Phoenix. It was the newcomers, the people attracted here by the promise of prosperity, who were remaking this city. Here were the faces of the future: poor and hungry, yes, but full of youth, energy, and dreams for a better life. Amid so many national and international conflicts, the new Nogales was struggling to be born.

At the dawn of the third millennium, the most striking thing about this city and many others on the border remained the contrast between the advanced, technological twenty-first-century world inside the factories and the nineteenth-century conditions that surrounded them. The 1996 opening of a new General Instrument (GI) plant in the San Carlos industrial park, just below the new housing project, made the contrast even starker. President Ernesto Zedillo came to inaugurate the plant, which he touted as the kind of industry Mexico wanted for the future. "The positive changes that the border region has experienced in the last three years have been incredible," he said. "The prosperity of the maquiladora industry has been a major contributor to these changes." The plant was impressive: clean and brightly lit, with state-of-the-art equipment and enough room to more than double GI's fifteen-hundred-person workforce. When I toured it a few months after it opened, personnel director Rick Mata told me it was one of the few facilities in Mexico built to U.S. standards. "With our method of operation, we could be anywhere in the world and be in compliance with all environmental laws and regulations." As Mata walked me out to my car, he gestured toward the employees' parking lot. "In a few years, we're going to need more educated and better-paid workers. The companies that are going to Mexico for low wages will die out." I looked at the beat-up cars of the current workers—the ones who had cars— and wondered, What's going to happen to them? Will their jobs go to southern Mexico, to Central America, to China? Or, more likely, disappear altogether?

On the other hand, the new GI plant was itself a powerful symbol of the company's commitment to Nogales. Management was apparently very satisfied with the quality of the workforce. Having been in Nogales for almost thirty years, GI was one of several local *maquilas* that consistently won productivity and excellence awards within their corporations. The sophisticated nature of maquilas such as GI and Otis were examples of how this industry, once just low-tech assembly, was developing into an important player in the Mexican economy. Maquilas were investing in advanced equipment, training their staffs to use it, and employing more Mexican managers and engineers, including all the top management at Otis. Maquiladoras were in Mexico to stay. They also were on the border to stay. Despite the movement of many companies inland, ease of transportation and communications as well as the advantage of managers being able to live in the United States ensured that cities such as Nogales would remain the industry's heart and soul.

Given the success of the maquiladoras, perhaps it was time for workers to begin to share in some of it. Some progress was made in establishing more workers' rights in Mexico in the 1990s—including a rise in the strength of opposition political parties, more dissident groups within the official unions, and, in a few industries, the growth of independent unions.

Maquila workers seized on these trends to press for independent unions of their own. In two well-publicized cases—a MaxiSwitch factory in Cananea, Sonora, which made computer keyboards and play stations, and Tijuana-based Han Young, which made truck parts for

Hyundai—workers waged successful, months-long organizing drives, only to have the local labor boards refuse to recognize their unions. Workers at these maquilas and others, including Sony in Nuevo Laredo, took their cases before a trinational labor rights board that had been set up to hear worker grievances under the North American Free Trade Agreement (NAFTA). Public airing of their claims of intimidation and persecution embarrassed both Mexico and the maquilas, and the workers were offered concessions in the form of jobs for fired protesters, back pay, and more power within official unions. After numerous appeals before Mexican courts, both the Han Young and MaxiSwitch workers eventually won the right to form their own unions, even though the one at MaxiSwitch was fairly powerless and not allowed to affiliate with anyone else. As of 1999, these unions were the only two independent ones in all of the nearly four thousand maquiladoras in Mexico.

In a number of cities, organizing was also under way outside the factories. Church-based community groups in Juárez, women's organizations in Tijuana, and the Comité Fronterizo de Obreras (CFO, Border Committee of Women Workers) in the Rio Grande Valley reached maquiladora workers in their homes, where they could learn to support each other and stand up for their rights without fear. Organizers conducted study sessions on the federal labor law, health and safety standards, and other issues, and they led role-playing games in which workers practiced confronting their bosses. These groups had many successes over the years—helping workers to collect money and benefits they were owed; to get fans, chairs, and safety equipment installed; to end preemployment pregnancy testing at some companies; and to achieve many other small but significant gains. As vital as this kind of organizing was, it did not lead to industrywide change and was hampered by the young and transient nature of the workforce. "The industry has no memory," said mural artist Alberto Morackis. "Every generation is new. The longest time they work is ten years—then they leave. They've seen that life, and it doesn't serve anyone except the maquilas."

One of the best hopes for maquila workers lay in the growing support they were receiving from American labor. In the past, U.S. unions had offered scant support to Mexican workers, whom they saw as competitors, not allies. But as it became clear that maquila jobs were never coming back and that employees of the same global corporations had interests in common, progressive unions in the United States and Canada joined religious, environmental, women's, and human rights groups calling for decent wages and working conditions in the maquiladoras. The same network that came together to oppose NAFTA began conducting worker exchanges, solidarity campaigns, and boycotts on behalf of striking MaxiSwitch and Han Young workers, among others.

Representing a variety of nongovernmental groups from both countries, the San Antonio–based Coalition for Justice in the Maquiladoras put forth a maquiladora code of conduct, and another organization— the Interfaith Center on Corporate Responsibility—sponsored shareholder proxy resolutions relating to health and safety conditions in the factories, wages, sexual harassment, pregnancy testing, and other issues. By calling public attention to the maquiladoras and demanding a place at the table when trade agreements were negotiated, these international worker-support networks became small but nettlesome thorns in the sides of governments and multinationals.

International networks also played a key role in getting the U.S. and Mexican governments to face up to environmental problems on the border. During negotiations over NAFTA, environmental organizations in Mexico, the United States, and Canada successfully pushed for the creation of two new binational agencies, the Border Environment Cooperation Commission (BECC) and the North American Development Bank (NAD Bank), to help local communities build water, wastewater, and sanitation systems. Over the next few years, the BECC and NAD Bank helped develop and finance dozens of desperately needed projects, including the first wastewater treatment plant in Ciudad Juárez, as well as a new water supply and distribution system for Nogales, Sonora. Although some projects, including the one in Nogales, were controversial, environmentalists praised the BECC and NAD Bank for taking steps in the right direction. They took advantage of the BECC's binational and relatively open approval process to push for more public control over the design, construction, and financing of infrastructure.

In Nogales, the controversy centered on the project's main component, an eight-mile-long *acuaferico* (aqueduct) intended to bring more water from well fields along the Rio Magdalena south of town. Mexican environmentalists warned that the Rio Magdalena aquifer was too shallow to sustain much more pumping. At the same time, Nogales, Arizona, officials worried that the plan's call for additional pumping along the Santa Cruz River threatened their city's water supply. People on both sides also raised questions about the financing, wondering how residents of Nogales, Sonora, would be able to afford the expected 20 percent annual increases in water bills needed to pay back the eight-million-dollar NAD Bank loan. In spite of these concerns, Nogales, Sonora, officials went ahead with the project. The acuaferico was completed by the spring of 1999, when President Zedillo again came to town to dedicate both it and a new truck highway that skirted the old *periferico,* as well as an expanded Mariposa port of entry. Water and sanitation systems may have been slowly improving in Nogales, but construction of infrastructure for human needs still lagged far behind construction of highways, ports, and other public works aimed at promoting trade.

In contrast to the rancor surrounding the acuaferico, work on the joint sewer system proceeded in the spirit of close cooperation on the environment historically demonstrated in Ambos Nogales. By the mid-1990s, the main issue had become how to divide up the increasingly valuable wastewater from Nogales, Sonora, which made up 70 percent of the flow into the treatment plant. Mexico wanted at least some of the water back to recharge the region's declining aquifers, but the U.S. side wanted to keep the water in Arizona, where it fed a thriving ripar-

A man drinks from a water pipe emerging from under the Nogales, Sonora, dump. The pipe supplied all the water for inhabitants of this *colonia*.

ian area along the Santa Cruz River north of Nogales. The two sides formed a binational planning committee to consider dozens of options—such as returning some of the effluent to the Mexican side, building another, smaller treatment plant in Nogales, Sonora, or some combination of the two. Once agreement was reached, they planned to approach the NAD Bank for funding.

Binational cooperation aside, questions remained whether there would be enough money to build a new treatment plant for Nogales, let alone operate and maintain it for many years. The same doubts that had arisen over repayment of NAD Bank loans for the water system were likely to arise over loans for the wastewater system as well. All along the border, people were concerned not only about the cost of NAD Bank loans, but about where they would find the billions needed to build infrastructure.

"Right now, both the U.S. and Mexican governments are directing a lot of grant money and other resources toward the border," said Placido Dos Santos, border environmental manager for the Arizona

Department of Environmental Quality. "What's going to happen when that ends?" Dos Santos and others believed that, sooner or later, border communities were going to have to turn to industry to bear some of the costs. "The maquiladoras are helping drive population growth on the border," he told me, "and they share responsibility for paying for it."

Since the very beginning, the U.S. and Mexican governments had held out maquiladoras as the long-term solution to unemployment and poverty in Mexico. But as long as maquiladora jobs paid so little that people couldn't afford a minimal standard of living, poverty and the resulting illegal immigration would continue. As José Torres from Casa de la Misericordia had once told me, "Someone should have told the poor people here that it was going to take a long time for free trade to work for them." Studies found that wages in Mexico wouldn't have to go up that much in order to have a big effect on illegal immigration— maybe one-third of what they were in the United States, rather than one-tenth. In the meantime, the Border Patrol did the job that maquiladoras and NAFTA failed to do.

Some analysts perceived a sinister relationship between the border crackdown and the maquiladoras, arguing that keeping Mexican workers cheap and easily exploitable was essential to the success of the industry. In his book *The Militarization of the U.S.–Mexico Border*, University of Texas researcher Tim Dunn wrote that although harsh border enforcement measures would seem to contradict the principles of free trade and NAFTA—a contradiction noted by many border residents—the 1980s and 1990s in fact saw the rapid and simultaneous expansion of both. "This suggests that border militarization and economic integration are not necessarily mutually exclusive developments." Dunn pointed out that the crackdown benefited business interests by forcing Mexican workers either to stay in Mexico or to live a fearful, illegal existence in the United States. Mexican workers remained controlled, powerless, and essentially unable to fight for higher wages and better working conditions on either side of the line.

Although the crackdown did serve to keep the demands of Mexican labor in check, it was at best a stopgap response to a complicated and deeply rooted problem. Many border residents believed it was unfair and ultimately unsustainable for law enforcement to have to shoulder the entire burden for illegal immigration. By the late 1990s, the crackdown seemed to have reached the point of diminishing returns. Border towns such as Nogales had been turned into virtual fortresses, more and more people were having their rights violated, more agents were being attacked, and more border-crossers were dying, yet there was no evidence at all that the overall flow of undocumented immigrants had been curtailed, let alone stopped. The border was paying a terrible price for the inability of the United States and Mexico to come to grips with the underlying causes of illegal immigration. Frustrated by national policies that didn't seem to recognize the costs and limitations of the crackdown on the border, local residents led the search for alternatives.

Border historians have pointed out that migrant Mexican labor has for generations been an integral part of the American agricultural and service economies, and will continue to be so in the future. Many have felt that the United States has a duty to acknowledge this longstanding relationship and to treat Mexican workers accordingly by, for example, signing and abiding by the United Nations convention on the treatment of migrant labor. Some scholars, including Jorge Bustamante of the Colegio de la Frontera Norte in Tijuana, have said it probably wouldn't be long before an aging U.S. population recruited young Mexicans to work here, just as we did during World War II and at other times in the past. Others, including many growers as well as border residents such as Mayor Ray Borane of Douglas, have called for a revival of the controversial bracero program.

Under the bracero program, hundreds of thousands of Mexican migrant laborers worked legally in the United States between 1942 and 1964. The program ended when U.S. labor unions complained that braceros were undercutting American farmworkers' already low wages.

Critics also attacked the program for legitimizing growers' abuse and exploitation of the Mexican laborers. These concerns were valid, yet it was difficult to see how U.S. farmworkers benefited from competing with workers who had no legal status or protection at all. Moreover, Mexican migrant workers could scarcely be more abused and exploited than they already were. The current situation is not much different.

In the fall of 1999, Arizona governor Jane Hull followed Mayor Borane's lead and announced she was willing to establish a pilot guest worker program. The idea was quickly endorsed by Texas governor (and presidential hopeful) George W. Bush, among others. Nevertheless, significant hurdles remained. For such a proposal to succeed, business interests would have to agree to accept certain standards on wages, housing, and working conditions, and labor would have to drop its bias for U.S. workers in favor of a broader vision of rights and dignity for every worker in North America. If these two groups could come together, a properly designed guest worker program had the potential to significantly reduce both illegal immigration and the pressure for more law enforcement on the border.

Like illegal immigration, America's drug problem stubbornly resisted law enforcement solutions, and nowhere was this resistance more clear than on the border. Despite a massive buildup of men and equipment, it was difficult to say what impact, if any, the crackdown was having on the nationwide availability of drugs. A couple of massive seizures in Nogales in early 1998 indicated how many drugs were continuing to come in, crackdown or no. In March, Customs officers found 1,313 pounds of cocaine in a car parked on a side street downtown, their largest seizure in more than two years. Two months later, inspectors at the Mariposa port of entry discovered 1,743.5 pounds of cocaine, estimated to be worth fifty-two million dollars, inside two diesel generators strapped to a flatbed truck. Coinciding with the new Nogales Customs director's first day on the job, the seizure was the second largest ever at that port.

Although marijuana smuggling continued much as it had in the old days, on mules through the desert, traffickers were apparently turning to the ports of entry to cross more valuable cargos. Corrupt inspectors made it easy. In early 1999, three Nogales Immigration and Naturalization Service (INS) employees were found to have been taking bribes to look the other way when drug-laden vehicles came through the port. The head of the Tucson FBI office called the arrests an indication of the "pervasive" corruption that exists among law enforcement on the border. "It's a national disgrace," he said. Traffickers were also buying up produce companies, warehouses, truck companies, rail lines, and other legitimate businesses involved in cross-border commerce in order to facilitate smuggling. A confidential 1998 Customs report highlighted the conflict between free trade and the drug war at the ports of entry, citing pressure on agents not to impede commerce as a main reason why fewer than 1 percent of trucks crossing the border were thoroughly inspected. One Drug Enforcement Agency official called the free-trade agreement "narco heaven."

Further evidence of the persistence and resourcefulness of drug smugglers came to light in early 1999, when authorities discovered two hand-dug drug tunnels in Nogales, Arizona. These tunnels were less sophisticated than some that had been found in other cities on the border, but they did have concrete flooring, wooden ceiling supports, lighting, and evaporative cooling, which made them far from amateur efforts. One of the tunnels ran from beneath a downtown house to a city storm grate next to the Grand Avenue tunnel, a distance of about 250 feet; the other tunnel ran from the same house about 400 feet to a crawl space under Sacred Heart Catholic Church. The owner of the house, an absentee landlord who lived in California, denied knowing anything about the tunnels and was not charged. Authorities also questioned people at the church, but found no evidence that they were involved. Sacred Heart had been a sanctuary church during the 1980s, and some locals wondered whether the tunnel dated from that time. Former sanctuary workers scoffed at the idea, pointing out that there was no need for tunnels in those days. Everyone just went through the fence.

It was clear that no matter what the U.S. government did to try to stop drug smuggling at the border, traffickers would figure out a way to get their goods to market. Corruption and bloodshed had escalated dramatically since the crackdown began, with no end in sight. For local residents, the war on drugs was no metaphor. It was a real war, complete with soldiers and automatic weapons, and it was being fought in their backyards and in their neighborhoods. They knew its costs firsthand. They had lost Dario Miranda Valenzuela, Alex Kirpnick, Esequiel Hernandez, as well as many more friends and family members from both sides of the line and from both sides of the law. Once again, the border was paying the price for the failure of the United States to take a realistic, responsible, and nuanced approach to a complex problem. And again, border residents took the lead in calling for new approaches.

"All these operations on the border, both sides—checkpoints, police—it makes me laugh," said Nogales, Sonora, businessman Marco Antonio Martínez. "How long is it going to take them to figure it out? They're going to have to become a fascist government. Even if they disappear drugs from the face of Earth, there will always be alcohol, Resistol, gasoline, banana leaves. . . . I don't say decriminalize, just reanalyze." Martínez and many others believe drug use should be approached more as a social and moral failure than as a crime. "There are three ways to regulate relations between people: law, custom, and morality. We usually go about it the opposite of the way we should. I don't believe there can be enough laws to regulate human behavior if there are no morals or customs to begin with." As he pointed out, drug use in Mexico was much lower than in the United States, and not just because people were poor. In Mexico, drug use was frowned on as an insult to the family, and people cared deeply about their families. Many Mexicans were willing to transport and sell drugs to gringos, however, and for similar reasons. "It's not the use of drugs that's spoiling our society; it's the money. People are so poor, the temptation is overwhelming. Who can resist? They have to weigh the morality of selling drugs against the morality of feeding their families," said Martínez.

Considering the money to be made from smuggling versus that to be made from working in the maquiladoras, it is a wonder why more young people in Nogales haven't ended up in the tunnels. The fact that they haven't is a testament to the loyalty and closeness of Mexican families, even in the face of tremendous poverty. The tunnel kids' chaotic homes, although more common on the border, are still the exception. The tunnel kids themselves, especially the girls, vowed not to let their own children end up like they had, and if Cristina was to be believed, her children were a motivating force for her to change her life. Good intentions and the efforts of Mi Nueva Casa notwithstanding, however, the tunnel kids I met seemed destined to repeat their parents' mistakes. In the spring of 1999, Cecilia Guzmán told me that Inez, Alma, and Cristina were pregnant again, Alma and Cristina for the third time. This news came just a few weeks after Cristina claimed to me that she was using contraception and didn't want any more children. The father, according to Cecilia, was a gringo gang member whom Cristina had met when she was in Tucson robbing houses.

Cristina may have been an extreme case, but she was hardly unique in being caught in the wrenching changes of the border, particularly in terms of women's sexuality and roles in life. Traditional Mexican culture and religion taught women like Yolanda to be sexually passive and to depend on men for support. The modern values of the border encourage women such as Yolanda's daughters to be more sexually and financially self-reliant. By giving young women access to health care, family planning, and independent income, the maquilas have been an important influence behind these essentially positive changes. Although still poverty-stricken, female maquila workers have more power than their mothers to decide when and how many children to bear, and they are bearing fewer. They are also achieving more equality in their marriages, including finding husbands who do housework and care for the children while they are at work. Some girls, like Cristina, keep falling into the chasm of conflicting cultures and values on the border. Most, however, have taken advantage of the opportunity to gain control over their lives and bodies. In this way, as in many others, the maquiladoras are a double-edged sword for Mexico and its people.

Although maquilas were beginning to take some responsibility for workers' living conditions and the environment by the 1990s, consensus was rising on the border that they needed to do even more. Local residents, including many politicians and business people, believed it was no longer enough for the companies to say they were benefiting the community just by being there. Managers such as Hope Torres and Tom Higgins as well as CEOs such as Doug Chapman have led the way in getting companies involved in individual and voluntary efforts, but as long as no large-scale or mandatory programs exist, conditions on the border are not going to improve.

Local communities have searched for ways to get money from the maquilas without targeting them specifically. One of the most promising ideas was developed in the state of Chihuahua and put into law there in 1994. It required every business with more than five employees—both Mexican and foreign—to contribute to a fund called the Chihuahuan Business Foundation, which was then used for locally controlled development projects. Receiving about thirty cents a month for each minimum wage paid, the foundation took in some $3.5 million a year, and through matching grants from Mexico City, the United States, Germany, Italy, and other places, raised the total to about $5 million. These funds were used not only to build and maintain the Salecinian youth centers in Juárez, but also to support community banks, hospitals, scholarships, and many other programs.

Following the foundation's success in Chihuahua, business and community leaders across Mexico, especially those in states where maquilas predominate, proposed similar ideas. Marco Antonio Martínez spearheaded the effort in Sonora. After more than a year of lobbying the Sonoran business community, state legislature, and governor, and after having received endorsements from the Juárez

Maquiladora Association, the InterAmerican Foundation, the Prince of Wales Business Leaders Forum, the Chicago Community Trust, and many other Mexican and foreign organizations, he was on the verge of success. One group that had yet to lend its support was the Nogales Maquiladora Association. "They said it should be a decision of individual companies," Martínez told me. "The maquilas are very concerned that the government will take the money." Martínez, a backer of the pro-business Partido de Acción Nacional (PAN), agreed that government involvement was a bad idea. "In Chihuahua, the model is that as soon as the government gets the money, they have to give it back to boards of business people. The government does not touch the money." If a well-run, truly nonpartisan foundation could be established, it had the potential to make a lasting difference in cities such as Nogales. Martínez was trying to keep expectations low, though. "Fighting poverty, paying attention to youth, these are good flags to use, and people in Mexico have been burned a lot by people who say they're going to do something and then nothing happens."

Given the overwhelming nature of the border's problems, it may be tempting to believe that not much can be done. Yet Martínez and the others described in this book have proven that change is possible. From the top of society to the bottom, in Ambos Nogales and all along the border, local people are working to gain control over the forces that affect their lives. They have had many successes. They fought to get labor and environmental standards inserted into NAFTA, and they continue to fight to make sure those standards are enforced and strengthened. They demanded more accountability from industry and government for environmental health, pushed the Border Patrol to better train and supervise its agents, rejected militarization, and organized transnational coalitions and charities to benefit maquiladora workers, the environment, immigrants, and youth. They have demonstrated that binational problems could be solved by reaching across boundaries and working together. Just as during the sanctuary movement, border residents have proved that, regardless of the forces brought against them, they can resist and will triumph.

On a deeper level, the people of Ambos Nogales are leading the way to a new relationship between the United States and Mexico. Forever linked by geography, the two countries are becoming increasingly intertwined economically, socially, and culturally. In Ambos Nogales, people have lived this way for generations. They know how to celebrate and find strength in difference. They know that when Americans fight for the rights of Mexicans to a decent standard of living, we fight for our own as well. People in Nogales have much to teach us about tolerating paradox and contradiction. They understand that it is important to seek balance, even though many tensions of the border may never be fully resolved. Most locals believe in free trade—after all, the border was built on trade—but they also believe in protecting the environment and the rights of workers. They want law enforcement not at all costs, but rather professional, well-trained, civilian law enforcement. They want a border that is neither open nor closed, but a safe and peaceful border, where commerce flows freely and where all people, regardless of status, are treated with dignity and respect. Local people's insistence on creating harmony in spite of everything is one of the many things that make Ambos Nogales such a powerful place.

Finally, on a personal note, although this book contains examples of reporters whose work has made a difference on the border, I was not one of them. I benefited much more from knowing the people of Ambos Nogales than they did from knowing me. The caring that Yolanda and Hope and so many others extended to me changed my life. I wasn't able to take Yolanda out of her cardboard house or Cristina out of the tunnels. I couldn't prevent Bobbi or Liana Teyechea or Margarita Tello or Hope from losing their loved ones. They, on the other hand, taught me what generosity is, what courage is, and what faith is. They showed me what it means to have hope and to believe in a better future. They showed me that it is possible to reach across the wall that divides us and to create lasting friendships. That is the meaning of Ambos Nogales.

CHAPTER NOTES

INTRODUCTION

Pages 3-4

Sources on the shootout include: Tim Steller, "3 Men Held in Border Slaying; Violence Leaves One Dead, 4 Hurt," *Arizona Daily Star*, Nov. 25, 1997; Francisco Castro, "'It Was Ugly, Really Ugly,'" *Nogales International*, Nov. 28, 1997; and Tim Steller, "Mexico Tightens Border Security at Nogales," *Arizona Daily Star*, Dec. 5, 1997.

Pages 5-6

Early settlement described in Nogales Centennial Committee, comp., *Nogales, Arizona, 1880-1980 Centennial Anniversary* (Nogales, Ariz: Pimería Alta Historical Society, 1980), 6 and 37-38; Alvaro Obregón quoted in Tim Kelly, "Ambos Nogales," *Arizona Highways*, Nov. 1964.

Page 8

History of the sanctuary movement in Nogales described in Miriam Davidson, *Convictions of the Heart: Jim Corbett and the Sanctuary Movement* (Tucson: University of Arizona Press, 1988).

Pages 10-11

Early maquila history from Milo Kearney and Anthony Knopp, *Border Cuates: A History of the U.S.-Mexican Twin Cities* (Austin: Eakin, 1995), 243-44, and from author telephone interview with Don Nibbe, Feb. 1997. Nogales workforce statistics in Kathryn Kopinak, *Desert Capitalism: Maquiladoras in North America's Western Industrial Corridor* (Tucson: University of Arizona Press, 1996), 39, 104.

Page 12

Nogales geography, binational environmental cooperation, and tunnel construction described in Helen Ingram, Nancy K. Laney, and David M. Gillilan, *Divided Waters: Bridging the U.S.-Mexico Border* (Tucson: University of Arizona Press, 1995), 51, 62-63, and in Alma Ready, *Open Range and Hidden Silver: Arizona's Santa Cruz County* (Nogales, Ariz.: Pimería Alta Historical Society, 1986), 142.

Page 13

Sources on the history of smuggling in Nogales include: Ready, *Open Range,* 41, 71; Charles Fowler, "Bootleggers 20's Customs' Target," *Nogales International*, Feb. 26, 1976; Tim Steller, "Border Agent Is Slain near Nogales," *Arizona Daily Star*, June 4, 1998; James

Maish, "Somozas Part Legend, Part Terrifying Reality," *Arizona Daily Star,* May 24, 1987; and Miriam Davidson, "Militarizing the Mexican Border," *The Nation,* Apr. 1, 1991.

Page 14
"Berlin Wall" quote by Nogales businessman Hank Tintos in Pamela Hartman, "Barrier between Nogaleses to Be 14 Feet Tall and in Blue," *Tucson Citizen,* Nov. 5, 1996.

Page 15
Mexican population figures from Sam Dillon, "Smaller Families to Bring Big Change in Mexico," *New York Times,* June 8, 1999.

Page 16
Don Nibbe quote from telephone interview with author, Feb. 1997.

CHAPTER 1
All the stories, descriptions, and quotes from Yolanda in this chapter are from author interviews and visits to her home in Nogales, Sonora, in 1997 and 1998, and from a trip the author and Yolanda took together to Bacobampo, Sonora, Apr. 1998. Interviews were conducted in Spanish and translated by the author. Yolanda's and Elias's last names were changed to protect their privacy.

Pages 24–27
Information on Dick Campbell and early maquila development in Nogales from Kopinak, *Desert Capitalism,* 37–38. Information and quotes also from author telephone interview with Dick Bolin, Oct. 1998; author interview with Duane Boyett, Tucson, Arizona, Oct. 1998; and author interview with Richard Bosse, Tubac, Arizona, Oct. 1998. Boyett was the source of the Campbell quotes. Local officials quoted in "Big Deal at the Border," *Newsweek,* Jan. 24, 1972.

Pages 32–33
Maquila workforce problems, Mexican government easing of labor laws, and 1981 CTM contract described in Kopinak, *Desert Capitalism,* 10–11 and 38–41; the maquiladora manager is quoted in John Dougherty and David Holthouse, "Bordering on Exploitation," *New Times* (Phoenix), July 9–15, 1998.

Pages 33–35
Alberto Morackis quotes from interview with author in Nogales, Sonora, Feb. 1999, conducted in Spanish and translated by the author. Information on maquila strikes and protests also from Ray Panzarella, "Lean Times Put Squeeze on Border Plants" and "Workers Follow Socialist Leader," *Arizona Daily Star,* June 20, 1982; and Kearney, *Border Cuates,* 260. Miriam Davidson, "Organizing in the Maquilas," *NACLA Report on the Americas,* May 1991, was the source for Eureka vacuum strike and Victor Clark Alfaro comments. Maquila growth in the 1980s in Kopinak, *Desert Capitalism,* 12, 38.

Pages 36–39
Author interviews with Yolanda's children, Nogales, Sonora, fall 1998, conducted in Spanish and translated by the author, were sources on conditions inside the factories; also, Tim Steller, "Factory Tests for Pregnancy in Mexico Draw Criticism," *Arizona Daily*

Star, Feb. 1, 1998. "See the moon" quote from author interview with Hope Torres, Tucson, Jan. 1997. Kopinak describes maquila workers smoking marijuana after their shifts in *Desert Capitalism,* 93. The scene at Coco Loco described by Dougherty and Holthouse in "Bordering on Exploitation."

Page 39
Juárez killings and arrests described in Sam Dillon, "Feminist Propels Outcry at Brutal Mexico Killings," *New York Times,* Feb. 28, 1999, and in AP, "Maquiladoras Draw Fire in Women's Killings," *Arizona Daily Star,* Apr. 4, 1999.

Pages 40–41
Gephardt visit described to author by Tom Higgins, Nogales, Sonora, Jan. 1997. See also Sandy Tolan, "The Border Boom: Hope and Heartbreak," *New York Times Magazine,* July 1, 1990. In "Bordering on Exploitation," Dougherty and Holthouse describe being followed and videotaped; "We get criticized" quote from author interview with Tom Higgins, Nogales, Sonora, Jan. 1997. Don Nibbe quotes from phone interview with author, Feb. 1997.

Pages 41–42
Impact of 1994–95 peso crisis on Nogales and Ken Lilley quote from Miriam Davidson, "Maquiladora Workers Hit by Mexican Peso Drop," *Christian Science Monitor,* Apr. 5, 1995. Nogales market-basket survey conducted by author in October 1996. Author interview with Roscoe Combs, Rio Rico, Arizona, Feb. 1997. See also AP, "Abducted Executive Free after Sanyo Pays Ransom," *Arizona Republic,* Aug. 20, 1996, and Sarah Tully, "Safeway to Shut Border Store, a Victim of Peso Drop," *Arizona Daily Star,* Feb. 22, 1995.

Pages 43–44
Borderlinks visits with Yolanda witnessed by author and also described by Janet Elwood in Borderlinks newsletter, *Loaves and Fishes,* summer 1998.

CHAPTER 2

Pages 50–54
Author interview with Jimmy Teyechea, Nogales, Arizona, Feb. 1994; author interview with Dr. George Comerci, Nogales, Arizona, Oct. 1997; author interview with Liana Teyechea, Nogales, Arizona, Aug. 1997; author interview with Sylvia Montañez, Rio Rico, Arizona, Aug. 1997. Fernie Espinoza's quote from Rubén Hernandez, "The Littlest Victims," *Tucson Citizen,* Oct. 21, 1993; Jimmy's scrapbook, the videos, and Liana's letter provided to author by Anita Teyechea, July 1997.

Pages 55–56
Sources on water and air pollution in Nogales include author interview with Susan Thomas Ramirez, Amado, Arizona, Aug. 1997; Ingram, Laney, and Gillilan, *Divided Waters,* 98–102; testimony given by Santa Cruz County Health Director Pat Zurick before a Congressional Subcommittee on Regulation, Business Opportunities, and Energy, Feb. 21, 1992; *Protecting the Environment and Health along the Arizona/Mexico Border,* Ari-

zona Department of Environmental Quality and Arizona Department of Health Services newsletter, Phoenix, Arizona, summer 1994; and author interview with Mike Alcala of the U.S. Public Health Service in Nogales, Arizona, July 1997.

Page 58

Quotes and information on disease rates in Nogales, Arizona, from author interviews in Nogales, Arizona, with Anna Acuña, Oct. 1995 and July 1997; Jimmy Teyechea, Feb. 1994; Anita Teyechea, July 1995 and July 1997 (the source on Jimmy's quote); and Dr. Comerci, Oct. 1997. Jessica Bell, "Death in a Small Town," *City Magazine*, April 1988, was an additional source on pancreatic cancer cluster.

Page 59

Edie Rubinowitz, "High Cancer Rates in City Well-Kept Secret" and "Teyechea's Humor Helps Fight Bone Marrow Cancer," *Nogales International*, Dec. 2, 1992, were sources of quotes and information on the founding of LIFE. Glenn Saavedra quote from author interview in Nogales, Arizona, July 1997.

Pages 59–61

Dr. Flood and state cancer figures quoted in Laura Brooks, "Cancer Rates in Nogales to Be Studied," *Arizona Daily Star*, Jan. 24, 1993. Edie Rubinowitz, "UA Team Interested in Possible Cluster of Cancer, Lupus," *Nogales International*, Dec. 23, 1992. Author interview with Dr. Larry Clark, Tucson, Arizona, Feb. 1994. "Killer tomatoes" quote in Rubinowitz, "Teyechea's Humor." Video of Jimmy at the reunion provided to author by Anita Teyechea.

Pages 61–62

Sources on toxic dumping in Nogales and elsewhere on the border include Sandy Tolan, "The Border Boom: Hope and Heartbreak," *New York Times Magazine*, July 1, 1990; Sanford J. Lewis, Marco Kaltofen, and Gregory Ormsby, *Border Trouble: Rivers in Peril*, National Toxics Campaign Fund report, Boston, Massachusetts, May 1991; and Roberto Suro, "Border Industry's Nasty Byproduct Imperils U.S.–Mexico Trade," *New York Times*, Mar. 31, 1991. Jimmy's quote from author interview, Nogales, Arizona, Feb. 1994. Phil Bernake quoted in *A Current Affair* segment called "Nightmare in Nogales," aired in 1993, video provided to the author by Anita Teyechea. Juárez example found in Holden Lewis, AP, "Maquiladora's Toxic Waste Producing Cheap Highs in Juarez," *Arizona Daily Star*, June 26, 1989, and Tijuana example in Ingram, Laney, and Gillilan, *Divided Waters*, 100.

Pages 62–63

Sources on birth defects in Nogales and borderwide include Eduardo Montes, AP, "High Rates of Fatal Defects at Birth in 2 Border Towns Baffle Doctors," *Arizona Daily Star*, July 13, 1992; Rubén Hernandez, "Brainless Babies" and "The Littlest Victims," *Tucson Citizen*, Oct. 21, 1993; author interview with Dr. Comerci, Nogales, Arizona, Oct. 1997; Mike Beebe, "Mallory Plant Is Long Gone; Some Say It Left a Grim Legacy," *Buffalo News*, Mar. 11, 1987; and Tom Barry and Beth Sims, *The Challenge of Cross-Border Environmentalism* (Albuquerque: Resource Center, 1994), 43–44.

Page 64

John Maggs, "GM Agrees to Treat Water at 35 Maquiladora Plants," *Journal of Commerce,* May 13, 1991. Jimmy's quote from author interview, Nogales, Arizona, Feb. 1994; Lewis Mitchell quote from author interview, Nogales, Sonora, July 1997. Mitchell told the author about giving the inspector an office in his maquila.

Pages 65–66

Sources on burning oil in wash and railroad spills include Barry and Sims, *Challenge of Cross-Border Environmentalism,* 35; Laura Brooks, "Railroad Tanker Derailment Forces Evacuation in Nogales, Sonora," *Arizona Daily Star,* Feb. 24, 1994; and Tim Vanderpool, "Daily Toxic Threat," *Nogales International,* Nov. 14, 1995. Information on UMI from author interview with Susan Ramirez, Amado, Arizona, Aug. 1997; UMI official quoted in Steve Yozwiak, "Polluters Get State 'Green' Awards," *Arizona Republic,* Sept. 21, 1997. Jimmy quotes from author interview in Nogales, Arizona, Feb. 1994, and from Gary Collins's *Home* show, aired in late 1993. Video provided by Anita Teyechea.

Pages 66–67

Quotes on controversy over Meister's and Clark's grant proposal reported in Laura Brooks, "Controversy Ends Nogales Cancer Study," *Arizona Daily Star,* Aug. 20, 1993, and Edie Rubinowitz, "LIFE Health Survey on Indefinite Hold," *Nogales International,* Aug. 20, 1993. Dr. Rivera-Claisse quote from Binational Task Force on Border Health meeting attended by author, Rio Rico, June 17, 1994. Also Pamela Hartman, "Study: Sonora Cancer Rates Normal," *Tucson Citizen,* Nov. 30, 1995. Susan Ramirez quote from telephone interview with the author, Feb. 1994.

Pages 68–69

William Joffroy Jr. quoted in Suro, "Border Industry's Nasty Byproduct." Commentary in *Nogales Herald,* Feb. 22 and 23, 1994. Jimmy's comments on backlash in Nogales made in author interview, Nogales, Arizona, Feb. 1994. Jimmy's quotes on fatalism from Rubinowitz, "High Cancer Rates," and Chris Coppola, "Cesspool at Our Border," *Mesa Tribune,* Aug. 29, 1993.

Page 69

Jimmy Teyechea, "Forget Border Patrol, 'I'll Take Steel Fence,'" *Nogales International,* Apr. 4, 1993. Anna Acuña quote from author interview, Nogales, Arizona, Oct. 1995.

Pages 69–70

Richard Price, "Nightmare on the Border," *USA Today,* Oct. 27, 1993. See also Russ Hemphill and Janet Perez, "Cancer Crisis in Nogales," *Phoenix Gazette,* Nov. 1, 1993, and Demetria Martinez, "Paying Pollution's Price," *National Catholic Reporter,* Jan. 7, 1994. Jimmy's quote from author interview, Nogales, Arizona, Feb. 1994.

Pages 70–71

Jimmy and Anita Teyechea described Jimmy's conversation with Governor Symington in interviews with the author, Nogales, Arizona, Feb. 1994 and July 1995. Jimmy's "lives devalued" and "grandstanding" quotes are from Tucson station KOLD-TV news coverage of the Symington visit, Dec. 1993. The "Hurricane Andrew" quote is from *Toxic Border*, a three-part documentary on border pollution that appeared on the Discovery Channel in early 1994. Videos provided to the author by Anita Teyechea. See also Laura Brooks, "Nogales Cancers Spur Official Action," *Arizona Daily Star*, Dec. 2, 1993.

Pages 71–72

Susan Ramirez quote from telephone interview with author, Feb. 1994. Pamela Hartman, "New Dump Eases Fears on Border," *Tucson Citizen*, Jan. 24, 1995. UMI information obtained during author-led Society of Environmental Journalists tour of UMI plant in Oct. 1997. Sources on NAFTA impact on border environment include *Environmental Protection along the U.S.–Mexico Border*, United States Environmental Protection Agency report, Washington, D.C., October 1994; Yozwiak, "Polluters"; and Frank Clifford and Mary Beth Sheridan, "Borderline Efforts on Pollution," *Los Angeles Times*, June 30, 1997.

Pages 72–73

Quotes from Dec. 1994 meeting at Nogales High School attended by author and reported in Miriam Davidson and Martin Van Der Werf, "Health Study in Nogales Confirms Ills," *Arizona Republic*, Dec. 14, 1994. Also Pamela Hartman, "CDC Questions Findings of UA Lupus Study," *Tucson Citizen*, Feb. 25, 1995, and Kathy Vandervoet, "Nogales Will Get CDC Specialist to Study Cancer, Lupus Troubles," *Nogales International*, Apr. 25, 1995.

Pages 73–74

Report on ADEQ study of Nogales air quality presented at meeting attended by author in Nogales, Arizona, on May 7, 1998. Water results reported in Keith Bagwell, "Nogales Water Contamination Up, Study Finds," *Arizona Daily Star*, June 20, 1998. Also Tim Vanderpool, "Dark Data," *Tucson Weekly*, June 12–18, 1997, on barriers to the release of binational study results. Dr. Comerci quote from interview with author, Nogales, Arizona, Oct. 1997. Author telephone interview with Dick Kamp of the Border Ecology Project in Bisbee, Arizona, Sept. 1997, was the source of the quote and of the information on CDC plans in Douglas.

Pages 75–76

Keith Bagwell, "Fumes Force Huge Nogales Evacuation," *Arizona Daily Star*, Feb. 18, 1994. Copy of letter to Symington provided by Jimmy Teyechea during interview with author, Nogales, Arizona, Feb. 1994. Settlement of lawsuit against Matamoros maquilas reported at border health conference attended by author at the University of Arizona, Tucson, Mar. 29, 1996. Mitchell quotes from author interview, Nogales, Sonora, July 1997.

Pages 76–79

Author interviews with Anita Teyechea, Liana Teyechea, Sylvia Montañez, and Anna Acuña in Nogales and Rio Rico, Arizona, July and Aug. 1997, were sources on the trip to Washington, D.C., and on Jimmy's last days. Tape of funeral mass and copy of Symington's eulogy provided to author by Anita Teyechea. Susan Ramirez quote from author interview, Amado, Arizona, Aug. 1997. Dr. Comerci comments from author interview, Nogales, Arizona, Oct. 1997. Information on LIFE play from author interview with Celia Concannon, director of the Santa Cruz Environmental Theater, by telephone and in Nogales, Arizona, Oct. 1998. Also, Sarah Tully, "Exchange Program Studies Pollution on

Border," *Arizona Daily Star,* Dec. 15, 1997, was source on student exchange program. Liana Teyechea quotes and essays obtained during interview with author, Nogales, Arizona, July 1997.

CHAPTER 3

Pages 80–87

The quotes and descriptions of Dario Miranda Valenzuela's death are a dramatic recreation that is based on Agent Tom Watson's version of events as given under oath at both of Elmer's trials; testimony of other agents on the scene and at the scene of Elmer's earlier shooting incident in Mar. 1992; author interview with Luz Castro and her daughter in Nogales, Sonora, May 1995, conducted in Spanish and translated by Catalina Spencer; and author interview with Jesús Romo Véjar, attorney for the Miranda family, in Tucson, May 1995. Luz Castro was the source of quote by Miranda's cousin. Copies of the trial transcripts were provided to the author by Tucson attorney Richard Gonzales, who also represented Miranda's family. Author interview with Teresa Leal, Nogales, Arizona, April 1998, was the source of the quote from Miranda's son.

Pages 87–88

In addition to author interview with Joe Pankoke, Nogales, Arizona, June 1997, sources on illegal influx and Border Patrol crackdown in Nogales and elsewhere include: *Border Patrol Strategic Plan 1994 and Beyond,* United States Border Patrol report, Washington, D.C., July 1994; *Building a Comprehensive Southwest Border Enforcement Strategy,* United States Immigration and Naturalization Service report, Washington, D.C., June 1996; Lourdes Medrano Leslie, "INS Aims to Stem Illegal Flow at Border," *Arizona Republic,* Oct. 18, 1994; Sebastian Rotella, "Putting the Squeeze on Nogales," *Los Angeles Times,* Jan. 30, 1995; José Palafox, "Militarizing the Mexico–U.S. Border," *Covert Action Quarterly,* Mar. 5, 1996; "Tucson Is Regional Headquarters for Newly Expanded War on Drugs," *Arizona Daily Star,* Dec. 4, 1997; and Tim Vanderpool, "The Real Drug Lords," *Tucson Weekly,* Apr. 30–May 6, 1998.

Page 88

See *Operation Blockade,* a report on the El Paso crackdown by the American Friends Service Committee's Immigration Law Enforcement Monitoring Project (AFSC-ILEMP), Philadelphia, Penn., July 1994.

Pages 90–91

Carlos Arias, "Illegals Help Hurt BP Agent," *Nogales International,* Aug. 7, 1998. Sources on Lopez shooting include author's telephone interview with Chief Sanders in Aug. 1995, and Ignacio Ibarra, "Border Agent 'Positive' Mexican Police Shot Him," *Arizona Daily Star,* Aug. 25, 1995. Jerry Kammer, "Policeman in Probe Kills Self," *Arizona Republic,* Oct. 17, 1995, was the source of the "Russian roulette" quotes.

Page 91

"Border Patrol Seizes Pot, Horse," *Arizona Daily Star,* June 7, 1997.

Page 93

The quote and description of the demonstration at port of entry are from Rubén

Hernandez, "Bond Refusal Satisfies Mexicans," *Tucson Citizen*, July 31, 1992. Sources on Border Patrol abuses include: *Human Rights at the U.S.–Mexico Border*, AFSC-ILEMP report, Philadelphia, Penn., March 1990; Miriam Davidson, "The Mexican Border War," *The Nation*, Nov. 12, 1990; and *United States Frontier Injustice*, Americas Watch report, New York, N.Y., May 13, 1993. Jesús Romo quoted in Maggie Rivas, "Border Agent's Acquittal Underscores the Need of Oversight, Groups Say," *Dallas Morning News*, Dec. 20, 1992.

Pages 93–97

Author interview with Luz Castro, Nogales, Sonora, May 1995, and trial transcripts were sources on the evidence of Dario Miranda's drug use and attire. Luz Castro quote comes from Tina Plaza, "America's Secret Police," *Spin*, Sept., 1993. Debbie Nathan, "Rodney King South," *LA Weekly*, Jan. 8–14, 1993, was an additional source on Miranda's childhood jobs. Patrick McDonnell, "Border Agent Was Accused of Stealing Cocaine," *Los Angeles Times*, July 24, 1992, was the source on Elmer's drug involvement. The trial transcripts were sources of quotes, descriptions of Mar. 1992 shooting, and other testimony, including Serrano's and Elmer's quotes. Elmer's ex-wife quoted in Tessie Borden, "Border Agent Was Boastful, Papers Say," *Arizona Daily Star*, July 22, 1992.

Pages 97–98

Sources on reaction to verdict, including quotes from Miranda's family, are: Tessie Borden, "Jury Clears Border Agent in Alien's Killing," *Arizona Daily Star*, Dec. 17, 1992; John Rawlinson and Laura Brooks, "Verdict Outrages Minority Groups, Victim's Relatives," *Arizona Daily Star*, Dec. 17, 1992; and Rubén Hernandez, Ann-Eve Pedersen, and Christina Valdez, "Elmer Relieved; Victim's Kin, Mexico Official Outraged," *Tucson Citizen*, Dec. 17, 1992. Irasema Coronado quoted in Laura Brooks, "Rape Charges against Border Patrol Agent Have Sonorans Fuming over Alleged Abuse," *Arizona Daily Star*, Oct. 4, 1993. Sources on calls for oversight board and civil suit include: Tessie Borden, "Trial Mars Border Patrol's By-the-Rules Image," *Arizona Daily Star*, Dec. 15, 1992; Mary Benanti, " 'Many Incidences of Abuse,' " *Tucson Citizen*, July 1, 1992; and Tessie Borden, "Shooting Victim's Family Sues Border Patrol Agents," *Arizona Daily Star*, Mar. 27, 1993.

Pages 98–100

Elvira's Restaurant owner Alicia Monroy quoted in Laura Brooks, "'Muro de Berlin,' Steel Sheet Marks Border in Nogales," *Arizona Daily Star*, Mar. 27, 1994. Additional sources on the wall include Louis Sahagun, "Unlucky Illegals Injuring Selves on Nogales' Wall," *Los Angeles Times*, reprinted in *Arizona Daily Star*, Sept. 9, 1994; and Jerry Kammer, "Good Fence Called Bad Neighbor," *Arizona Republic*, May 31, 1995. Quote on bordercrossers breaking into houses from author interview with Steve Colantuoni, director of the Santa Cruz County Economic Development Association, Nogales, Arizona, Jan. 1997. Sam Howe Verhovek, "Tiny Stretch of Border, Big Test for a Wall," *New York Times*, Dec. 8, 1997, was a source on the "decorator" wall.

Page 100

Quotes from Nogales immigration official and from Harlan Capin are from author interviews in Nogales, Arizona, Feb. 1996, for Miriam Davidson and Graciela Sevilla, "Hassles on Upswing at Border," *Arizona Republic*, Feb. 18, 1996.

Page 101

Sources on controversy over checkpoints and vehicle stops include: Howard Fischer, "Ruling Allows Suits over Border Patrol Stopping Motorists," *Arizona Daily Star,* Jan. 13, 1999; Tim Steller, "Border Patrol Accused of Bias from Within," *Arizona Daily Star,* Jan. 16, 1999; Miriam Davidson, "Border Patrol Catches Flak at Arizona Checkpoint," *APF Reporter,* Feb. 1998; and Julia Bishop, "Rio Rico School Board Taking Checkpoint Argument to State," *Nogales International,* June 12, 1998.

Pages 101–103

Sources on high-speed chases include Pamela Hartman, "Border Chases Turning Fatal," *Tucson Citizen,* May 9, 1997, and Tim Steller, "One of Three Killed While Fleeing Border Agents Was Mom of 2 Kids," *Arizona Daily Star,* Sept. 24, 1997. University of Houston study and Rodriguez quote in Sam Howe Verhovek, "'Silent Deaths' Climbing Steadily as Migrants Cross Mexico Border," *New York Times,* Aug. 24, 1997. Sources on deaths in Arizona and California include: Mark Shaffer, "Dying for a Dream," *Arizona Republic,* June 18, 1996; Ignacio Ibarra and Sarah Tully Tapia, "Six Drown in Douglas Floodwaters," *Arizona Daily Star,* Aug. 7, 1997 (two more bodies were later found); and "Migrant Death Toll Due to Cold Now at 10," *Arizona Daily Star,* Apr. 8, 1999. Immigrants quoted in Mark Shaffer, "Tensions Rise along the Border," *Arizona Republic,* Jan. 15, 1996, and in Rubén Hernandez, "Bond Refusal Satisfies Mexicans," *Tucson Citizen,* July 31, 1992.

Pages 103–104

Sources on the second verdict and the reaction to it include Mark Shaffer, "Acquittal Is Met with Indignation, Disbelief on Border," *Arizona Republic,* Feb. 4, 1994. Luz Castro and Jesús Romo quotes from Tucson press conference attended by author, Feb. 3, 1994. Author telephone interview with Wallace Kleindienst, summer 1996, was the source of the content of jury's note.

Pages 105–106

Watson quoted in Sebastian Rotella and Patrick McDonnell, "A Seemingly Futile Job Can Breed Abuses by Agents," *Los Angeles Times,* Apr. 23, 1993. Luz Castro quote from author interview, Nogales, Sonora, May 1995. Sources on Elmer plea and impact on Nogales station include Pamela Hartman, "Elmer Found Guilty of Felony," *Tucson Citizen,* Sept. 8, 1994; Ann-Eve Pedersen, "3 Nogales Agents Fired by Patrol," *Arizona Daily Star,* Sept. 19, 1995; and Angélica Pence, "3 Border Cops Fired in Elmer Case Regain Jobs," *Arizona Daily Star,* June 5, 1996.

Pages 106–107

Sources on misbehavior of Tucson-sector agents and on Selders case include Sebastian Rotella and Patrick McDonnell, "Renegade Agents at Border Outpost," *Los Angeles Times,* Apr. 23, 1993, part of a week-long series on the Border Patrol; Edie Rubinowitz, "Nogales Border Patrol Agent Faces Rape Charges," *Nogales International,* Sept. 10, 1993, and Mary Bustamante, "Ex-Agent's Sentence Criticized," *Tucson Citizen,* Oct. 8, 1994.

Pages 107–108

Border patrol spokesman Steve McDonald quoted in Mark Shaffer, "Acquittal Is Met with Indignation, Disbelief on Border," *Arizona Republic,* Feb. 4, 1994. *Citizens' Advisory Panel Report to the Attorney General,* Washington, D.C., Sept. 1997, was the source on the panel's recommendations. Jim Kolbe quote from telephone interview with author, May 1997. Mike Piccarreta quoted in Gregory Gross, "Migrant Hit in the Back; Officer Accused of First Degree Murder," *San Diego Union,* July 5, 1992.

Pages 108–109

Thaddeus Herrick, "Reno Urges Putting Brake on Border Patrol Buildup," *Houston Chronicle,* Mar. 10, 1999, was source on the Border Patrol growth statistics. Sources on the Kirpnick killing include: Tim Steller, "Border Agent Is Slain near Nogales," *Arizona Daily Star,* June 4, 1998; Tim Steller, "Reno Joins Crowd in Mourning Victim of Border Shooting," *Arizona Daily Star,* June 16, 1998; and Tim Steller, "Mexico Agrees to Extradition in Agent's Slaying," *Arizona Daily Star,* Oct. 15, 1998. Local television news coverage of the funeral was the source of Reno quotes.

Pages 109–110

Sources on border violence after June 1998 include: Tim Steller, "Enforcement Is Heating Up Border Mood," *Arizona Daily Star,* June 14, 1998; Tim Steller, "Man with Rock Is Shot Dead by Border Agent," *Arizona Daily Star,* Sept. 11, 1998; and AP, "Border Agent Shoots, Kills Crosser," *Arizona Daily Star,* Sept. 28, 1998. Sources on arrests and vigilantism in Douglas include: Tim Steller, "Border Patrol Set Record with 60,537 March Arrests," *Arizona Daily Star,* Apr. 2, 1999; "600 Migrants Try Mass Border Crossing," *Arizona Daily Star,* Apr. 15, 1999; Tim Steller, "Landowner Charged in Assault on Illegals," *Arizona Daily Star,* Feb. 10, 1999; and Ignacio Ibarra, "Rancher Detains 27 Illegal Entrants," *Arizona Daily Star,* Apr. 6, 1999. Mayor Borane quoted in Ignacio Ibarra, "Group Wants Guard to Patrol Border Area," *Arizona Daily Star,* Apr. 21, 1999. Also AP, "Bill OKs Troops on Mexican Line," *Arizona Daily Star,* June 21, 1997.

Pages 110–111

Sources on Esequiel Hernandez shooting include: Julia Prodis, AP, "Border Shooting Pits Town against Military," *Arizona Daily Star,* June 29, 1997; *San Antonio Express News,* "Panel Refused to Indict Marine in Border Killing," reprinted in *Arizona Daily Star,* Aug. 15, 1997; Ignacio Ibarra, "Use of Troops along Border Dead for Now," *Arizona Daily Star,* June 19, 1998; Monte Paulsen, "Collateral Damage," *Tucson Weekly,* Dec. 10–16, 1998; also, author interviews with members of the Redford citizens' committee at ILEMP-sponsored border strategy conference, Tucson, Jan. 1998.

Pages 111–112

Sources of the information on the use of the military on the Mexican side include Tim Steller, "Mexican Soldiers Shoot at 11, Killing One," *Arizona Daily Star,* Jan. 7, 1998, and author interview with José Marrufo, director of the Partido Revolucionario Democrático (PRD) migrant-assistance office in Nogales, Sonora, May 1998. Sources on Border Patrol hiring problems include: Tim Steller, "Border Patrol Wants to Grow Despite Reno," *Arizona Daily Star,* Mar. 13, 1999; Tim Steller, "Border Patrol Buildup Cut

Back," *Arizona Daily Star,* Apr. 28, 1999; and AP, "Arizona Lawmakers among 61 Blaming Clinton for Shorting Border Patrol," *Arizona Daily Star,* May 13, 1999.

Pages 112–115

Sources on Miranda family settlement include author interviews with Margarita Tello, Luz Castro, and Miranda's sister in Nogales, Sonora, May 1995; author interview with Jesús Romo, Tucson, May 1995; and phone interview with Mike Piccarreta, May 1995. Hernandez settlement reported in AP, "U.S. to Pay $1.9 Million in Border Killing," *Arizona Daily Star,* Aug. 12, 1998. Margarita Tello quotes from author interviews in Nogales, Sonora, June 1997 and May 1998, conducted in Spanish and translated by the author.

Pages 115–117

The lyrics and music for "Cañon Mariposa" were written by Victor Franco of Culiacán, Sinaloa, Mexico, and performed by Adalberto Gallegos of Tucson. David Valdez, director of the video, provided a copy to the author, Tucson, Mar. 1999. Translation of lyrics by Karen Valdez. English lyrics condensed and arranged by the author.

CHAPTER 4

Pages 118–122

Sources on tunnel kids include author interviews with Cristina in Jan. and Feb. 1998, Dec. 1998, and Jan. 1999; author interview with Cecilia Guzmán in Jan. 1999 and numerous informal interviews between 1996 and 1999; also numerous author visits to Mi Nueva Casa and informal interviews with kids and staff between 1995 and 1999. All interviews were conducted in Nogales, Sonora, in Spanish and translated by the author. Due to the personal and criminal nature of the tunnel kids' stories, their names have been changed.

Pages 122–127

Sources on Grupo Beta include author interview with Adán Leal, Nogales, Sonora, Feb. 1998, in Spanish and translated by the author; chapter 3 of Sebastian Rotella, *Twilight on the Line* (New York: W. W. Norton, 1998); Pamela Hartman, "Mexican Police Patrolling Border," *Tucson Citizen,* Aug. 6, 1994; and Sarah Tully, "Mexican Police Proving Their Worth on Border," *Arizona Daily Star,* Apr. 12, 1995. Photo of Cristina taken by Yoni Pozner appeared in Rubén Hernandez, "Dark Lives," *Tucson Citizen,* Apr. 8, 1994. Angélica Pence, "Mexicans Unsure of 'Reformed' Grupo Beta," *Arizona Daily Star,* May 28, 1996, was the source on 1996 Grupo Beta firings. Cecilia Guzmán also confirmed the rape story in an interview with the author, Nogales, Sonora, Jan. 1998, in Spanish and translated by the author.

Page 127

Mark Shaffer, "Lost Boys of Nogales Tunnels," *Arizona Republic,* Dec. 5, 1993, was source of Nogales, Arizona, crime statistics and of the quotes and descriptions of the kids' impact on local businesses.

Pages 128–132

Jan Smith Florez quotes from author interview, Tucson, Arizona, Jan. 1999. Additional sources on Mi Nueva Casa are Mi Nueva Casa newsletters between 1994 and 1998, also the source on the Carlos Santana donation; Rubén Martínez, "Notes from the Underground," *Hope,* Jan.–Feb. 1997; and author visits and interviews for Miriam Davidson, "Job Skills, Not Handouts for Mexican Tunnel Kids," *Christian Science Monitor,* Mar. 16, 1995. Sources on tunnel kids' stories include author interviews with Cecilia Guzmán in Jan. 1998 and Jan. 1999, with Alma in Jan. 1998, and with Cristina and Manuel in Feb. 1998—all in Nogales, Sonora, in Spanish and translated by the author.

Pages 132–135
Author interview with Alejandro Guzmán, Nogales, Sonora, Feb. 1998, in Spanish and translated by the author. Guzmán was the source of Nogales, Sonora, juvenile crime statistics. Nogales, Arizona, crime statistics are from Harold Kitching, "Major Crimes in City Drop Dramatically," *Nogales International,* Feb. 17, 1998. Author interview with Mayor Cota, Nogales, Sonora, Feb. 1998, in Spanish and translated by author, and Fabian Hernandez, "Se pierde la juventud," *Diario de la Frontera,* Feb. 4, 1998, were additional sources on the Rescate program. Portions of this story originally appeared as Miriam Davidson, "Nogales Plans to Rescue Children from Border Underworld," *APF Reporter,* Sept. 1999.

Pages 135–137
Sources on Mi Nueva Casa include author interviews with Cecilia Guzmán, Teresa Leal, Ron Rosenberg, Gilbert Rosas, and Jan Smith Florez in Tucson and Nogales between 1995 and 1999.

Pages 137–141
Sources on police officers' murders and Adán Leal arrest include: Tim Steller, "2 Nogales, Son., Cops Slain; Border Officer Held," *Arizona Daily Star,* July 3, 1998 (source of Adán Leal quote); Tim Steller, "Rocked by Cops Slaying, Nogales, Son., Loses Police Chief," *Arizona Daily Star,* July 9, 1998; and "Grupo Beta Leader Quits after 41 Days," *Arizona Daily Star,* Oct. 16, 1998. Cecilia Guzmán quote from author interview in Feb. 1998; Alberto Morackis quotes from author interview in Feb. 1999. Both interviews in Nogales, Sonora, conducted in Spanish and translated by author. Marco Antonio Martínez quotes from author interview in Nogales, Sonora, Feb. 1999. Martínez was the source on Mexican social statistics.

Pages 141–144
Author interviews with Cecilia Guzmán and Cristina, Jan. and Feb. 1998, Dec. 1998, and Jan. 1999, Nogales, Sonora, conducted in Spanish and translated by the author.

CHAPTER 5

Pages 145–151
Author interviews with José Torres and visits to Casa de la Misericordia in Nogales, Sonora, Jan. 1997, and author interview with Hope Torres, Tucson, Jan. 1997.

Pages 151–153
Sources on the maquila housing project include author telephone interview with Tom Higgins, Nov. 1996; author interview with Tom Higgins in Nogales, Sonora, Feb. and Apr. 1997; author interview with Marco Antonio Valenzuela, Nogales, Sonora, Feb.

1997; and telephone interview with Doug Chapman, Feb. 1997. This story was originally published in different forms as Miriam Davidson, "Maquiladora Workers Get Homes of Their Own," *APF Reporter,* Sept. 1997, and "A Dream Realized," *Arizona Republic,* Oct. 21, 1997.

Pages 154–155
Information on Juárez maquila tax from Miguel Angel Díaz Marin, "Juárez Tax Relief Maquilas Win Judgments," *Twin Plant News,* Aug. 1996. Francisco Trujillo quotes from author interview, Nogales, Sonora, fall 1996, conducted in Spanish and translated by Marisol Guzmán. Mayor Zaied quotes and budget figures from author interview in Nogales, Sonora, Mar. 1997, conducted in Spanish and translated by the author. Brochure provided by the Nogales Maquiladora Association. Information on lease renegotiation from author interview with Mayor Cota, Nogales, Sonora, Feb. 1998. Roscoe Combs quotes from author interview, Rio Rico, Arizona, Feb. 1997.

Pages 155–159
All of Hope Torres's stories and quotes are from author interviews in Tucson and Nogales, Sonora, between Jan. 1997 and Jan. 1999; "At least they don't have to dig in garbage" quote from Miriam Davidson, "Women of the Maquiladoras," *Agni 36* (fall 1992).

Pages 159–161
Don Nibbe quote from telephone interview with author, Feb. 1997. Sources and quotes on housing project include author interviews with Tom Higgins, Nogales, Sonora, Feb. and Apr. 1997, and with Doug Chapman (by telephone), Feb. 1997; author interview with project developer Nikita Kyriakis, Nogales, Sonora, Feb. 1997; author interview with Chamberlain personnel director Rene Moreno, Nogales, Sonora, Mar. 1997; and telephone interviews with other Nogales maquila managers between Mar. and Oct. 1997. Alfredo del Mazo quotes from "Maquila Housing GM and Infonavit Join Forces," *Twin Plant News,* Aug. 1996.

Pages 161–165
Author visits and interviews with José and Hope Torres, Dec. 1997 and Jan. 1998; also interviews with Hope in Aug. 1998 and Jan. 1999, when she gave me copies of her poem and other writings.

Pages 165–168
Sources on San Carlos include author interviews with Tom Higgins, Marco Antonio Valenzuela, project developer Nikita Kyriakis, and residents of San Carlos in Feb. and Mar. 1997. Brochures and other written information on San Carlos also were provided to the author by Tom Higgins, Nikita Kyriakis, and the Nogales Maquiladora Association. The information on housing program expansion is from "Maquila Housing GM," and from author interview with Marco Antonio Valenzuela, Nogales, Sonora, Feb. 1997.

Pages 168–170
Author interviews with Hope Torres in Aug. and Oct. 1998, and Jan. 1999, Nogales, Sonora.

CONCLUSION

Pages 171–172

Folklorist Jim Griffith was a source of the story of the shrine to San Ramón Nonato and the industrial park accident. Teresa Leal also told me the accident story. Reporter Rubén Hernandez was first to use San Ramón's birth as a metaphor for Nogales in "Boom Is Bust for Nogales, Son.," *Tucson Citizen,* Dec. 31, 1990.

Pages 172–173

Zedillo quoted in Angélica Pence, "Zedillo Praises Tying Economy to Environment," *Arizona Daily Star,* Dec. 20, 1996. Author tour of GI and interview with Rick Mata, Mar. 1997; author tour of Otis in Oct. 1996; and Mónica Gambrill, "Labor Policy in the Maquiladoras," *Voices of Mexico* 45 (Oct.–Dec. 1998), were additional sources on maquila modernization.

Pages 173–175

Sources on organizing in Mexico after NAFTA include: Carlos Heredia, "Downward Mobility," *NACLA Report on the Americas,* Nov.–Dec. 1996; *U.S. National Administrative Office North American Agreement on Labor Cooperation Public Report of Review,* U.S. Department of Labor report, Washington, D.C., Apr. 11, 1995 (on the Sony case); Communications Workers of America press releases on the MaxiSwitch case, Apr. 16, 1997; "Maquiladora OKs Independent Union," *New York Times,* published in *Arizona Daily Star,* Dec. 14, 1997; also author conversations with Tucson activists involved in these cases, especially sociologist Leslie Gates, the source on current status of independent unions, May 1999.

Sources on the CFO and other community-based organizations, cross-border labor organizing, the Coalition for Justice and other U.S.-based worker support groups include: author research for "Organizing in the Maquilas," *NACLA Report on the Americas,* May 1991, as well as research for several unpublished papers written during University of Southern California master's degree program, 1992–93; Mary McGinn and Kim Moody, "Labor Goes Global," *The Progressive,* Mar. 1993; *Six Years of NAFTA: A View from Inside the Maquiladoras,* Comité Fronterizo de Obreras report, in cooperation with the AFSC Mexico-U.S. Border Program, Piedras Negras, Coahuila, Mexico, and Philadelphia, Penn., Oct. 1999; and author participation in AFSC maquiladora-organizing project in Agua Prieta, 1996–99. Alberto Morackis quote from author interview, Nogales, Sonora, Feb. 1999.

Pages 175–178

Sources on BECC, NAD Bank, and Nogales water controversy include author interviews in 1997 with Teresa Leal, BECC spokesman Gonzalo Bravo, and Ambos Nogales water officials. Zedillo visit reported in Tim Steller, "Zedillo, on Tour, Sees What Works in Nogales, Sonora," *Arizona Daily Star,* Mar. 6, 1999. Placido Dos Santos quote from author interview, Tucson, Sept. 1997. A more detailed version of this story appeared as Miriam Davidson, "Bridging Troubled Waters in Ambos Nogales," *APF Reporter,* Dec. 1998.

Page 178

José Torres quote from author interview, Nogales, Sonora, Jan. 1997. Sources on impact of wage differential on illegal immigration from author research for "Pact Called 'Only Solution to Immigration Problem,'" *Arizona Republic*, Nov. 7, 1993, especially work done by Sidney Weintraub of the University of Texas at Austin. Dunn quote from Timothy Dunn, *The Militarization of the U.S.–Mexico Border, 1978–1992: Low Intensity Conflict Doctrine Comes Home* (Austin: University of Texas Press, 1996), 164. Also "U.S. Unable to Verify Border Crackdown's Effectiveness, GAO Says," *Arizona Daily Star*, Dec. 16, 1997.

Pages 179–180

Sources for historical perspectives on migrant labor include: Oscar J. Martínez, *Troublesome Border* (Tucson: University of Arizona Press, 1988); talk by Martínez and Guadalupe Castillo attended by author, Tucson, May 1995; and author interview with Jorge Bustamante in Tijuana, spring 1993. Additional sources on controversy over bracero program and other perspectives on illegal immigration include: Ignacio Ibarra, "Let Mexican Workers in Legally, Douglas Mayor Urges U.S.," *Arizona Daily Star*, Mar. 26, 1999; Manuel Garcia y Griego and Andres Jimenez, "Legislation Would Allow Farm-Worker Exploitation," *New York Times*, reprinted in *Arizona Daily Star*, Oct. 18, 1998; and Howard Fischer, "New Guest Worker Plan of Hull's Gains Support," *Arizona Daily Star*, Sept. 11, 1999.

Pages 180–181

Sources on drug seizures include Harold Kitching, "$42 Million in Cocaine," *Nogales International*, Mar. 6, 1998, and Tim Steller, "Huge Coke Seizure Greets Customs Boss," *Arizona Daily Star*, May 7, 1998. Tim Steller, "Bribe-Taking INS Inspectors Let Coke, Aliens in, Feds Say," *Arizona Daily Star*, Feb. 3, 1999, was the source on arrest of Nogales border inspectors. Tim Steller, "FBI Official Calls Border Corruption Widespread," *Arizona Daily Star*, Feb. 7, 1999, was source on the "pervasive" and "national disgrace" quotes. See also David Johnston and Sam Howe Verhovek, "Drug Trade Feeds on Payoffs at Mexico Line," *New York Times*, Mar. 24, 1997. Tracey Eaton, "NAFTA Aids Drug Gangs, Report Says," *Arizona Daily Star*, May 11, 1998, was source on the Customs report and the "narco heaven" quote.

Pages 181–182

Sources on Nogales drug tunnels include Ignacio Ibarra and Tim Steller, "Nogales Drug Squad Discovers Two Tunnels," *Arizona Daily Star*, Jan. 21, 1999. Marco Antonio Martínez quotes from author interview, Nogales, Sonora, Feb. 1999.

Pages 183–184

Author interview with Cecilia Guzmán, Tucson, Feb. 1999. Additional research on cultural impacts on Hispanic teenage sexuality conducted by author for "The Teenage Mothers of East L.A.," unpublished paper, May 1993.

Pages 184–185

Written information and quotes about the Chihuahuan Business Foundation and efforts to establish one in Sonora provided to author by Marco Antonio Martínez, Nogales, Sonora, Feb. 1999.

SELECTED BIBLIOGRAPHY

Arreola, Daniel, and James Curtis. *The Mexican Border Cities: Landscape Anatomy and Place Personality.* Tucson: University of Arizona Press, 1993.

Barry, Tom, and Beth Sims. *The Challenge of Cross-Border Environmentalism.* Albuquerque: Resource Center, 1994.

Barry, Tom, Harry Browne, and Beth Sims. *The Great Divide: The Challenge of U.S.-Mexico Relations in the 1990s.* New York: Grove, 1994.

Davidson, Miriam. *Convictions of the Heart: Jim Corbett and the Sanctuary Movement.* Tucson: University of Arizona Press, 1988.

Dunn, Timothy. *The Militarization of the U.S.-Mexico Border, 1978–1992: Low Intensity Conflict Doctrine Comes Home.* Austin: University of Texas Press, 1996.

Fernández-Kelly, María Patricia. *For We Are Sold, I and My People: Women and Industry in Mexico's Frontier.* Albany: State University of New York Press, 1983.

Flores García, Silvia Raquel. *Nogales: Un siglo en la historia.* Hermosillo, Sonora: Secretaria de Fomento Educativo y Cultura del Estado de Sonora, 1987.

Ingram, Helen, Nancy K. Laney, and David M. Gillilan. *Divided Waters: Bridging the U.S.-Mexico Border.* Tucson: University of Arizona Press, 1995.

Kearney, Milo, and Anthony Knopp. *Border Cuates: A History of the U.S.-Mexican Twin Cities.* Austin: Eakin, 1995.

Kopinak, Kathryn. *Desert Capitalism: Maquiladoras in North America's Western Industrial Corridor.* Tucson: University of Arizona Press, 1996.

Langwiesche, William. *Cutting for Sign.* New York: Pantheon, 1993.

Martínez, Oscar J. *Border People: Life and Society in the U.S.-Mexico Borderlands.* Tucson: University of Arizona Press, 1994.

———. *Troublesome Border.* Tucson: University of Arizona Press, 1988.

Mercado, Priscilano. *Historias y recuerdos de Ambos Nogales.* 2 vols. Nogales, Sonora: Didigraf, 1996.

Miller, Tom. *On the Border: Portraits of America's Southwestern Frontier.* New York: Harper and Row, 1981.

Nogales Centennial Committee, comp. *Nogales, Arizona, 1880–1980: Centennial Anniversary.* Nogales, Ariz.: Pimería Alta Historical Society, 1980.

Ready, Alma. *Open Range and Hidden Silver: Arizona's Santa Cruz County.* Nogales, Ariz.: Pimería Alta Historical Society, 1986.

Richardson, Chad. *Batos Botillos Pochos and Pelados: Class and Culture on the South Texas Border.* Austin: University of Texas Press, 1999.

Rotella, Sebastian. *Twilight on the Line.* New York: W. W. Norton, 1998.

Ruíz, Ramón. *On the Rim of Mexico: Encounters of the Rich and Poor.* Boulder, Colo.: Westview, 1998.

Tiano, Susan. *Patriarchy on the Line: Labor, Gender and Ideology in the Mexican Maquila Industry.* Philadelphia: Temple University Press, 1994.

Urrea, Luis Alberto. *Across the Wire: Life and Hard Times on the Mexican Border.* New York: Anchor, 1993.

Voices from the Pimería Alta. Nogales, Ariz.: Pimería Alta Historical Society, 1991.

Weisman, Alan. *La Frontera: The United States Border with Mexico.* New York: Harcourt Brace Jovanovich, 1986. Photographs by Jay Dusard.

ACKNOWLEDGMENTS

I am deeply indebted to all the people who gave so much of their time and attention during the years it took me to write this book. The maquiladora workers and managers, the business people and the environmentalists, the lawyers and the journalists, the government officials and the activists, the professors and the scientists, the Border Patrol agents and the border-crossers, the teenage gang members and the youth advocates, as well as many others in Ambos Nogales and elsewhere are too numerous to mention by name. A few, however, deserve special thanks for opening their hearts, being my friends, and sharing their stories. Yolanda and her family, especially her daughters, Guadalupe and Bobbi, as well as Hope and José Torres, helped me in ways I can never repay. I would also like to thank the Guzmán family—Cecilia, Kiko, Chuy, and Marisol—for teaching me so much about Nogales and for extending the hospitality of their little apartment. Other people in Ambos Nogales who went out of their way to help include Anita Teyechea, who loaned her son Jimmy's scrapbooks and videos to me; Cookie Bundy at the Nogales Public Library; the staff at Mi Nueva Casa and at the Casa de la Misericordia; Teresa Leal; and many more.

I am grateful to the law firms of Jesús Romo Véjar and Richard Gonzales for giving me access to the transcripts of and other information about the Elmer trial. I also would like to thank songwriter Victor Franco for writing "Cañon Mariposa" and for granting me permission to reproduce it. David Valdez generously shared a copy of the "Cañon Mariposa" video that he directed. Special thanks to Karen Valdez for painstakingly translating the lyrics.

I owe a great deal to my colleagues in journalism and academia who supported and encouraged me during my years of study and preparation. They are again too numerous to mention, but I'd particularly like to thank Murray Fromson, director of the University of Southern California Journalism School, and my fellow students in the 1992–93 class of the University of Southern California Center for International Journalism. It was during that wonderful year that the idea for this book began to take shape. I also would like to thank Margaret Engel, Sandy Close, and the other judges at the Alicia Patterson Foundation for choosing me as a 1997 Alicia Patterson fellow. The foundation's support was invaluable in allowing me the time to research and write the book.

Thank you as well to Scott Baldauf at the *Christian Science Monitor* and to my colleagues at the *Arizona Republic,* particularly editors Venita James and David Fritze, as well as reporters Jerry Kammer, Mark Shaffer, and Graciela Sevilla. They are all fine editors and reporters who taught me a great deal. I'd also like to thank the other reporters whose work is cited in the book, especially freelancer Sandy Tolan and Tim Steller of the *Arizona Daily Star.*

I would like to thank my agent, Patricia Van der Leun, for her wise and judicious attention to the manuscript in its early stages. Her suggestions were excellent, and her care and attention inspired me to keep going. I also am grateful to my editor at the University of Arizona Press, Patti Hartmann, and to the other UA Press readers and editors who made suggestions for the improvement of the manuscript.

My friend Catalina Spencer helped me a great deal. She held a reading for me at her house, accompanied me to Nogales to interview people, and made fine editorial suggestions, including the title for chapter five. Carol Freundlich, another good friend, read the manuscript and offered some excellent ideas about how to make it better.

I also would like to express my appreciation to photographer Jeffry Scott for all the great work he has done documenting the changes in Ambos Nogales over the years. It has been a pleasure to work with Jeff, and I am grateful that he generously donated his photographs for the book.

A big *abrazo* to my friends at Borderlinks and the American Friends Service Committee's maquiladora-organizing project in Agua Prieta, especially Rick and Kitty Ufford-Chase, Jenny Johnson, John Ostermann, Kate Griffith, Leslie Gates, Susan Gallegos, Pola Pantoja, and Elisa Ortega. They made this book possible by teaching me about the border, by helping with my Spanish, and by introducing me to Yolanda, Cecilia Guzmán, and many others.

Finally, I would like to thank my father, William Davidson, for being the first to tell me about Nogales and La Caverna and for inspiring my love of Mexico; my father's cousin, William Weber, for understanding and supporting my desire to write; and my mother, Florence Davidson, for offering her love and encouragement.

To my mate, David, thank you for being there every step of the way. I couldn't have done it without you.

INDEX

Dabdoub (family), 24, 26, 140, 154
DeConcini, Dennis, 98
del Mazo, Alfredo, 161
Delphi Automotive Systems. *See* General
   Motors
Delta (maquila), 36, 37, 38, 45, 159
Dos Santos, Placido, 177–78
drug smuggling, 3–4, 13, 88; incidents in
   Nogales, 43, 90–91, 108–9, 121, 180–
   81; policy on, 182–83
Dunn, Tim, 178

Elmer, Michael, 14–15, 69, 80–86, 94–97,
   103–5
Elvira's restaurant, 98
environment, 6, 11–12, 176-77. *See also*
   maquiladoras, NAFTA, Nogales
Environmental Protection Agency (EPA),
   71, 72
Esperanza Foundation, 153, 159, 166
Espericueta, Andres, 166–67
Espinoza, Fernando, 53, 78

Flipper, Lt. Henry, 6
Flood, Tim, 59, 75
Florez, Jan Smith, 127–28, 135–37
Foster Grant (maquila), 26, 28, 36

General Instrument (maquila), 10, 16, 145,
   160, 168, 172–73
General Motors, 35, 64, 66, 167
Gephardt, Richard, 40
Grupo Beta, 122–26, 128, 132, 137–38,
   141
Guzmán, Alejandro, 132–35
Guzmán, Cecilia, 129–32, 135–36, 138,
   183

Habitat for Humanity, 136, 167
Hasta Mex (maquila). *See* Otis Elevator
Hernandez, Esequiel, Jr., 110–11, 182
Higgins, Tom, 17, 151–53, 159–61, 165–
   68, 184

Holy Cross Hospital, 51, 77, 164
House of Mercy. *See* Casa de la Misericordia.

illegal immigration, 13, 87–89, 99–100,
   101–3, 109; policy on, 178–80
industrial park, 25, 61, 171–72
Infonavit, 161, 166–67
Interfaith Center on Corporate Responsibility, 175
International Boundary and Water Commission, 73–74

Jefel (maquila), 22–23, 28, 33
Joffroy, William, Jr., 68

Kirpnick, Alex, 108–9, 123, 182
Kleindienst, Wallace, 104
Kolbe, Jim, 101, 107

La Caverna restaurant, 5–6, 172
La Paz Agreement, 74
Leal, Adán, 122–26, 137–38
Leal, Teresa, 128, 136
LIFE (Living Is For Everyone), 58–59, 60,
   66–67, 75–76, 78, 162
Lilley, Ken, 41
Lopez, Art, 90
Los Encinos (colonia), 29–32, 44, 149, 153

maquiladora managers, 16–17, 32, 40–42;
   charitable involvement of, 145, 153–
   54, 156, 184; on environmental conditions, 62, 64–65, 172; on workers
   and corporate social responsibility,
   25–27, 154–55, 158–59, 173
maquiladoras: allegations of toxic dumping
   by, 61–63, 75–76; founding and expansion of, 5, 10, 24–27, 35, 41, 172–
   73; housing program, 17, 151–55,
   159–61, 165–68; in Juarez, 34, 39, 62,
   167, 184–85; in Matamoros, 63, 75–
   76, 167; media coverage of, 27, 40–

XENY, Radio, 86, 93, 137, 168

Yerba Buena Wash, 95–96
Yerena, Enrique, 82–85, 104
youth, 15–16; crime by, 120, 132–33, 143–44; crime prevention and drug treatment programs for, 128, 134, 138–41; drug use by, 39, 121, 130, 135, 144, 182; education of, 38, 131, 134, 140–41; environmental interest of, 78–79; religious interest of, 45–46, 54, 139–40; sexual attitudes of, 36, 38–39, 121–22, 130, 135, 142–43, 183–84; *see also* maquiladora workers, tunnel kids

Zaied, Abraham, 154–55
Zedillo, Ernesto, 172, 176

ABOUT THE AUTHOR

Miriam Davidson has studied and written about the U.S.–Mexico border for almost twenty years. She has worked as a reporter, editor, journalism professor, and freelance writer. Her writing on border issues has appeared in the *New York Times*, the *Christian Science Monitor*, *The Nation*, the *NACLA Report on the Americas*, *The Progressive*, and many other newspapers and magazines. From 1993 to 1996, she covered Tucson and Nogales as a correspondent for the *Arizona Republic* in Phoenix. She is also the author of the critically praised *Convictions of the Heart: Jim Corbett and the Sanctuary Movement* (University of Arizona Press, 1988). She holds a B.A. in English from Yale University and a master's degree in international journalism from the University of Southern California. Davidson has received several grants and awards for her writing, including a 1997 Alicia Patterson Fellowship. She lives in Tucson, Arizona.